Breakthrough Quality Improvement for Leaders Who Want Results

Also available from Quality Press

Untangling Organizational Gridlock: Strategies for Building a Customer Focus
Michele L. Bechtell

Management by Policy: How Companies Focus Their Total Quality Efforts to Achieve Competitive Advantage
Brendan Collins and Ernest Huge

Creating a Customer-Centered Culture: Leadership in Quality, Innovation, and Speed
Robin L. Lawton

Integrated Process Management: A Quality Model
Roger Slater

Ethics in Quality
August B. Mundel

Quality Management Benchmark Assessment
J. P. Russell

A Guide to Graphical Problem-Solving Processes
John W. Moran, Richard P. Talbot, and Russell M. Benson

Benchmarking: The Search for Industry Best Practices That Lead to Superior Performance
Robert C. Camp

QFD: A Practitioner's Approach
James L. Bossert

To request a complimentary catalog of publications, call 800-248-1946.

Breakthrough Quality Improvement for Leaders Who Want Results

Robert F. Wickman
Robert S. Doyle

ASQC Quality Press
Milwaukee, Wisconsin

Breakthrough Quality Improvement for Leaders Who Want Results
Robert F. Wickman and Robert S. Doyle

Library of Congress Cataloging-in-Publication Data

Wickman, Robert F.
    Breakthrough quality improvement for leaders who want results/
Robert F. Wickman, Robert S. Doyle
      p. cm.
    Includes index.
    ISBN 0-87389-213-5 (alk. paper)
    1. Total quality management.   2. Benchmarking (Management)
I. Doyle, Robert S.   II. Title
HD62015.W53   1993
658.5'62—dc20   93-13578
                                                                            CIP

© 1993 by ASQC

All rights reserved. No part of this book may be reproduced in any form or by any means, electronic, mechanical, photocopying, recording, or otherwise, without the prior written permission of the publisher.

10 9 8 7 6 5 4 3 2 1

ISBN 0-87389-213-5

Acquisitions Editor: Susan Westergard
Production Editor: Annette Wall
Marketing Administrator: Mark Olson
Set in Galliard and Avant Garde by Montgomery Media, Inc.
Cover design by Montgomery Media, Inc.
Printed and bound by BookCrafters, Inc.

ASQC Mission: To facilitate continuous improvement and increase customer satisfaction by identifying, communicating and promoting the use of quality principles, concepts, and technologies; and thereby be recognized throughout the world as the leading authority on, and champion for, quality.

For a free copy of the ASQC Quality Press Publications Catalog, including ASQC membership information, call 800-248-1946.

Printed in the United States of America

Printed on acid-free recycled paper

ASQC
Quality Press
611 East Wisconsin Avenue
Milwaukee, Wisconsin 53202

Contents

Introduction vii

Part I: Quality Defined . . . Its Meaning, Environment, and Elements 1
   1   The Meaning of Quality 3
   2   The Environment of Quality 35
   3   The Elements of Superior Quality 51

Part II: Quality Implemented . . . The Tools of Breakthrough Quality Improvement 83
   4   Quality Awareness and Management 85
   5   Data Gathering and Interpretation 103
   6   Work Process Analysis 129
   7   Problem Solving 147
   8   Decision Making 165
   9   Project Management 181
  10   Team Building and Leadership 195

Summary 219

Index 223

Introduction

Let us admit the case of the conservative: if we once start thinking, no one can guarantee where we shall come out; except that many ends, objects, and institutions are doomed. Every thinker puts some portion of an apparently stable world in peril, and no one can wholly predict what will emerge in its place.

—John Dewey

Quality. This simple word has become the rallying cry of the American workplace. Almost all companies have begun some initiative on quality. (In this book, the phrases *total quality management* or TQM, *quality*, and *quality management* will be used interchangeably.) Many companies have multiple efforts in place, with a steadily growing number of dedicated quality professionals within those companies. Enough books have been written to fill a small library. Topics cover an extremely wide range, from deadly serious works aimed at fourth-year calculus students, to lighter reading for people simply interested in the concepts. Quality consultants, speakers, and program experts are everywhere, expounding on the importance and methodologies of quality.

Yet few companies are seeing the results they expected or should be achieving, considering the time and expense represented by their efforts. In our consulting work, we have met many quality professionals, CEOs, and managers of every type who can talk for hours about the programs they have implemented and sometimes, in frustration, have ended. *But too often they cannot point to measurable results.* A common phrase we hear is "We haven't seen too many results yet, but we've only been at this for a year!"

Our title promises breakthroughs in quality improvement. One dictionary definition of *breakthrough* is a strikingly important advance or discovery. To some, this phrase might bring such historic advances as penicillin or personal computers to mind. But breakthroughs can occur every day. Some are small improvements while others are large. Individually and together, though, all these changes are indeed strikingly important. They will take a business to places it has never been before. They require the skills we've described here, and the belief that "if it ain't broke, let's fix it anyway!"

We have written this book in the belief that a properly planned and executed quality initiative can and should produce immediate measurable results. It isn't easy. It doesn't happen without change, and sometimes considerable change, especially in the attitudes of senior and middle management. But it is possible. More important, it is necessary for success in our future of worldwide competition. Good quality is an investment, not an expense. It will provide lasting dividends to the visionary leaders who make the tough choices and move forward toward total quality management in their companies.

> *Ah, but a man's reach should exceed his grasp—or what's heaven for?*
> —Robert Browning

The Plateaus of Quality Efforts

The seriousness with which a company views its or others' quality efforts tends, in our opinion, to fall onto one of three plateaus. These plateaus describe a broad range of commitment, from not very much to totally committed. Virtually every company we've researched or worked with falls into one of them. Our objective in this book is twofold: (1) to motivate the move from the lower and middle plateaus to the highest plateau, where immediate measurable results are achievable; and (2) to show how that can be done.

Plateau 1: Studied Indifference, or "Quality Is for Them"

It might be hard to believe that we have reached the 1990s and still find companies and entire industry groups that think quality is for the other guy—that it has no relevance to them. A common indicator of a company residing on the studied indifference quality plateau is the presence of the lonely inspector, standing at the end of the production line (sometimes literally) making yes and no decisions about the product. The percentage of rejected product is carefully calculated, but not thought of as terribly high.

Customer needs are usually assumed by the company, and certainly the actual needs of the customer are never sought. Quality is viewed as a production activity and never finds its way into the service areas of the company, such as accounts payable or marketing.

Since they are doing little to control what is happening within themselves, the survival of these companies depends on events or variables outside of their control. For example, survival might be the result of a lack of serious competition. Or the company's product is presently so important to the customer that some degree of tolerance of manufacturing imperfection and poor service is acceptable. If you believe it is reasonable for any modern business to stay at this plateau, and hope for some support for that position in this book, you might want to stop reading.

Plateau 2: Externalized Appreciation, or "We Know All About Quality"
If you have read this far and know there are two other plateaus to be described, you might have already mentally reviewed all the efforts of your company and decided you'll be found in the third plateau. Before you congratulate yourself though, you should know that the vast majority of companies with which we have become familiar reside fully in this second plateau.

A lot of training activity characterizes companies in this plateau. Usually, a high level quality position is evident, such as vice president of quality assurance. Often this job begins with an intense roundup of all the quality providers out there, such as ourselves. An in-depth research into the company's offerings follows, with the objective to determine which is the right choice for its culture and needs. Decisions to do anything take a very long time. When quality teams are finally formed, they are pointed to with pride as proof of management's commitment; after all, they come with no small expense in lost time and production. We find four-color glossy books describing the quality philosophy and mission, and the walls are festooned with quality exhortations.

Senior management often refuses to embrace a single philosophy or approach, deeming that "each department knows what is best for it." As a result, multiple and often poorly integrated efforts are implemented.

These multiple quality efforts can also result in an attitude that "since we've tried just about *everything*, we pretty much have all the quality know-how we need. After all, who knows our company better than us?" Yet, the quality director or manager or vice president often complains that other senior people poke fun (sometimes in jest, sometimes not) at the efforts. "Aren't there better things to do than this?"

Results? "Well, they're undoubtedly there, but you know, we've really only been at this for a year."

How are the teams working? "Hmm, they are kind of frustrated. After all, they do have other work and other priorities as well."

And that sums up companies at this plateau. The good effort is viewed as additional responsibilities and tasks which have been added to the real job of getting product out the door. When push comes to shove in a company in this plateau, quality efforts are often the first to go, or at least to be put on a back burner.

Plateau 3: Internalized Understanding, or the New Job *Is* Quality

Plateau three companies don't appear to be much different from their neighbors one plateau below. The same efforts are in place (although usually fewer in variety). Similar posters adorn the walls. And four-color brochures might cover the reception area tables. The difference is solely in the genuine support given by senior and middle management. Quality activities are not seen as another intrusion on the real task of the company. They *are* the real task of the company. The management of these companies believe that their investment in time, money, and effort is never ending, and that it is absolutely essential to the long-term success of the company. Companies that have reached this plateau are the sort that win the Malcolm Baldrige National Quality Award.

These three plateaus are shown in Figure I.1. Plateau three generally requires more effort and time, but the advantages to the company far outweigh these requirements. Often the plateau occupied by a company can be discerned by the statements one commonly hears about quality in the workplace. Some of the more common statements for each plateau are shown in Figure I.2.

Unfortunately, results can be elusive, even in plateau three. What makes the entire effort work best is the combination of beliefs we find in plateau three companies and the application of the appropriate tools.

That's the purpose of this book—to demonstrate the importance of the beliefs and the nature of the right tools to use in the quest for total quality.

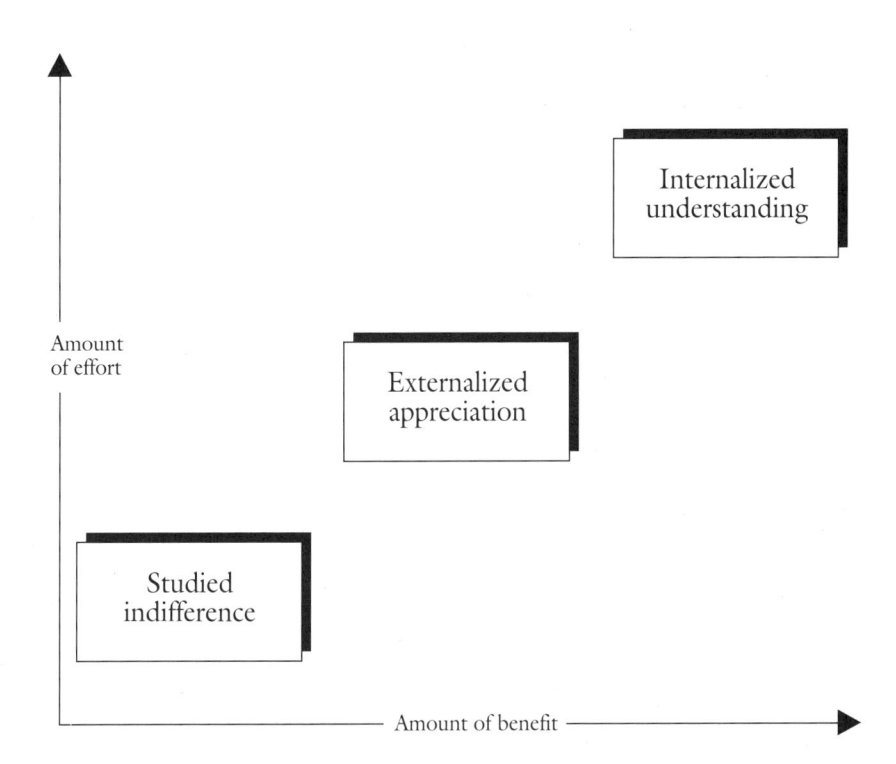

Figure I.1. The three plateaus of quality.

> *Most human organizations that fall short of their goals do so not because of stupidity or faulty doctrines, but because of internal decay and rigidification. They grow stiff in the joints. They get in a rut. They go to seed.*
>
> —James Gardner

Why Quality Is So Important

We see at least four reasons that compel any company, whether its primary focus is manufacturing or service, to fully embrace a total quality effort now. None of these are new, but together they create an almost overwhelming urgency to excel in quality management.

Studied indifference	Externalized appreciation	Internalized understanding
Quality programs are not for us.	Quality is important. We'll just have to find time for it!	Quality is the new job around here
Quality programs don't do much. They are here today and forgotten tomorrow.	Quality process implementation is tough. There is never enough time.	Quality is exciting!
We've always done it this way.	We're doing all kinds of great new things in quality.	We're not doing anywhere near enough as much as we should.
The cost of quality is too high.	The cost of quality is high, but necessary.	Quality is our best investment.
We haven't looked into this quality stuff, because it doesn't apply here.	We have learned just about all there is to know about quality, at least for our company.	All in all, we don't know very much as all. We're always learning.
Our inspectors handle quality problems.	We have dozens of teams and committees.	Everybody is doing quality work. It's part of every job.
We have always known what's best for our customers.	Our customers demand ongoing quality efforts.	Our customers deserve that we be the best we can be.
Our management's job is to hold spending to a minimum.	Our management supports quality, but will demand hard results to justify the costs.	Our management is leading the charge. They know that results will justify the costs.
We expect our people to do the job they are assigned.	People can be managed to do even better, even if they complain about it.	People want to do the best job possible.
We've survived this long, and with luck we'll be around for a lot longer. We don't see any growth.	Our survival is very likely. We'll wait and see about growth.	Our survival and growth are assured!

Figure I.2. Common statements of companies in each of the three plateaus of quality.

First, global competition will continue to increase. Our products and services cannot be viewed any longer as secure because they are made in the United States. As the world shrinks, our businesses must find new and innovative ways to compete within markets dominated by companies with lower wage rates, longer working hours, and sometimes more highly skilled employees. And the result is a domino effect. Our customers, as they gain an awareness of the importance of quality, have begun to demand quality efforts that are real, not just words. The auto industry is a good example. One major domestic manufacturer expects that auto parts be received at the assembly line just in time, which means that the supplier must now paint the parts in the order that cars are rolling down the assembly line! Such demands create considerable need for solid quality management in the supplier companies.

Second, CEOs and other senior management want more out of their employees. "Lean and mean" is a rallying cry of the boardroom. Give-backs are expected more frequently at the bargaining table, and the days of automatic pay increases without an increase in worker productivity are disappearing. Another phrase we often hear is: *People need to learn to manage that which they do not know.* That is, people are expected to broaden their responsibilities into areas in which they may not be fully skilled. The result in many companies is a considerably higher level of stress among employees.

At the same time, employees are beginning to feel that enough is enough. The percentage of professionals willing to sacrifice almost anything to achieve career success is decreasing. A balanced life-style, with more attention paid to family and a social life, is becoming important. People see their careers as the means to an end, not as the ends themselves.

What is needed to deal with these seemingly conflicting needs is the ability to work *smarter*, not harder. Easily said, less easily done. But effective total quality management processes help companies do just that.

The third reason to embrace total quality is that the expectations of our employees are changing considerably. We may think of "buying a worker's back" as a phrase from the coal mines of the turn of the century. But in fact that approach, perhaps with somewhat less literal meaning, continues in a surprisingly high number of U.S. industries. Today, this approach may take form as a belief that a person should be grateful for the employment and to do the job he or she is told to do, without complaint and certainly without bothersome suggestions for change. Labor unions continue to find inroads into companies largely because of this management attitude, despite the fact that a well-run company concerned with issues of welfare and growth for its employees should be able to deal with these issues without the mediation of an outside party.

Employees want more of a say in what they do and how they do it. They need to feel a part of the company, to belong. "Buy my mind, if you need to feel you've bought something. I'll throw my back into the work when it is necessary, but my back is not the only thing that I offer."

Smart companies recognize that almost all employees nurture these feelings in some way or another; that it is not a feeling specific to professionals or degreed people. Smart companies know that each employee has the best vantage point to identify and recommend improvements to the job, given the necessary information and skills. And smart companies install a framework to manage those efforts most effectively—a framework of total quality management.

Finally, our customers are becoming much more discriminating. No longer are most customers willing to put up with shoddy merchandise or poor service. Their sophistication demands that they have more of a say in what the product or service will be, and that it better meets their present and future needs. We'll talk about customer needs in more detail later in the book. Successful companies recognize the new roles that their customers are playing, and mobilize their efforts through total quality processes to enable them to understand and meet these new demands.

> *If business leaders had channeled one-tenth of the energy they devoted to fighting this bill [Nader's consumer protection bill] into improving their products and services they would not find themselves in this fix. The subcommittee had analyzed the warranties of 51 leading manufacturers. Only one of them provided the customers with a warranty free of loopholes.*
>
> —James J. Kilpatrick

What Must Be Done

Success into the next century demands new and comprehensive approaches to the way we do business. Our companies must recognize the absolute importance of total quality, not as another program but as a new way of life. Leaders with vision about the future must be found, and they must be given the means to make the necessary changes. Success comes about when *all* customers, both external and internal, can continually, clearly, and fully describe their changing needs, and the work done within the business completely satisfies those needs at all times.

In general, three things must be done. First, a new set of values must permeate our businesses, from the boardroom to the loading dock. These values must result in an insistence that quality no longer be a stand-alone novelty, but be completely linked with the purpose, strategy, tactics, and work activities of the business.

Second, everyone must be given the right tools to do the quality job correctly. For some employees, the right tools are those that enable them to identify and solve problems on the production line as they occur and where they occur. For others, a process whereby they can continually analyze the efficiency and effectiveness of their nonmanufacturing function is appropriate. Managers and supervisors must learn these techniques and more. They must also become fully adept in all the skills of team management, motivation, social styles recognition and adaptation, and other leadership skills. In fact, we see a future in which quality management is an essential part of any manager's skills, just as planning, controlling, delegating, and organizing are today. We envision a day in which there are no people in the company titled quality coordinator, vice president quality assurance, or manager of quality programs, because *everyone* will be responsible for quality.

Finally, quality must be a win for everyone. Shareholders must gain their win through enhanced stock performance and dividends. Employees must see their win as greater job security resulting from better performance. They must also see their win in receiving training in a new set of skills that are applicable not just on the job, but at home as well. Employers will win through increased profits which will enable long-term capital investment and perpetuation of the business.

This book can't overcome a lack of leadership. But we'll give the leaders of our businesses some effective ways to achieve their quality goals.

Part I
Quality Defined...
Its Meaning, Environment, and Elements

1 The Meaning of Quality

"Getting Close to the Customer" is not close enough. Glue yourself to customers, distributors, and suppliers; make "relationship management" your motto.

—Tom Peters

What is this concept we refer to as quality? We all have a sense of its definition as Webster might state it. Quality experts use phrases such as *fit for use* or *conformance to requirements*. These definitions are good, and relate in a few words an entire philosophy of quality in American industry. While we certainly accept the overall meanings of these familiar definitions, we've decided to expand the definition, for three reasons: (1) to provide managers and employees a more detailed and more immediately understood definition, usable on a day-to-day basis; (2) to capture in the definition the likely prospect that the requirements with which we wish to conform are in a state of perpetual change; and (3) to specifically suggest the tools that employees need to implement such a philosophy of quality. What do people do to achieve quality? How do they make it happen?

The impossible is often the untried.

—Jim Goodwin

A New Definition of Quality

Companies invent and implement numerous programs, processes, and procedures. They modify and massage them. And then they try to teach and motivate their people to apply them, all in the quest for perfection in the things that they do, whether those things are the manufacture of tangible goods or the provision of services.

Some very significant questions often remain unasked: Are we just trying to do the things we already do right, or are we trying to do the right things right? How do we know what the right things are? If there's a change in what are the right things to do, can we react or adapt to the change quickly and still remain competitive? How can we learn to anticipate or even initiate the changes with which we'll have to contend?

Any definition of quality, indeed any *process* of quality that will be usable by everyone in the company, should be able to answer these questions. A frame of mind must be developed among all employees that causes them to recognize and truly believe that quality is not only doing things right, but that quality is doing the right things right.

Such a definition of quality might be: Quality in the workplace comes from understanding, and then fully meeting, the needs of all your internal and external customers, now and into the future, with continual improvement in efficiency and effectiveness. Let's look carefully at each part of this definition.

Meeting the Needs of Your Customers

From whose point of view is quality measured? Too often, the quality of our work is defined from our perspective. It is based on what we think is best for our customers. But much more important is what your customers, those inside and outside of the company, think is best for them. Doing anything that does not meet the needs of a customer is of no value to the organization. Those customers may be the external buyers of your goods or services, or may be the group of employees next on the assembly line. Either way, all of the things that are done must meet those customers' needs.

There are some ways in which a company or its employees might distort this simple truth. Most serious is the mistake of assuming customers' needs or, in a similar vein, doing the job in a certain way because it is more convenient to do so. Recently a major automobile manufacturer decided that one criterion of its definition of quality was to achieve the most rear seat headroom to be found in a certain size class of automobiles, a size class in which it competed. This certainly sounds like a laudable effort, probably one that a sizeable number of its customers would ordinarily applaud. However, the manufacturer made the extra headroom possible by lowering the backseat!

Headroom certainly was increased. The manufacturer congratulated itself on achieving the highest level of quality in the class. But this definition of quality was its own. Customers soon found that a more important criterion of quality to them, namely reasonable backseat comfort, had diminished. How do you suppose the buying public, the most important customer of all, felt about the manufacturer's sense of having achieved high quality?

In another example, a bank decided that it could increase its customer satisfaction index (which it carefully measured through questionnaires and other means) by reducing the time customers had to spend in line waiting for a teller. The goal was to reduce to two minutes a time that then averaged closer to eight minutes. Studies were conducted. Experts mulled the data. Changes were made. Data were again collected. And indeed the new average time was reduced significantly, to under three minutes. In many branches, the customer satisfaction index rose, much to the delight of the bank's management. But in one branch the customer satisfaction index plummeted. How could that happen? Surely everyone wants to spend less time waiting for a teller! Closer inspection revealed that this branch's clientele were largely retired people. They enjoyed waiting in line for a teller, because it represented an excellent opportunity to see friends and catch up on the recent news of the retirement community. The bank had met its criteria for quality, but had not met its customers' needs, at least not at that particular branch.

We occasionally hear an interesting complaint about this requirement to meet customers' needs. It goes something like this: "I am a professional (engineer, manager, accountant, and so on), and I am not paid to just do what anyone else asks me to do. I must lead, be creative, and do things that my customers may not even be aware that they need." That is, of course, an appropriate and necessary part of the job for many professional people. But it doesn't diminish the importance of meeting customers' needs. Customers will always expect the outputs to them—whatever those might be—to meet a need. Sometimes those needs are expressed in general terms; for example, customers may expect their suppliers to lead, create, and do the right things right, even though they may not know exactly what those right things are. One of our definitions of professionalism is effectively working with customers to discover their needs and to perhaps influence those needs in ways beneficial to the customers.

Understanding the Needs

Companies are not likely to meet their customers' needs if they are unaware of them. Too often, especially within a company, there is very little if any effort made to find out what customers expect. Employees are left to decide for themselves what those needs must be and then try to fill them. Who among us has never been in the position of feeling we've done a great job, only to have our boss tell us that it didn't measure up? In most of these cases, these differences between our action and the needs of our customer (the boss) are caused by not understanding the needs in the first place.

A manager was describing his new role, that of a liaison between a service and a manufacturing organization within his company. The service organization was implementing some new and significantly different ways of providing their service, and the manufacturing organization was going to be one recipient of that service. The liaison's role was to ensure that manufacturing's requirements were being met by the service organization. Although manufacturing was very clear about its expectations of the service it was to receive, manufacturing was not clear at all to the liaison manager about its expectations of him. He received some advice from a co-worker, who suggested that the manager write a list of his needs from the organization, needs that would allow him to do his job, and present those needs in a meeting. His list would likely contain items like timely information, advance knowledge of scheduled meetings, certain data, changed requirements, and the like. Good advice, if not carried out in a heavy-handed way.

We added some additional thoughts. Why not also write a second list, one that contained a proposed set of needs that the organization might want to consider of him? Why not give the *quid pro quo* that would allow both parties to completely understand the expectations of the other? Unreasonable needs could then be negotiated, and everyone should be more effective. The manager prepared and presented both lists much to the astonishment of the organization's management group, which was not accustomed to dealing with customers' needs in this nonmanufacturing, internal role. The needs were negotiated, agreed upon, and implemented, and the liaison role immediately became clear and effective.

Internal and External Customers

We are continually surprised that so few companies have achieved a deep sense of the importance of satisfying all their customers, not just the ultimate external ones who pay the bill. A little later in this chapter we'll expand on the idea of customers and suppliers within the company, and show that each of us is a customer and supplier to many others within our company. For now, though, our definition of customers includes anyone who receives output of a work process, be it a finished widget, data, information, reports—whatever. The customer may be your secretary, whose needs might include an accurate and timely schedule for your upcoming business trip so that your reservations and travel can be properly orchestrated. The customer may be your boss, who may have some very specific needs about the report you are preparing.

By the way, it is very useful to break the overall word *needs* into its component parts, *musts* and *wants*. *Musts* are those needs that are nonnegotiable, mandatory, and measurable. *Wants* are negotiable, often subjective, and usually weighted. That is, on a scale of 1 to 10, 10 being very important, one want might be a 5 and another want might be an 8. For example, the very reasonable desire to increase employee morale should not be considered a must, because there are no certain ways of objectively measuring employee morale, but it certainly could be a strong want. An appropriate must might be to reduce the waste rate on line six from 4 percent to 2 percent weekly average by January 23. This must is measurable, and if deemed reasonable, becomes a mandatory and nonnegotiable must.

Sometimes, of course, a customer can demand an impossible must. In some recent work, we dealt with a group of skilled repair technicians who had a need for many diverse parts to enable them to do their job, the diagnosis and repair of a large variety of equipment. Some parts were almost never needed, but even their occasional unavailability cost the technicians time and money. A classic confrontation with the parts department ensued. Learning that a must was mandatory and nonnegotiable, the technicians quickly established one of their musts as "the parts department must constantly inventory all parts for all conceivable needs." To meet the technicians' must, the parts department would have had to more than double staff, build onto the parts storage area, and tie up a significant amount of money in inventory. The technicians' must was in this case unreasonable and couldn't be met without serious financial burden to the company. Furthermore, it wasn't really necessary to inventory all possible parts.

This must might be negotiated into a series of weighted wants. Then a remaining must might be "the parts department must have a system whereby the perceived parts requirements of the technicians, both now and two months into the future, are factored into the final decisions about what and how many parts will be inventoried." In this case, the system and its use are mandatory, and easily measured. Is such a system operating or is it not? Over time, with experience operating such a system, we would expect a restating of musts and wants to become much tighter.

Now and into the Future

Satisfied customers usually decide that more can be received from you, and they tend to upgrade their needs. We've all heard variations of the phrase *What have you done for me lately?* Many customers today are vigorously examining and rating the quality abilities of their suppliers, demanding shipment direct to inventory, just in time, better quality products, and the like. In many cases, customers have announced to long-term suppliers that a continuation of the business relationship will require significantly stronger efforts in applying principles of quality in the business, and improvements in the things that are done, as well as the way they're done.

Customers change their needs for other reasons, of course. Sometimes their strategies have changed, and they need different outputs from you to achieve their new goals. Or, they may have found a competitor who offers them a comparable or superior product or service, more quickly and at a better price. Whatever the reason, companies today must be able to first recognize and then accept the fact that customer needs will change. What is done today to meet those needs will not be acceptable later. Then, companies must implement the means by which to continually change the things they are doing, and the ways of doing them, to adjust to the changing needs.

Continually More Effectively and Efficiently

As we'll talk more about later, meeting the musts and wants of your customers is the first priority of any business or employee. To worry about the effectiveness or efficiency of the way you are doing your job, when in fact you are not meeting your customers' needs, is like deciding to beautify the barn with a fresh coat of paint when broken stall and door latches are allowing all the animals to escape!

Meeting customer needs, though, is not reason to rest on our laurels. Once we're doing the right things, we must ask ourselves over and over again, are we doing them right? Is there a better way, using less time, resources, money, or effort? Can we streamline the work processes that we are performing to achieve the same or better outputs more quickly? Can we identify ways in which our suppliers (because we too are a customer of one or more suppliers) can modify their outputs to us so that we can better meet the needs of our customers? Can we suggest to our customers, either internal or external, changes to our outputs to them that might better meet their needs and at the same time make us more cost effective?

These and others are the questions we will ask again and answer later in this book. They will form the foundation of an effective quality process that will work for all your employees.

So far, we've seen the importance of recognizing that we have many customers. They are our co-workers as well as the more obvious purchasers of our products or services. Establishing criteria of our work that meet our sense of quality is fine, except that our criteria often do not match those of our customers. Our customers' needs will inevitably change over time, not because they are capricious but because conditions and needs do indeed change. We have to understand and meet their needs of today as well as their needs of tomorrow. Finally, it does us no good to meet those needs with no profit. It violates the purpose of being in business. Continual improvement of the way we do our jobs must happen! Competitors are everywhere, and one certainty is that they are trying to get a larger market share at your expense!

Faced with the choice of changing one's mind and proving there is no need to do so, almost everyone gets busy on the proof.
—John Kenneth Galbraith

The Multiple Role of Each Employee

We were once talking about meeting customers' needs in a workshop. (It was the management group responsible for the repair technicians and their parts woes that we mentioned earlier.) We had said that everyone in any company simultaneously plays three roles, that of supplier, work processor (getting the assigned job done), and customer. We then stated that most supplier-customer relationships work both ways: the customer can also be a supplier of things back to the person or organization from which the product or service is received. "Baloney!" cried one of the participating managers. "My repair technicians are always the customers of the parts department. Parts does what we tell them to do, and don't you forget it! To use your words it's *their* (parts') responsibility to meet the stated needs of their customers!"

"Well," we said, "would you agree that if parts *did* have some musts and wants of you, that would mean they are your customer?"

"Sure, but that's just not the case!" He was adamant.

"OK," we said, "that means that if you headed the parts department you would never expect any input from the technicians, input that would establish you as their customer?" He nodded emphatically. "Then, as a technician, any of us in this workshop could come up to your parts window and demand the correct part without telling you the part number, or describing the piece of equipment that we are working on?" He frowned. "Also, you would expect no input from any of us on what we felt was the correct inventory and yet you would not expect any technicians to complain when the part we need, a part which by the way we might think is a common sense item to stock, was not available?"

"I see your point," he grumbled.

There are three roles that organizations and individuals play in the world of work.

- **Supplier.** Any person or organization who provides inputs of some form (materials, information, reports, and the like) to a work process.
- **Processor.** Any person or organization that takes inputs and performs work processes, or throughputs, on them, with the intention of adding value and satisfying the needs of one or more customers.
- **Customer.** Any person or organization who receives outputs from processors.

Of course, from the supplier's perspective, our processor is a customer, receiving the outputs of the supplier. And from the customer's perspective, our processor is a supplier, providing inputs. So far, this idea is fairly simple and is depicted in Figure 1.1.

For a simple work process, such as selling hot dogs, it's easy to figure out who is playing the various roles. The processor would be the one cooking

```
┌──────────┐  Inputs  ┌──────────┐  Outputs  ┌──────────┐
│ Suppliers│ ───────► │   Work   │ ────────► │ Customers│
│          │          │processors│           │          │
└──────────┘          └──────────┘           └──────────┘
```

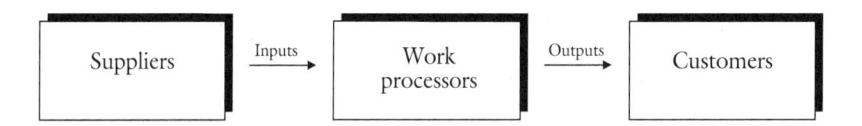

Figure 1.1. Supplier/processor/customer.

the wieners, steaming the buns, piling on the goodies, and taking the money. The suppliers would include the meat company, bakery, condiment distributors, and, at least in the beginning, the seller of hot dog stands and cooking equipment. Customers are all the lucky folks who get to eat the culinary masterpieces.

But in the more complex and multifaceted organizations found in most larger companies, customers and suppliers are everywhere and very often much less easily identified! Consider this example. You are the supervisor of several accountants, one of whom is Ann. On Monday morning you call Ann into your office and give her this assignment: "Ann, I want you to put together a report, by product line, on sales volume over the past quarter and projected sales volume for the next quarter. Show and analyze the data separately for each of the four marketing regions, but also show the combined results and recommend next quarter's inventory levels for our Chicago and Pittsburgh distribution centers. Have the report ready in one week. I want a copy sent to me and 22 copies each to the distribution centers. I also want two copies of the report as overhead slides, in case we're asked by senior management to give a presentation."

Ann leaves your office, and being a diligent employee, gets right to work. She calls the heads of the four marketing regions to relay your request, asking for the necessary information to be sent in two days. She then calls computer operations to get a quick program written to help arrange and analyze the expected data. A call to the office supply store results in the order of overhead slide blanks. Ann's immediate chores are completed with a call to the print shop (to alert them that she'll need a job done quickly in the week).

We can easily identify some of the customers in Ann's project. Certainly her boss is one. And the distribution centers in Chicago and Pittsburgh are others. We might call these her final customers, since they will receive the final output, the completed report. Her suppliers seem likewise apparent. The marketing regions, print shop, office supply store, and computer operations will all give Ann some input that will allow her to add value and satisfy the needs of her customers.

But are her boss and the two distribution centers the only customers that Ann has to satisfy? Certainly not! In fact, all of the groups that will be involved in Ann's project can be considered customers! Let's go back to our definition of customers—people or organizations who receive outputs from processors—and look at the other groups in Ann's project. Ann must give accurate, complete, and timely information about her requirements to the marketing regions. Without it, they will be reduced to guessing what it is she has asked for, and only with luck be able to later provide her with the information she really needs. In a similar way, Ann must describe to the office supply store her exact specifications for blank overhead slides. Her input to them might be a purchase order detailing timing, quantity, stock number, and/or other relevant descriptors that will enable the store to properly fill the order. Computer operations will work best if they too don't have to guess about Ann's expectations. In this case, of course, Ann may delegate some additional discretion of detailed design to the professionals, but they still need to know her basic needs. Even the best architect cannot design a good bridge without knowing which river it has to cross!

Each of these groups receives an output of some form from Ann. When they receive Ann's output, they are her customers. That output must satisfy their needs if they are to perform their work properly, be it the design of a program, the compilation of quarterly data, or the printing of the final report. Only then can they put on their other hats, first adding value as processors, and then performing the more immediately obvious roles as suppliers. We'll explore this idea in more detail later in this chapter. For now, though, remember: Everyone that Ann has dealt with in this project has been, at least for awhile, Ann's customer. As such, each has musts and wants of Ann that she must discover (or acknowledge if expressed by the customer)

Actually, in our earlier hot dog example the vendor is a customer too. The vendor needs accurate outputs from the buyer (how much mustard, onions, and so on) to properly meet the buyer's expectations. Unlike more leveraging work situations, though, all you as the buyer need to do is ask for more mustard!

Ann's project and all of the various relationships are shown in Figure 1.2.

Most American workers, like Ann, are diligent, hardworking, and loyal. They commonly do their jobs in the manner they see best, and are usually viewed by themselves and others as effective. But too often they recognize only a limited number of customers whose needs must be satisfied: themselves, the immediate recipient of their outputs, and perhaps their boss. Because of these unintentional blinders, they fail to recognize the critical importance of providing accurate information, instructions, insights, specifications, or deadlines to all those people on whose inputs they will eventually depend. Communication with suppliers is haphazard.

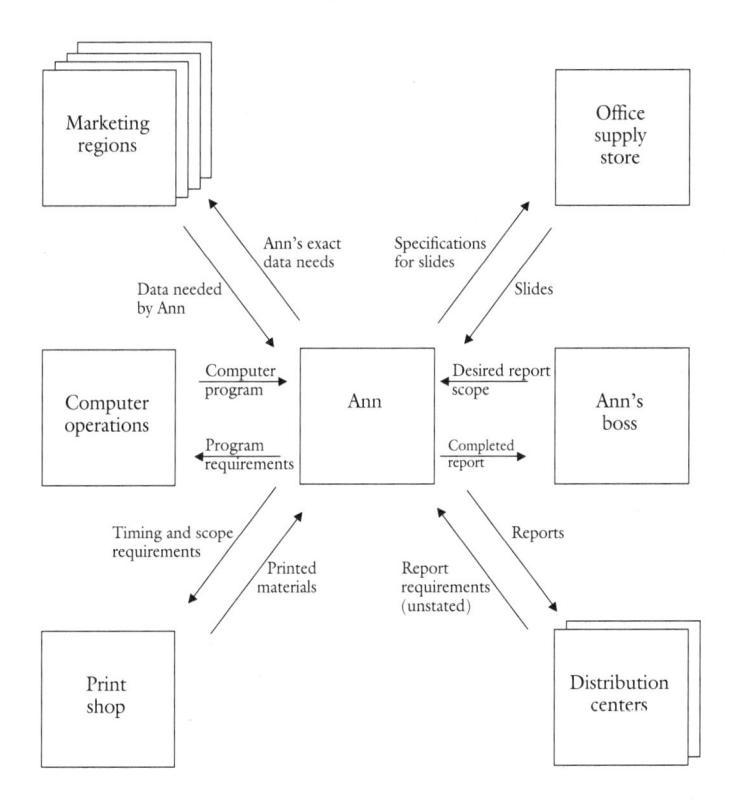

Figure 1.2. Ann's project.

Assumptions are made about what these suppliers need to know to do their jobs. ("They better know what I want without me having to do half their job for them!")

And so, the inputs that our workers do receive are inferior. And with inferior input, Ann's efforts to process them (create an acceptable report) will result in one of two unwanted outcomes. She might not be able to satisfy her final customers—her boss and the distribution centers. Or more likely, she will satisfy her final customers, but only after adding far more value to the inputs than should be required—by reworking the numbers, calling for more information, conducting extra meetings with computer operations, personally picking up office supplies at the last minute; in short, processing the inputs to death. Time better spent on other activities is wasted. Quality has failed. Unknowingly, Ann has in her haste been a major cause of the failure. But Ann's most likely reaction to her boss is "those #*!^&%$ people in the regions screwed it up again!" Sound familiar?

We have found that everyone in an organization is simultaneously a supplier, a customer, and a processor. Everyone is a processor because everyone does some sort of job, receiving inputs of various types, adding value to them by the job they do, and providing some form of output. Since they receive inputs, however, they are also customers, and should ensure that their musts and wants of those inputs are accurately and completely communicated to the input supplier. Finally, since they generate value-added outputs, they are also suppliers and must satisfy the musts and wants of those to whom they provide the outputs. The organization that can recognize all of its myriad customers, fully understand the complete needs of each, and then fulfill those needs in the most effective and efficient way, has found the path to quality. In chapter 4 we will show some of the tools and procedures that can make this happen.

We can now expand our simple view of supplier/work processor/customer that was shown in Figure 1.1 to include these new ideas (see Figure 1.3).

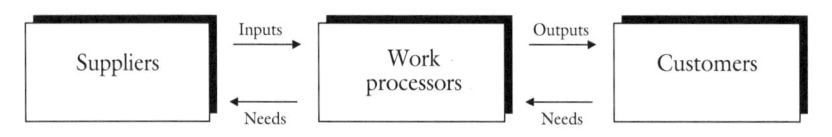

Figure 1.3. Supplier/processor/customer.

[Conformity] abandons evolution, repudiates the once popular concept of progress, and regards America as a finished product, perfect and complete.

—Henry Steele Commager

A Quality Definition for Everyone

Let's look again at our definition of quality. Quality in the workplace comes from understanding, and then fully meeting, the needs of all your internal and external customers, now and into the future, and doing so with continual improvement in efficiency and effectiveness.

We have seen that the key to continual improvement in quality begins with the identification of your customers, and their needs. Your customers typically supply you with information about what they want from you, which if complete and accurate, meets your needs from them. Next, your suppliers must be identified. You should be able to provide to them an accurate and complete list of your needs, and in this sense they are your customers. In almost every transaction in business, each party to the transaction is at one point or another a customer. Which is simply to say, "let me know your needs, and I'll endeavor to fill them!"

Can this definition apply to any job or organization that may exist in a company? From manufacturing to engineering, from accounting to marketing, and from personnel to customer service? Al Bigelow, the president of SlowSpoke Bicycle Company, a manufacturer and direct marketer of fine bicycles, wanted to find out. He called a meeting with three of his employees, Lois, the vice president of marketing, Jack, the production superintendent, and Bill, the customer service supervisor.

"People," he said, "I want to see what all this fuss about wants and musts means. Seems that everybody's talking about their needs. Who's getting any work done? I want each of you to clear this up for once and for all. Each of you deals with a lot of people, that's why I asked you to this meeting. I want each of you to figure out who your suppliers are, and what your musts and wants of them might be. Then, do the same for your customers. Let me see the results a week from today!"

The three decided to meet for a few extra minutes to decide on a format for the results. Bill, the customer services supervisor, decided to meet with his boss to talk about the assignment. Jack scheduled a meeting with his production foremen to occur between shifts later that day. And Lois decided to think, by herself, about marketing's suppliers and customers before she solicited the input of her marketing managers.

After a week of writing, thinking, and meeting with their respective department staffs, Bill, Jack, and Lois were ready to present their findings to Mr. Bigelow. He had asked Norm Burns, SlowSpoke's quality assurance manager, to join the meeting as an observer. Norm had been one of the proponents of formally determining musts and wants. Lois was first. She handed the president her results, which are shown in Figure 1.4.

"My list is pretty straightforward," she began. "We rely on three organizations as suppliers. Production, of course, creates the product that we sell. And then we get support from several advertising agencies and ACME, who prints our brochures. We know what we need from them, and all I had to do was think about those needs in terms of *musts* and *wants*. You can see our thoughts on that sheet. I frankly can't think of any other customers except the obvious ones: the people who buy the bicycles, and you, Al. After all, you give us an annual revenue goal, and expect us to meet it within our budget. We don't have any problem understanding what you want of us, Al, and the customers certainly vote with their sales."

"Good," said Al Bigelow. "That seems complete. Thanks for a good job." He turned to the others. "Gentlemen, who's next?"

"My production foremen and I came to the same conclusion, Al," said Jack while handing his report to the president (see Figure 1.5). "The report you're holding is straightforward. We know who our suppliers and customers are, and everyone has a firm understanding of their needs, or musts and wants if you prefer."

"Likewise with customer service, Mr. Bigelow," chimed in Bill. "Here's our report. Nothing new that we could uncover." And Bill handed the president his report, shown as Figure 1.6.

"Hmmm. I see. Well, I conclude that there is some value in this must and want business, but it certainly appears that here at SlowSpoke we've got the situation well in hand." And with that Bigelow dropped the three reports on his desk and turned to his quality assurance manager. "Norm, don't you agree?"

Norm reached over the front of the desk and picked up the reports. "Well, Al," he began while looking at the reports, "I would agree that Lois, Jack, and Bill did a fine job of determining their suppliers and customers,

Work process:	Establish marketing strategy, advertising, selling of company products
Suppliers:	Production *(product)* Advertising agency *(marketing themes)* ACME Printing Company *(sales brochures)*
Customers:	Retail customer *(product)* President *(department goals)*
Marketing's musts and wants of our suppliers	*Production:* They must manufacture all standard products within specifications and projected timetable. Want special orders completed within two weeks. *Advertising agency:* They must respond to all requests for marketing themes within six working days. Must be within 5% of established budget. Want 5%/year revenue growth attributed to marketing strategy. *ACME Printing:* They must prepare printed materials according to specifications, within two hours of agreed-upon time. Defectives must not exceed 1:10,000.
Customers' musts and wants of marketing:	*Retail customers:* We must sell a product fully meeting brochure specifications. They want maintenance-free cycling for at least five years. Want good styling and value. Must deliver within two weeks of order. *President:* We must achieve revenue goals for budget year, and stay within 2% of department budget. Must replace and train any departing salespeople within 60 days of opening. Want 5% growth above budget. Want improved department morale.

Figure 1.4. Suppliers and customers of marketing.

18 Breakthrough Quality Improvement

Work process:	Manufacture of standard and custom company products.
Suppliers:	Engineering *(design)* Suppliers *(parts, materials)* Scheduling *(production schedule)*
Customers:	Quality assurance *(specifications met)* Marketing *(product)* Production vice president *(goals)*
Production's: musts and wants of our suppliers	*Engineering:* They must provide accurate design and manufacturing specifications. Want technical support to upgrade manufacturing capabilities. *Suppliers:* They must provide ordered materials exactly to specifications. Parts must be available no later than one shift prior to use. Want new ideas on substitute materials. *Scheduling:* They must meet each Wednesday with production superintendent to ensure production's input schedule. Must provide final weekly schedules by 8 A.M. the preceding Friday.
Customers' musts and wants of *production:*	*Quality assurance:* We must manufacture bicycles that meet all QA specs. Waste must remain below 1% on total materials. Must reduce rework time by 25% this budget year. *Marketing:* We must manufacture bicycles that meet brochure specs. Must produce all special orders within two weeks. *Production vice president:* We must manufacture within +/−5 units of weekly scheduled production. Must be within 1% of budget. Must reduce third shift by two employees; want three. Want maintenance costs and downtime reduced by 10%.

Figure 1.5. Suppliers and customers of production.

Work process:	Liaison with past and prospective customers on questions of product use, warranty, and customer accounts.
Suppliers:	Accounting *(customer account information)* Marketing *(customer demographics)* Engineering *(technical information)* Scheduling *(availability information)*
Customers:	Retail customer *(product)* Administration vice president *(goals)*
Customer service's musts and wants of our suppliers:	*Accounting:* They must update computer entries on customer accounts daily by 10 A.M. *Marketing:* We want data on customer demographics within one month of sale. *Engineering:* They must provide accurate technical data and parts lists for each model within one week after its introduction. *Scheduling:* They must provide production schedules and inventory levels each Tuesday by 9 A.M.
Customers' musts and wants of customer service:	*Retail customers:* We must answer phones within five rings. Information requiring research must be called back within 24 hours. *Administration vice president:* We must receive no more than 10 customer complaints per quarter. We must conform to within 1% of budget. Want 5% staff reduction.

Figure 1.6. Suppliers and customers of customer service.

and the respective musts and wants. Especially for a first effort. There are, however, a few points I'd like to make.

"First, I see that Bill identified marketing as a supplier of information about customer demographics to customer service."

"That's right," interrupted Lois. "We send them information so that they have a better idea of the typical age, likely bicycle usage, and other data that helps them do their job better."

"I see," Norm continued. "But that means that Bill and his customer service people are one of *your* customers, and I don't see that on your report, Lois."

"How can that be so important? We've been sending them that information for years. It's no big deal, Norm!"

"Well, I'm sure your system of sharing data works just fine . . . in this case," Norm answered. "Often though, an organization I'll call A, thinks that organization B is supposed to supply it with something. But B doesn't see organization A as its customer. It might mean that B just doesn't agree that A should get the input. Or, it may mean that B doesn't know that A expects the information. You'd be surprised how often these problems arise in real organizations, even though it would seem pretty easy to work through them."

Lois nodded slowly. "So by making sure that both sides of a supplier-customer relationship such as ours with customer service are identified, we can avoid misunderstandings and missed deadlines, things like that?"

"That's right," said Norm. "We're much more likely to meet our customers' needs if everyone recognizes the respective roles, and both the suppliers and customers define musts and wants of each other. If both see the needs the same way, fine. If not, something has to change to correct the situation."

"Yes," said a thoughtful Bigelow. "I see your point. What other comments do you have, Norm?"

"So far, it has been fairly easy to see these customer-supplier relationships, even though both sides are sometimes accidently omitted, as was done by Lois. But we also have to recognize that each customer-supplier relationship is also the reverse, a supplier-customer relationship, if you will."

"I don't follow you," said Jack, puzzled.

"Jack, you identified one of your customer-supplier relationships as production-engineering. Production, the customer, expects engineering, the supplier, to supply design and other technical specifications so that you know what it is you're supposed to build, right?"

"That's right, Norm."

"We want both you and engineering to agree on the specific musts and wants. That is, your musts and wants of your supplier, engineering, should exactly match engineering's view of the musts and wants of their customer, you. But that's only half the story, Jack. What kinds of things do you have to tell engineering that help them do their job?"

Jack thought a minute. "Let's see. They should have an idea about limits in our manufacturing capability, for example, so that they don't give us an impossible design. I guess in a similar way they need to know how many units we expect to make in a week. If a new design is being planned for introduction, say, in March, we need to have the specifications three months earlier to ensure we can have product ready on time. Things like that."

Norm looked triumphant. "So Jack, while it's easy to see engineering as your supplier, you can now recognize that they need outputs from you to do that job. So although they are your supplier, they are at the same time your customer!

"For example, one of their musts of you might be to provide them with whatever information might be necessary to help them in their design work. Or, to let them know that you need three months lead time for a design to become a finished bicycle. That kind of information is an output to them: they're your customer. It may seem like a nit-picking detail, but in my view it's those details that result in genuine and continual improvement in quality around here."

"You know," said Bigelow taking back the reports from Norm Burns, "none of you showed the reverse of the relationships on these reports. But it makes sense to do so. I want each of you to return to your organizations, and add to your reports those reverse musts and wants that Norm's talking about. Then let's meet again, say, same time tomorrow?"

The next day, Lois, Jack, and Bill came into the president's office, and handed him and Norm Burns copies of their expanded reports (see Figures 1.7, 1.8, and 1.9). Bigelow spoke first. "These are really interesting. Norm, what do you think?"

"Just quickly looking at this, I'd say everyone has done a great job! For example, look at the marketing and production groups reports. Their original view of themselves as supplier-customer, with marketing being the customer in this case, led to a set of musts and wants that are virtually identical. I would guess," Norm continued, looking up at Lois and Jack, "that you two aren't surprised by that?"

"Well, no. We did meet to share our respective input," said Lois.

22 Breakthrough Quality Improvement

Work process:	Establish marketing strategy, advertising, selling of company products.
Suppliers:	Production *(product)* Advertising agency *(marketing themes)* ACME Printing Company *(sales brochures)*
Customers:	Retail customer *(product)* President *(department goals)*
Marketing's musts and wants of our suppliers:	*Production:* They must manufacture all standard products within specifications and projected timetable. Want special orders completed within two weeks. In return, we must provide accurate and complete product requisitions within established delivery expectations. *Advertising agency:* They must respond to all requests for marketing themes within six working days. Must be within 5% of established budget. Want 5%/year revenue growth attributed to marketing strategy. In return, we must provide a marketing liaison to answer any questions within one hour, or meet within one work day. *ACME Printing:* They must prepare printed materials according to specifications, within two hours of agreed-upon time. Defectives must not exceed 1:10,000. In return, we must provide camera-ready originals to their specifications. Also, they want us to deliver rush projects Wednesday through Friday.
Customers' musts and wants of marketing:	*Retail customers:* We must sell a product fully meeting brochure specifications. They want maintenance-free cycling for at least five years. Want good styling and value. Must deliver within two weeks of order. In return, we want customers to provide feedback on good/bad aspects of our product. *President:* We must achieve revenue goals for budget year, and stay within 2% of department budget. Must replace and train any departing salespeople within 60 days of opening. Want 5% growth above budget. Want improved department morale. In return, we want support when requested and timely information on changes that may affect strategies and goals.

Figure 1.7.   Suppliers and customers of marketing.

Work process:	Manufacture of standard and custom company products.
Suppliers:	Engineering *(design)* Suppliers *(parts, materials)* Scheduling *(production schedule)*
Customers:	Quality assurance *(specifications met)* Marketing *(product)* Production vice president *(goals)*
Production's musts and wants of our suppliers:	*Engineering:* They must provide accurate design and manufacturing specifications. Want technical support to upgrade manufacturing capabilities. In return, we must share changes in manufacturing capability within one week of making them. We must specify exact lead-time requirements for new designs in each product line. *Suppliers:* They must provide ordered materials exactly to specifications. Parts must be available no later than one shift prior to use. Want new ideas on substitute materials. In return, we must provide accurate and complete purchase requisitions at least three weeks prior to desired shipping date. *Scheduling:* They must meet each Wednesday with production superintendent to ensure production's input schedule. Must provide final weekly schedules by 8 A.M. the preceding Friday. In return, we want to be flexible in scheduling, recognizing that scheduling often must deal with conflicting demands.
Customers' musts and wants of production:	*Quality assurance:* We must manufacture bicycles that meet all QA specs. Waste must remain below 1% on total materials. Must reduce rework time by 25% this budget year. In return, we must have feedback on worsening quality statistics within one day of their discovery. *Marketing:* We must manufacture bicycles that meet brochure specs. Must produce all special orders within two weeks. In return, we want an extra week of production time when possible. *Production vice president:* We must manufacture within +/−5 units of weekly scheduled production. Must be within 1% of budget. Must reduce third shift by two employees; want three. Want maintenance costs and downtime reduced by 10%. In return, we want biweekly attendance at production staff meetings to facilitate the sharing of production problems and opportunities.

Figure 1.8. Suppliers and customers of production.

Work process:	Liaison with past and prospective customers on questions of product use, warranty, and customer accounts.
Suppliers:	Accounting *(customer account information)* Marketing *(customer demographics)* Engineering *(technical information)* Scheduling *(availability information)*
Customers:	Retail customer *(product)* Administration vice president *(goals)*
Customer service's musts and wants of our suppliers:	*Accounting:* They must update computer entries on customer accounts daily by 10 A.M. In return, we accept that during month-end closing, computer entries may be delayed one day. *Marketing:* We want data on customer demographics within one month of sale. In return, we must provide them with monthly reports on complaint trends. *Engineering:* They must provide accurate technical data and parts lists for each model within one week after its introduction. In return, we must provide them with monthly reports on complaint trends. *Scheduling:* They must provide production schedules and inventory levels each Tuesday by 9 A.M. In return, we must not make scheduling promises to customers that we know cannot be achieved.
Customers' musts and wants of *customer service:*	*Retail customers:* We must answer phones within five rings. Information requiring research must be called back within 24 hours. In return, we want them to be courteous. *Administration vice president:* We must receive no more than 10 customer complaints per quarter. We must conform to within 1% of budget. Want 5% staff reduction. In return, we want clear goals and support when requested.

Figure 1.9. Suppliers and customers of customer service.

"That's good. That's exactly what you should have done. And now you've added more. Lois, you now recognize that Jack is your customer too. And that in return for his meeting your needs, or I should say to enable him to meet your needs, you have to provide some outputs to him, and when you do, he's your customer. Jack, you've done the same thing."

Bigelow looked pleased as he turned to Norm. "So, that's pretty much it, then?"

"I'm afraid not, Al," responded Norm. "Now the real work begins. There are at least three steps that should be taken right away. First, all these mutual expectations need to be polished. Are they complete? Are the musts really measurable? Are they specific? For example, do we really know what the phrase 'a complete and accurate requisition' means? Then, each group needs to sit down and make sure that each of these musts and wants between suppliers and customers, both the first ones we did and the 'reverse' ones, is agreeable to each group. If they aren't, some negotiation might be needed."

"How do we do that with our retail customers?" Bigelow wondered aloud.

Lois looked up from the reports. "We do some of that now, Al. Our market research, for example, includes customer questionnaires that in effect tell us their musts and wants."

"I see," nodded Bigelow. "OK, Norm, what else?"

"Well, I'm not going to question whether these musts and wants are the best we can achieve, at least not today. We will talk about that in the next few weeks. For now, though, I can tell you that I'm going to want to poke at these some when they're all polished up and negotiated. Some of them, such as customer service's acceptance of late data at month-end closing, don't seem at all necessary to me. We should strive for perfection. But as I say, that's a subject for another meeting."

Bigelow stood up, signaling the end of the meeting. "Well, I'm convinced this is doing us some good. Frankly, I must confess I'm a bit surprised. I thought we really had things completely figured out. I want each of you to follow Norm's plan, and then schedule a follow-up meeting. Norm, I'm going to meet with each of the other departments to get them started on this kind of project. I'll want to review my approach with you before then, to make sure I'm covering all the bases."

"That would be just fine, Al!"

SlowSpoke Bicycle Company thus began its journey toward continual improvement in all facets of its business. A lot of work remained, but a firm recognition of who its many customers were, and that their needs must be satisfied, was a great start.

In a later chapter, we'll show how employees in any organization can apply a tool called *work process analysis* to identify customers and suppliers and their respective musts and wants. Even more important, we'll look at the steps needed when those musts and wants are *not* being met.

> *If the government was as afraid of disturbing the consumer as it is of disturbing business, this would be some democracy.*
> —Frank McKinney Hubbard

The External Customer

As we talk about the importance of customers, both internal and external, it is useful to pause for a while and consider some of the interesting aspects of the external customer, and how organizations with strong quality beliefs view the external customer.

Figure 1.10a depicts an organization of any company in a typical hierarchical manner, with a CEO or other organizational head at the top and the workers at the bottom. Often, this pyramid is viewed in two ways. First, it is thought to show the importance to the organization. The CEO sets the strategy that determines the future of the enterprise, and if one views the relative compensation paid to each of the levels, the CEO is said to be the most important member of the organization. Second, the pyramid shows the typical interactions within the organization. On a day-to-day basis, the CEO usually interacts with his or her executives or senior management. The workers usually interact with their managers and supervisors.

Where, then, does the external customer fit on this diagram? The external customer most frequently interacts with the workers, such as salespeople, customer service, billing, and so on. So we might show the external customer as in Figure 1.10b, according to the typical interactions within the organization. But Figure 1.10b, when viewed as showing importance to the organization, places the external customer as the least important element of

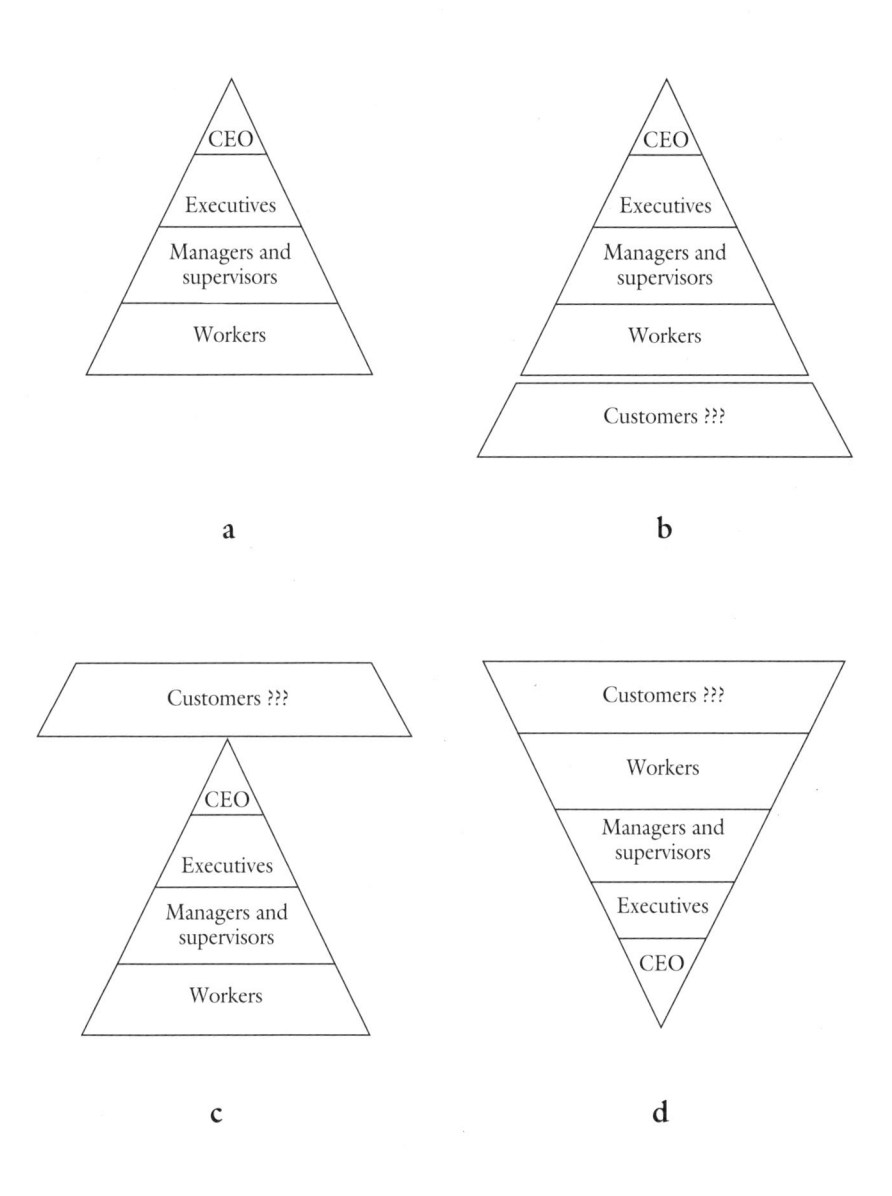

Figure 1.10. Looking at a company's structure and its customers—some old ways and a new way.

the business. Only the most unenlightened of companies would accept such a view.

Well, perhaps if the external customer is, in fact, the most important element of the organization, we ought to show the relationship as in Figure 1.10c. But now we must assume that typical interactions with the customer occur with the CEO. Except for a few very important customers, or with very complex or expensive projects, that is not usually the case.

Quality-conscious companies often solve this enigma by depicting themselves as shown in Figure 1.10d. The external customer *is* the most important element in the organization. The correct interactions are shown. Workers are a very important part of the organization, since they interact most frequently with the external customer.

Is the CEO position relatively unimportant? Not at all, but the importance to the organization is considered differently. Organizations that embrace Figure 1.10a see the CEO as leader; someone to follow. Organizations that embrace the situation shown in Figure 1.10d, however, see the CEO and other senior levels of the organization as the *foundation* that supports the workers' efforts. Support comes from ensuring that the organization's strategy, tactics, and work are all consistently aimed at a common goal. It comes from the provision of necessary resources (tools, space, skills) to the workers. Without the senior levels, the edifice would crumble. But without the workers, nothing of importance to the external customer can occur.

> *Our plans miscarry because they have no aim. When a man does not know what harbor he is making for, no wind is the right wind.*
> —Seneca

A New Way to View the Role of Any Organization

In the course of working with many organizations, at all levels, we have often asked people about their perceptions of their roles and that of their organization. Questions are usually fairly straightforward: What do you do? What is the role of your organization? What is your job?"

The typical answer would probably surprise no one. The content of the answer would, of course, reflect the kind of job or organization about which we asked; engineers do different things than secretaries, for example. So we hear things like the following:

- "I inspect our products to approve them for shipment."
- "My organization is responsible for the maintenance of this facility and its production equipment."
- "I perform secretarial duties for Ms. Smith."

All of these statements are quite reasonable. At one level of detail or another, they all describe the basic duties, responsibilities, and activities—the role, of an employee or organization. Yet it became more and more apparent to us that these kinds of role descriptions are flawed! They automatically perpetuate a culture that makes quality improvement very difficult if not impossible. How can that be true? In fact, these *are* the things that these people do every day. What could be wrong?

The structure of the answers is almost always the same, and each has two common characteristics that can cause problems. First, these responses tell the tasks being performed: inspection, equipment maintenance, various secretarial duties, and so on. This is what I do. Such descriptions do nothing to suggest that those tasks may or may not be the right things to do. They do not force employees or organizations to continually recognize their obligations to meet the needs of their customers.

The second troublesome characteristic of these responses is that they are all rooted in the present. This is what I do now. But since no reference is made to a future that may be different, one can assume that the role is locked in cement. It will never change because no language of change is used. As customer needs change, which they inevitably will, the old ways of doing things will just continue.

We believe that extremely detailed job descriptions should be thrown away. They perpetuate standardized work done by inflexible workers and organizations. They demand that something be done right, but not necessarily that the right things be done right. Instead, establish broad areas of responsibility for your people and organizations, and then communicate your current musts and wants as the manager responsible for those organizations. The role of the organizations and their employees then becomes a simple modification of our quality definition. The role of our employees and their organizations is to array themselves and their resources to understand, and then fully meet, the needs of all their internal and external customers, now and into the future, and to do so with continual improvement in efficiency and effectiveness.

The nature of the duties performed by an organization and its employees are then defined by its broad area of responsibilities, or its *function*, be that the provision of computer services, personnel activities or equipment maintenance. But the specific things that are done on a daily basis to fulfill those duties will be determined by the needs of the many customers that we have seen exist within and outside of each organization. Those specific things will change as the needs of customers change. And the organization and its employees will begin the journey toward genuine quality in the workplace.

So, recognition of the inevitability of change is important. When combined with the flexibility to adjust to change, significant improvement occurs. But such recognition of inevitable change, by itself, may not be enough. Changes may be made that seem to satisfy organization's many customers, of an organization, but are, in fact, not the best solutions to implement. To explore this idea further, let's look at how we define an organization's function. We had said earlier that function defined the broad area of customer needs that an organization and its employees serve. Systems analysts serve data processing needs, whereas electricians serve the company's needs for electrical power.

Often, an organization makes a serious mistake by defining its function too narrowly. For example, let's take the case of the dissatisfied warehousing manager, George. George was responsible for six warehouses in the New England area. The warehouses received and then inventoried a wide array of materials from manufacturers, and later supplied them as requested to a chain of 14 retail department stores. George had been concerned for some time about growing problems within his operation. As a result, he called a meeting of his six warehouse supervisors.

The group quickly quieted down when they saw the stern look on George's face. "People," he said, "I want to talk about some concerns that have been keeping me awake at night. Our costs have been skyrocketing. This year alone, I think we're going to be 10 percent over budget. That's a real problem, especially since I promised that we'd find a way to reduce costs this year. On top of that, I'm getting more and more complaints from the stores about mistakes in shipments. You know as well as I that those complaints don't just come to me. We're going to hear plenty more about them. And then there's this," and he held up a memo. "Management has decided to open a new section in each store specializing in fine sporting gear. I've done some quick calculations, and this decision will require at least another 6 percent storage capacity in our operation."

"George," one of the supervisors piped up. "Most of us can't store our current inventory with the space we have available."

"I know. That and these other problems are why we're here. We need some solutions, and we need them right now! We're going to run the best warehousing operation in the business, or I'm going to know why. My boss, and the store managers, aren't going to put up with this situation for very long, I guarantee you. Now, let's get to work and figure out what we're going to do about this mess!"

The meeting continued, with ideas and arguments being shared by all. George had begun the session by demonstrating the importance of satisfying their customers' needs, especially those of his boss and the store managers. He was aware that his organization was not meeting those needs, and had decided to do something about it. George has also kicked off the meeting by defining the purpose of his organization—to run the best warehousing operation in the business. And with this definition of purpose, George had, without realizing it, defined the nature of acceptable suggestions and proposals from his group: all should be targeted at the optimum performance of that purpose. All should deal with warehousing. Let's return to the meeting, about an hour later.

"Now," said George, looking up from several pages of notes he had taken. "Let's see if I can summarize all of this. First, I'll put together a request for capital expense for the purchase and installation of six of these new technology conveyor systems. I think the system that Hank recommended is the right one for us. Oh, by the way, Hank, nice job of comparing available systems. I have no doubt that there might be some trouble getting management to consider this request, considering our budget performance to date. On the other hand, we've all agreed that we can each reduce three loaders as a result." He scribbled some quick figures on his pad. "The payback on the cost looks like it might be about two years, which is pretty good.

"Next, we'll move one of the displaced loaders into a new job, called shipment inspector. Gene, I want you to put together the actual description of this job. You know what we're taking about. This new person will be an additional check to ensure that the shipments going out to stores match the request.

"Finally, I guess we're not going to get too far in requesting additional construction to deal with our space problem. But your idea, Susan, about using some of the older trailers as temporary storage space, might just work. Put a pencil to paper and let me know in a day or two how you'd actually suggest we do that."

George concluded the meeting feeling better than he had for weeks. Three problems had been raised, and three pretty good solutions developed. Sure, he wasn't excited about trying to get more money for the new conveyor systems, but he hoped management would be able to see a good short-term payout on that. And the idea of letting people go had never appealed to him. But after all, his supervisors would have to face that unpleasant task, and it was their idea. George mused out loud. "Darn good group of people! All I had to do was ask, and they didn't let me down."

All the solutions, of course, were targeted at the warehouses. George had made it very clear at the beginning of the meeting that the purpose of the group was to run a good warehousing system. Try as they might, they had been unable to generate any better ideas than these, restricted as they were to improvement of the current system.

What if George had started the meeting differently? Let's give him another chance.

"That and these other problems are why we're here. We need some solutions, and we need them right now! One thing before we start, though. I want to make sure we consider every option we have. You know, I've given a lot of thought to why we're here. The quick and obvious answer is to 'run warehouses'. But then I realized that our ultimate customers, the retail buyers, don't care whether we run warehouses or slice bread. All they really expect is that the store is not out of whatever it is they want to buy. So, I guess our purpose is to make sure that doesn't happen. Let's keep that thought in mind as we consider our options, and see where it takes us. We've got to do something, because my boss and the store managers aren't going to put up with this situation for very long, I guarantee you. Now, let's get to work and figure out what we're going to do about this mess!"

Good for George! He has managed to set the tone for considerably expanded thinking by his supervisors. They are no longer restricted to running a warehouse system. Their purpose is now much broader: to ensure that inventory is always available to the retail buyer at the point of purchase. (Of course there may still be some reluctance to suggest solutions that might cause the demise of their jobs!) Two hours later, this second version of the meeting was just winding up.

"Now," said George, looking up from several pages of notes he had taken. "Let's see if I can summarize all of this." George proceeded to review the same ideas of new conveyors, reduced staff, an inspector's job, and the use of old trailers as emergency storage space. "Those ideas look good," he continued, "but I'm really interested in some of these other approaches that we've generated. Maria, I'm giving you the job of detailing your idea of negotiating more frequent shipments from manufacturers directly to the stores. Bypassing our operation on some key items would certainly help both our storage problems and their inventory gaps. Then, I'm going to make a few calls to store managers and set up some time to talk with them about increased levels of inventory at the stores. I think there's some room to negotiate there, and that should help everybody out.

"Finally, this long-term plan we've batted around might have some merit." George shuffled his notes. "Here it is. Consolidation of our six warehouses into two major distribution centers, here and here." George stood and tapped the wall map with his pencil. "Yes, I think that's beginning to look like a solid long-term plan. Certainly not something to propose for now, but it may guide us in thinking about our options. It should certainly slow down our enthusiasm for those new conveyor systems for our present operation. I want to meet again in two weeks and go over what we've learned. Then we should be ready to make some sensible recommendations."

George's people were not restricted to warehousing when their purpose was more broadly defined. Though they still developed the alternatives that might be expected, they now in addition saw a bigger picture which included several other and new ways to satisfy their customers' needs: having product available at the stores at the time of purchase.

> *The greatest discovery of my generation is that human beings, by changing the inner attitudes of their minds, can change the outer aspects of their lives. . . . It is too bad that more people will not accept this tremendous discovery and begin living it.*
>
> —William James

The Meaning of Quality

We began this chapter with a new definition of quality. Quality in the workplace comes from understanding, and then fully meeting, the needs of all your internal and external customers, now and into the future, and doing so with continual improvement in efficiency and effectiveness.

Simply put, quality is the meeting of your customers' needs. Those customers are everywhere, as we have seen with SlowSpoke Bicycle Company's efforts. And George has demonstrated the value of expanded thinking of purpose when deciding how to meet those needs.

Some years ago, Friden was a major manufacturer of mechanical calculators. Theirs was one of the best on the market. But Friden made a classic business error. They viewed their purpose as manufacturing mechanical calculators. They assumed that their customers would continue to need mechanical calculators. They were wrong. Customers wanted quick, reliable, and accurate calculating ability, without great cost. The advent of the silicon chip was destined to eliminate the mechanical calculator market just as the advent of the internal combustion engine ended the buggy whip market. Two simple acts might have prevented Friden's fall from this market: finding out what the customers' needs were, perhaps by thorough market surveys and customer focus groups; and proper definition of its purpose, not to provide the best mechanical calculators, but rather to place into the general public's hands the power to calculate arithmetic values quickly and accurately.

Skepticism about quality still exists in too many of our companies. Quality antagonistic environments, of which senior managers are sometimes unaware, promote the policies of "do what you're doing until we tell you to stop or change," or "we know what is best for our customers," or "we've always done it this way." A quality supportive environment, coupled with the specific skills that will enable people to perform this job of meeting customers' needs, will greatly enhance quality within both manufacturing and service sectors.

In the next chapter we'll look more closely at quality antagonistic environments and quality supportive environments.

2 The Environment of Quality

We trained hard—but it seemed that every time we were beginning to form up into teams, we would be reorganized. I was to learn later in life that we tend to meet any new situation by reorganization, and a wonderful method it can be for creating the illusion of progress while producing confusion, inefficiency, and demoralization.

—Pretonius Arbitier

Quality cannot happen without the absolute commitment of management. It is not enough to agree to let it happen. It is not enough to promote it through slogans and posters. The management of a company must first reorder its thinking, to find within itself the ability to change old ways of thinking about and running the business. It must genuinely believe that in this changing world, quality equals profitability, and that no other way will do. It must insist on the conversion of all the company's employees to the complete belief in quality.

Often, management installs a quality program of some sort while lacking a genuine belief that such a program is right. Managers *let* their people get some training, work on some teams, and make some suggestions. They skeptically await the results, knowing deep inside that this new cost of doing business is most likely a waste of time, and will inevitably die out. Of course, such prophecies are always self-fulfilling. Employees who might recognize the need for change, and who might want to do a superior and continually improving job, are punished in many subtle ways for doing so. They might be considered too slow or unable to take directions. Their judgments might be questioned. And in one way or another, managers will perpetuate its beliefs by promoting those people who think the same way they do.

The environment of quality begins with management. Management's commitment to and drive toward quality must be genuine. Halfway measures do not work for very long.

Stupid men, knowing the way of life, and having once laughed at it, laugh again the louder. If you need to be sure which way is right, you can tell by their laughing at it.

—Lao Tzu

The Nonquality Environment

Here is a speech given before the Society of American Companies Resolved to Keep the Old Ways (SACRED KOWS), presented by C. Roland Dugan, president of Dugan Manufacturing, on June 12, 1985.

"Committee members, distinguished ladies and gentlemen of the Society, I want to thank you today for inviting me to this important meeting of your Society. We face difficult times in American companies, and I am honored by this opportunity you have given me to say a few words about what I believe will keep the United States as strong as it has always been. You know, it used to be that we could point to the label *Made in the U.S.A.* with a lot of pride. People all over the world knew that when a product, any kind of product, was made by American workers, it would be the best available. Well, ladies and gentlemen, that's now all changed, I'm afraid. And I think you know why. Competition from other countries, you know who they are, who work their people almost nonstop and pay almost no wages, is completely unfair!" *(Applause)*

"Now, I could easily talk for another hour about why American workers ought to be protected by new and tougher tariffs and other restrictions on these unfair competitors. But that's only part of the story, and not the reason you've invited me to speak today. Today I want to talk about a subject that is fast becoming unfashionable. What really *is* a company in business for? Who is it *responsible* to? Why do we think that the old ways *can't still work?* Ladies and gentlemen, I for one am getting sick and tired of people pushing American companies around! We've done it right for over 200 years, and by golly we'll continue to do it right for the next 200!" *(Applause)*

"I'm the president of a medium-sized company. We manufacture and sell office furniture, maybe even the chairs you're sitting on right now. I'd know if my glasses were up to snuff." *(Laughter)*

"Now, I've been around a long, long time, and if there's one thing I've become sure of, it's what my job is as the president of my company. Put very simply, my job is to make a profit, year after year. We're a publicly held company, and our shareholders have a right to expect a profit. And our employees also have a right to expect a profit! They have a right to keep their jobs!

"Let me tell you about some of the things I have to do every day to protect my employees' and my shareholders' rights. Every day the mail is filled with brochures talking about all kinds of ways I can spend my employees' and my shareholders' profits. Every day the phone rings at least five times, and do you know who the caller is? Somebody who wants me to spend my employees' and my shareholders' profits. On what? On programs that guarantee nothing, take a lot of time and money, and give absolutely no return on my investment.

"The mail goes in the wastebasket unopened. The calls are not returned. That's what the role of the American senior manager has become. Fighting off predators selling useless junk. The last thing I need to do is spend my profits on useless junk.

"What is this junk, as I call it? It all has to do with the new seven-letter buzzword in America, *quality*. You know, you would think that the people pushing these programs on us believe that we, all of us, don't know what quality is! Well, I say we do know what quality is. Its what American companies have been churning out for 200 years. And I don't need a consultant to tell me otherwise!" *(Lots of applause)*

"Let me be more specific. Quality is doing your job, that's what it is. And making a good profit by doing it. It is *not* fixing things that are not broken! It is *not* pretending that our customers have somehow gotten smarter than us in running our business! It is not pretending that perfection is possible, because as long as people do jobs, they will make mistakes. It is not sitting around wringing your hands over mistakes. After all, all that can ever do is lower morale. To err, ladies and gentlemen, is human. And I don't think any of those consultants who call and write every day have figured out how to change men and women to make them perfect!

"There's another thing I hear all the time. People are always telling me that I have to meet my customers' needs. Well, that's exactly what we *are* doing! I said before that I certainly don't expect my customers to have to become experts in my business. That's why I'm where I am! But now it's 'the customer wants this or the customer wants that'. Our customers cannot know exactly what they want. We spend many, many dollars on development of new office furniture designs, and that expenditure keeps us ahead of anyone who never worries about such things.

"Frankly, my grandfather, my father, and I have been running Dugan Manufacturing the same way for almost 70 years now. It has worked for us so far and will continue to work for us into the future. Our customers don't have that kind of experience. How did customers get so different? How did they come to expect to run my company *for* me? Well, again I'm not going to name any countries, but we all know that when our markets are flooded with products that are made in sweatshops overseas, those companies make so much profit they can afford to ask their customers a lot of questions. And it's a good thing for them, because they don't have the experience to do a good job like we do without a lot of that kind of research. Our customers have become unnecessarily spoiled, ladies and gentlemen. They have come to equate companies that have to ask the customer how to do a good job with quality! And I for one am sick and tired of it." *(Applause)*

"We know what our customers need because we've been at this a lot longer than these market-bashing countries! And the last thing our customers need is for me to spend a lot of money, and lose a lot of profit, and get no measurable benefits, to learn what I *already know!*

"I once visited a company in my city which had put in a so-called quality program. Let me tell you what they found out. By the way, if that president had been working for *me*, he'd have been shown the door in short order, I'll tell you! This company hired a consultant who convinced them to do some training of the work force and then set up something called quality teams. The workers loved it, and do you know why? They got four hours a week free time, to sit in some classroom and, for all I know, sleep. These teams were then let loose on company time to 'solve problems'. Let me read to you some of the problems that were 'solved'. A new color for the men's room was decided on. The cafeteria menu was rewritten. None of us would call those anything but silly. But at least they didn't cost a lot of money, except of course the value of lost time and production.

"There was more, though. By far the worst was a recommendation to install a new piece of equipment that would reduce defects in the product this company manufactures. Sounds good, doesn't it? The problem is, the company is now, and has been for a long time, making money hand over fist with its product just the way it is. Is its product perfect? No, of course not. But their customers accept it *just the way it is*. And here's a company spending its employees' and its shareholders' profits to improve something that nobody wants improved! Ladies and gentlemen, if that's what this so-called quality movement is all about, you can keep it!" *(Applause)*

"Yes, there have been some stories about companies who, unlike us, were really in trouble. Companies who didn't know their business. And some of them seem to have had some success after doing some programs with their employees. I read a lot, and I'm aware that there are some things I don't know. So I actually considered trying one of these programs once. My plan was to put together eight employees, train them in some of these ideas, and then let them get together at lunch time to see what they might come up with. Of course, they'd be closely monitored by a member of my management team, who knows the business.

"As I said, I was ready to give it a try. Seemed to be the way many companies are going. But then I thought about what I was doing, and ladies and gentlemen, the mistake in my thinking became crystal clear. I pay my workers handsomely, you see, but I pay them to work, not to party, or make suggestions, or even to think beyond what it takes to do their job! Their job is to put in an honest day's work, making office furniture, for an honest day's pay.

"I have another group of people that I pay a lot more. They're my managers, and I pay them a lot more because they are the ones who think and make suggestions about the future of the company. By the way, even they can't party too much!" *(Laughter)*

"But seriously, we hire managers with college degrees and workers with high school or even less education. Who do you think should make the decisions? After all, in my experience, give the workers too much authority, and what do you get? An unhappy group of managers we can't afford to lose, and a militant bunch of employees who might just reward me with a union!

"Ladies and gentlemen, let me summarize my remarks to you today, because I see that it is almost cocktail hour. Our job is profits, and we in American businesses have been good at that for a very long time, thank you. If we're unable to stop foreign competitors from influencing our customers with all sorts of silly thinking about running our businesses, at least we don't have to spend all our profits in response to it. And let's stay proud! Sure, my company's profits have been down recently, but I know one thing. When the economy comes back up, so will we! After all, it has been our tradition for 70 years!

"Thanks again for inviting me this afternoon, and best wishes to all of you!" *(Applause)*

In his effort to shed light on the "truth," Dugan seems to prove some important points about company environments that are *not* conducive to quality activities. He worships at the altar of profits, not realizing that the real source of his profits is continued customer satisfaction with defect-free products and services. He is perfectly willing to blame others (countries in this case) for the woes of his business. He shows little, if any, respect for the wisdom and desires of his customers or employees. And he strives to prove his vision by carefully finding and citing the results of quality efforts that, in his view, have failed.

C. Roland Dugan suffers from a syndrome that we have seen over and over again in quality-poor companies: he has an *illusion* about his knowledge of the business and how it can remain profitable and grow in the face of increasing global competition. This illusion blinds him to facing reality, to learning that the business has in fact changed, and to recognizing that within his workers resides a wonderfully rich and valuable amount of information on how the business might be better run. If his business were in its death-throes, a panicky Dugan might in some halfhearted way try some quality initiative. But it will inevitably fail unless he looks deep within himself and recognizes his need to forever change his basic attitudes toward his role, his customers, and his employees.

Let's now jump forward a few years, and listen to another point of view about quality in the workplace.

Take care of the means, and the end will take care of itself.
—Mohandas K. Gandhi

The Quality Environment

A speech given before the National Organization of Reliable Manufacturers and Service Companies (NORMS) presented by Lillian Siemans, president of Somestate Insurance Company, on November 25, 1989.

"Thank you for that fine introduction. It is a great privilege to address you NORMS people this morning. It has been especially gratifying to talk with quality-minded professionals these past five or so years, because you all have become so much more sophisticated.

"I remember about 20 years ago I happened to be working with a U.S. auto manufacturer at one of its assembly plants. There was some training of new quality inspectors going on. One of the new people had the task, among others, of inspecting whether the turn signals worked. She was standing in front of a car as it came off the line, and a co-worker turned on the signal. She watched intently: It works. No it doesn't! It works. No it doesn't! It works. No it doesn't!" *(Laughter)*

"So you see what I mean about the current level of sophistication in quality.

"In thinking about what I wanted to say this morning, I realized that there is really only one message that is of critical importance, and it is this: *For your businesses to survive and prosper, you and the management of your company must be completely and irreversibly committed to total quality.* Nothing less will do, because anything less will soon derail any efforts you may begin. And derailed efforts result in unbelieving, unmotivated, and perhaps even distrustful employees. I'll talk about a few ways you might recognize such a level of commitment, why it is so critical, and what these kinds of committed people do about it.

"First, what is this kind of commitment? Well, it is many things, certainly, but first and foremost it is a basic change in management thinking and behavior. That is sometimes very hard to do. Many of our senior people got to where they are today by applying a set of learned skills and behaviors that are not as applicable in our current global economy. But they might find it hard to discard those very methods and beliefs that resulted in their career achievement.

"How can you tell when this behavior change—a change brought about by new fundamental managerial values—has occurred? Again, there are probably many ways. But one test I use when I visit other companies, and certainly within my own, is this. I look for managers who walk around making comments like: 'No! We are not going to do things that way, because it is not good enough!' 'Would you be happy with that product if you were our customer?' 'How do we know this is the best we can do?'

'What is your opinion about different and better ways to do this?' 'I'd like your help to solve this problem.' 'Keep looking.' 'There is a better way!' These are committed managers!

"Much has been said in recent years about 'acceptable quality levels'. Most quality people would agree that there is no such thing. Some talk about 'zero defects' as the only rational target. I believe that a truly committed management team does not tolerate some acceptable level of quality. But I submit that the best of these managers don't even find zero defects to be enough! *All* things can improve. If the managers on the team cannot make the things they are doing any better, they change the things they are doing. If someone convinces them that zero defects of the company's products has been achieved, they change the product's specifications. They make the specifications tougher. They strive to meet new customer demands or even customer wishes that couldn't have been met a year ago. In short, they are never satisfied with the phrase 'good enough'.

"Why does someone become so zealous? Many people really feel that behavior of that type can be counterproductive—that more than good enough simply drains away profitability. I've found that committed management typically believes in its approach because of two fundamental convictions.

"One, they have invariably linked profits to quality. They see that better quality equals better profits, without limit! Quality to them is sound economics. Whatever kind of investment that might be made to improve quality, it differs from more familiar investments in plant, property, and equipment only in that it is usually more profitable. They see ongoing work in quality improvement as an investment in the future of the company.

"Two, our committed managers have an abiding faith in the collective wisdom, skills, and innate desire of our people to help, not hurt, the company. Our employees are seen more as associates, each of whom can at any moment retrieve from his or her experience and knowledge a new idea that can significantly improve quality. These managers translate their beliefs into ongoing training of, and communications with, their people, to give them the tools and the desire to apply their experiences. These managers provide a role model for the people around them.

"How do they do it? How do they translate these beliefs into action? I have nine rules. They are simple to say but sometimes hard to apply. You might find them useful.

1. Recognize and make sure everyone understands that continual improvement is a *process*, not a program. That it is a *journey*, not a destination.
2. Become a *practitioner*, not an *observer*. Learn what your people are learning, not only to give them an example and earn their respect, but also to be able to talk the same language with them. Make your senior managers participate as well. For example, have them sponsor a quality team, to help it deal with its issues, properly network with others, and construct solid recommendations for action.
3. Manage the quality journey. Quality will come bubbling up from the bottom of your organization, but must be managed from the top. See that proper teams are established and well trained. Make sure they have real, meaningful problems to work on. Hear their recommendations and give honest feedback whatever the decision may be. Follow up. Visit teams. Show your dedication.
4. Continually communicate the need for quality improvement. Never let your message die.
5. Involve *everyone*. There is a problem-solving network in your business. It includes everyone who might have some data, fact, observation, or idea about something that is not being done as well as possible. So, folks, your problem-solving network includes every employee from the lowest to the highest level. Give them the tools, language, and motivation to enable them to share their considerable wisdom with you. By the way, there is something of a corollary to this rule. If you must have a cadre of multiple-degreed quality engineers and experts with computerized statistical systems using advanced calculus, by all means do so. But don't expect them to give you anywhere near as much benefit as you'll derive from your workers.
6. Invest in continual training of everyone. Don't just train people in the theory or 'religion' of quality. Give them usable tools that will not only help your business, but will help them in their everyday lives. Make the journey a win for them as well as for you.
7. Make sure the training is not only associated with 'quality' things, but also includes the skills needed to harness the power of teamwork. Train people in social style recognition, interpersonal skills, team leadership, and so on.

8. Create measurement systems so that people have a clear idea of the results of their work and know at all times where they are and where they are going.
9. Recognize the achievements of your people, and set up systems that ensure that they are well rewarded for their efforts on your behalf.

"These rules form the backbone of the quality journey at Somestate Insurance. Profits are up 23 percent from last year, turnover is dramatically reduced, and our customer complaints are less than 10 percent of two years ago. Those numbers do two things: they make me proud, and they tell me we still have a lot of work to do. In fact, our work to continually improve will never end.

"Folks, thanks again for the chance to speak with you this morning. If there are any questions, I'll be happy to answer them."

Lillian Siemans understands what it takes. She realizes the power of her people, and their ability and willingness to make the company prosper and grow. She knows who her customers are and makes sure all of her employees know it also. She knows that an ongoing investment in her people is assurance of the future viability of her company. And she realizes that it is not a one-time effort. It is a way of life, a culture of constant analysis, problem solving, and change.

Get your facts first, and then you can distort them as much as you please.
—Mark Twain

Getting Management's Attention

We have talked about the management attitudes that represent an environment hostile to quality, and those that represent an environment supportive to quality. For an individual, and especially an entire company management team, movement from the one to the other is often difficult. This change is usually completed only after a significant amount of introspection; talk with others knowledgeable in the quality arena; observation of the benefits of quality programs; and sometimes plain faith in plans that might, by their apparent high cost versus lack of immediate benefits, seem to contradict all prior beliefs in what constitutes good management practice.

What catalyst begins this process of change? Managers don't often just wake up one morning and see the light. In our experience, trouble in the company more likely brings on more of the same behaviors that probably contributed to the trouble in the first place. We've got to work harder around here! We need to cut staff . . . get lean and mean! A hiring freeze is now in effect! Or, in companies proud of their high tech image: This state-of-the-art computer system will really help our engineers figure out what's going on!

And the problems continue. At the worst, profits are further squeezed. Rework levels climb. Complaints grow. Old, valued customers are lost. Or at the best, another period of relative complacency begins. Printers are spewing forth stacks of four-color charts and graphs that only the engineers can really understand, but at least they're happy. Morale in the company is obviously heading down while turnover is skyrocketing, but after all, that's business, isn't it? The troops will get over it. We've got to get that profit level back.

In many companies, it has become what we call the *American business cycle*. Run the business as we've always done, until the problems become so acute that they can no longer be ignored. Assume that the problems are caused largely by outside influences, such as the economy, foreign competition, and temporary changes in buying trends. Do something dramatic to shake up the troops. Laying off a few is a good move. Lay out a schedule of training that fits the budget (that is, it is so modest that it would take 10 years to cover the entire company). The thoroughly shaken but still largely untrained troops will then do what they've always done, but they will do it harder and we'll be OK. Until, of course, the problems again become so acute that they can no longer be ignored.

Occasionally, something comes along that is so compelling or frightening to senior management that it is forced to question its tried-and-(not-so)-true modes of operation. Such a catalyst helps to begin or accelerates the change to a healthy quality environment. Many of these catalysts are related to genuine crises, such as impending bankruptcy or the decision by a major customer to go elsewhere. But we have found one that can engage the attention of management at any time, even when the business seems to be running effectively. It is called a *cost of quality audit*.

Cost of quality concepts have several names, among them *quality cost* and *cost of nonquality*. A full review of the concept is a book by itself and we will not get into much detail here. Most practitioners of quality define cost of quality as an expense to the business; that is, a lower number is better. The measurement of the expense consists of three cost categories.

1. **Prevention costs.** These are the costs of things done to prevent quality problems in any product or service that the company delivers. There are many components, including such things as product development, operations methods, quality training, supplier capability surveys, and all of the labor and fringe costs associated with these activities.

2. **Appraisal costs.** These are the costs incurred to ensure that products and services are defect-free. They include inspection and/or testing of purchased supplies, manufacturing or service operations, and finished product. Again, associated labor and fringe costs are included.

3. **Failure costs.** When prevention and predelivery appraisal fail to eliminate or find defects in products or services, failure costs apply. They include evaluation, correction, and replacement, plus the necessary labor and fringe costs. Failure costs may occur before delivery of product or service (internal) or after delivery to a customer (external).

The extent to which appraisal and failure costs are incurred depends largely on the size of the prevention cost initiatives a company is willing to implement.

- High prevention costs will, in time, allow moderate (and decreasing) appraisal costs, and very low failure costs. Waste is low, and the customer is satisfied with the product or service. In time, prevention costs will also diminish somewhat (but never disappear)—as the more serious problems are solved. This is, of course, the desired situation.
- Low prevention costs can be coupled with high appraisal costs—a situation common in many companies with large inspection organizations. Failure costs can be low and the customers fully satisfied, since

defective products or services are not released. But waste materials and time can severely cut into profitability.
- Low prevention costs can also be coupled with low appraisal costs. Now the failure costs can become astronomical, with significant loss of profitability and customer goodwill.

Many companies have calculated their costs of quality, and express the results as a percentage of their annual revenues. Thus a $100-million company with a cost of quality of 12 percent recognizes that $12 million dollars is annually spent on activities designed to make sure that quality problems don't happen when it does something; to make sure that they didn't happen when it finished doing something; and to fix the problem when what the company has done fails anyway.

Using data from the many companies that have undergone this exercise, a few simple statistics can be derived. Companies that have made little or no effort to implement consistent, integrated, and ongoing quality efforts find a cost of quality as high as 25 percent. One-fourth of their revenues are being used to deal with defects, usually in the appraisal and failure cost categories. These are the companies with very high waste levels, significant numbers of customer complaints, and squadrons of customer service people forever fixing the product in their customers' homes or workplaces.

At the other end of the scale, companies that have made a strong effort to implement consistent, integrated, and ongoing quality efforts find a cost of quality as low as 2 percent. Much of their expense is related to the preventive cost category, especially employee quality education and training. As much as 23 percent of annual revenues can be saved, and thereby effectively generated, by applying sound quality principles.

By the way, there's an interesting multiplier in these statistics. Quality-poor companies endure a cost of quality which is a high percentage of often-declining revenues, whereas quality-rich companies enjoy a cost of quality that is a low percentage of often-increasing revenues. Customers vote with their buying dollars.

These kinds of numbers should get the attention of any senior management group in the country, and be a very effective catalyst for change to a genuine quality-supportive environment. Surprisingly, they sometimes don't, and that shows us the steepness of the road ahead. Management sometimes prefers to deny the data, rather than face its enormous consequences, which might include some embarrassing questions about what management has been up to all this time. Because of this, we have redefined cost of quality in a way that has helped bring some heads out of the sand. Read it a few times, and see if it applies to you or your company.

Cost of quality is a number that is often too high to be believed by senior management and too low to be real!

Two stories illustrate the differences a quality practitioner might find when generating a cost of quality value. Both companies and their data are real, but will not be identified here.

You would all recognize the first company. It has been active in the quality arena for years and aggressively looks for new ways to apply education, training, and techniques to better its products and services. Its annual revenues are well into 11 figures—more than $10 billion. But after all its work in quality, its calculated cost of quality still exceeds 15 percent! Despite this, the company's management not only believes it, but feels that 15 percent probably understates the true value! We'd buy its stock any day.

The second company is much smaller, with revenues about $10 million. Quality efforts have included hiring inspectors and recently installing computer terminals near the production line so that a record of what the inspectors find can be quickly immortalized. The cost of quality audit done by this company included only the production area, not the equally important service organizations, such as accounting, marketing, engineering, and personnel. Yet it feels its agreed-upon cost of quality of 9 percent is probably too high! And the thought of more preventive activities, like employee training, is dismissed as unnecessary and not cost-effective. Such activities would only deplete already squeezed profits. If we had any stock in this outfit, we'd sell it!

Two companies; two very different viewpoints, and thus quality environments. The larger is not afraid of the data, but uses the data as one form of motivation to push harder. The smaller sees more effort as too costly, yet its true cost of quality probably approaches 25 percent. It could afford a lot of effort.

Read our definition of cost of quality again. If you have not done such an audit, do so. There is plenty of help available through the American

Society for Quality Control and other independent quality consultants. Decide that the number will probably be too low to be real. And use the data as catalyst for change, a way to break the American business cycle and the start of a truly productive, employee-participative, and continually improving workplace.

Change is not always improvement, as the pigeon said when it got out of the net and into the pie.
—Charles Haddon Spurgeon

The Environment of Quality

The right environment, one that will support an effective quality effort far into the future, can be difficult to achieve. It requires much more than lip service. It cannot be viewed as something acceptable to try because we have little to lose if it doesn't work. It does require a firm dedication to the belief that a new quality culture is essential to the long-term health, even life, of the company. It does require management's excitement in the idea that all workers will participate in the company's improvement, and that now there will be effective ways to tap the incredible store of knowledge they've been carrying around with them.

Finally, management sometimes needs a painful rap on the head to knock it out of its reverie. Cost of quality audits, properly conducted, can be a very effective way to get management's attention.

3 The Elements of Superior Quality

The lame man who keeps the right road outstrips the runner who takes the wrong one. Nay, it is obvious that the more active and swift the latter is the further he will go astray.
—Francis Bacon

Chapters 1 and 2 demonstrated that a good understanding of the meaning of quality coupled with a healthy environment for quality are essential to the success of a quality effort. Understanding and proper environment ensure that we will begin to do things right. They ensure that when training, quality processes, or some other initiatives are introduced within a company, people see clear objectives and find management totally supportive of their efforts.

But with all of this, the story is still incomplete. Understanding quality as meeting the needs of your customers is important, but not enough. Supportive management—which understands that quality equals profits, and that quality comes from the work force—is great. But nothing useful derives from support alone. We must also endeavor to do the right things right.

We have talked with many companies that seem to have done things right. Their commitment to quality is strong, or at least it was in the beginning. They had envisioned a future of fully meeting the needs of their internal and external customers. They vigorously began and continue training and communications. And after a time, many have become disillusioned. Perhaps without consciously being able to verbalize it, they have begun to sense that wanting to achieve superior quality does not make it automatically happen.

We detect disillusionment with quality processes when we hear comments like these.

It's hard to expect our management group to wait two years or more before they see a significant return on this investment we've made in quality. My job is to try to somehow sustain their commitment.

—QA manager

We've overspent our quality training budget by 20 percent this year. The last thing we need is 'another program'.

—Production supervisor

Those quality programs are not designed to meet the special needs of this department. They're really oriented to the shop floor, I guess.

—Head of marketing

We've gone with a guru. These things take time to work, and we don't want to do anything else that may jeopardize a consistent approach to quality.

—QA vice president

We put together quality teams a year ago. They started out real strong, but it seems now that they are stuck. Not much is happening.

—Vice president, manufacturing

We're going to continue this effort, because our customers demand it. But it has become a drain on time and budgets.

—Company president

Our teams are active, and they really enjoy the opportunity to participate. I'm just not sure they're working on the right problems, though.

—QA manager

These and similar comments show quality efforts gone astray and in trouble. None of the efforts would be in trouble if the participants had matched their positive attitudes about quality (doing things right), with the proper elements of a quality process (doing the right things). A company's quality activities may be designed by the company for itself or an externally available process, modified or not. In either case, certain elements must be present to make the process one of doing the right things right. Both parts of the equation are necessary for success.

We have identified nine key elements of superior quality. These include specific skills that should be mastered by each employee. They also address such things as good implementation technique, molding of the company's quality culture, necessary managerial mind-sets, management's control systems of quality activities, and effective training techniques. Together, they provide a company with the right things to do.

Here is what you need.

- A good start
- Usable tools of quality
- Flexibility for varying department needs
- A common language
- Involvement of the problem-solving network
- A system of top-down management
- Effective training for adult learners
- Quick results . . . not a quick fix
- A process that becomes yours

Let's look at each of these elements more closely.

Today is the tomorrow you didn't plan for yesterday.
—Anonymous

A Good Start

Once an organization's leadership has firmly concluded that a strong quality process needs to be implemented, it must begin to convey that to the entire organization. If the culture is one of fear, or contains any other negative factors that may impede the progress of implementation, the culture must be changed. In general, three techniques can help an organization get off to a good start on its quality journey.

Meet with Everyone

Meetings between management and all employees must be held, and employees must be given the chance to voice concerns and questions. The tone of these sessions is important: they should be more like conversations with colleagues and not announcements from your management. Specific content can and should be yours, but certainly ought to include some key points.

1. Tell everyone exactly what is planned, why it is being done, the role they will play, and the benefits they might expect. Explain the company's quality policy fully.
2. Tell everyone that the road ahead is going to be difficult at times. Don't make light of the change. Sometimes otherwise strong communication efforts are negated by unfortunate word choices. One example frequently heard is "This is just common sense!" Rather, tell employees that what they are going to learn and do is not just common sense, but a new way of dealing with the issues of the business. If it is just common sense, employees will not treat it as something important.
3. Tell everyone that perfection is the only goal. When norms or specifications are reached they will be made tougher.
4. Tell everyone that the company's management is not going to just give this process a try, but instead is committed to making continual quality improvement a way of life in the business. If there have been false starts before, openly acknowledge them and the reasons they failed. Then explain why this time is different. You will gain tremendous respect from this sometimes difficult act.
5. Tell everyone how their work lives may change. You might, for example, tell workers that they will no longer have the quality inspectors as their nemeses and scapegoats. Workers will be the new inspectors! Tell them that the company is moving from a work style interested largely in results (with less concern about the processes employed to achieve them), to a work style that is largely interested in process (from which desired results will be obtained).
6. Tell everyone that teamwork will be applauded and rewarded. Explain that the great American hero, the rugged individualist who does things his or her own way, is no more.

7. Tell everyone that you need their help, and that you believe the process will be a personal win for each of them. Tell them that they will get new skills applicable to everyday life, and that the company's enhanced profitability will enrich them through new reward and incentive programs. Then tell them about those programs.
8. Finally, believe completely everything you've told them!

Keep Communicating

The importance of the commitment and change to continual quality improvement must be stressed, either through more meetings, or by walking around and talking to workers, or both. Find leaders from all over the organization who can incorporate the quality concepts and plans into all of their interactions and conversations with employees. Make sure that everyday examples that are easily visualized and remembered are used. For instance, many companies paint a very graphic picture of a quality-poor environment using something like this.

What if everyone did his or her job correctly 99 percent of the time? Sounds pretty good, doesn't it? But is it good enough? If everything in this country operated at a 99 percent perfection rate, television stations would not transmit for 3 days, 15 hours, and 36 minutes each year! There would be nine misspelled words on every page of a magazine! The U.S. Postal Service would lose almost 500,000 pieces of mail every day! Your car would fail to start in the morning once every 14 weeks! The space shuttle would be hopelessly grounded, because far too many parts would fail at liftoff!

One U.S. automaker claims that its cars start 99.9 percent of the time. Not bad, until you think about it. Owning the car for five years, during which you start it four times a day, will result in a car that refuses to start seven times during its life. Almost all cars are more reliable than that, and if they were not, customers would complain loudly. Even 99.9 percent reliability isn't enough!

Find other companies that have implemented successful quality processes and invite their employees to come in and talk with your people to show them the benefits they are likely to gain. Start a newsletter designed to catch people doing things right—so unlike the common management role of catching people doing things wrong! There are dozens of other ways to keep the quality message, its importance, and your commitment to it fresh in the minds of all employees. Find the ways that fit your needs and the company's needs, and use them.

Start Right Now

So far, a lot of talking has occurred. And talk alone, without swift actions that match the message, soon loses its effectiveness. Implementation of the quality process should begin right after the first meetings. Later, we will discuss in more detail how training should proceed. For now, the most important lesson for a good start is to begin training at the top of the organization. Insist that the president (or facility equivalent) and immediate staff be the first to learn the quality concepts. Only in this way can workers begin to recognize a genuine commitment through direct actions. Only in this way will the workers' natural feelings of skepticism about management's motives erode over time. And only in this way will management learn the language with which they will be able to communicate with everyone in the company.

> *When the only tool you have is a hammer, you tend to treat everything as if it were a nail.*
> —Abraham Maslow

Usable Tools of Quality

Posters, videotapes, slogans, and other devices are often used to communicate to employees the need for quality. These efforts are intended to generate a zeal for quality, and usually succeed, at least in the beginning. Employees come to recognize that their management really believes that this quality thing is essential for the company's future success. And in time, they begin to believe it too.

With such zeal, however, comes a moment of truth. The employees now want to do something about the company's quality problems. Their support and participation has been requested, and they are ready to give it. Now their skills and capabilities must be up to the task.

Employees need a set of skills that will enable them to deal with the company's quality problems. We call these skills quality tools. These must not be chosen at random, but in such a way that a comprehensive and usable capability of each employee to fully engage in the pursuit of perfection results. The set of tools that an individual or department receives may differ somewhat from those of another individual or department, as we will see later. But everyone's tools should satisfy two basic guidelines.

They must be immediately usable. Theory must be used very sparingly, if at all. Adult learners don't often care to know the elegant underpinnings of a concept. They simply want to know why a concept is used, to ensure that it isn't pointless in their minds, and in what ways the concept will help them. In fact, adult learners are most likely to believe that tools are of value if they can be used in everyday life. The special needs of adult learners are sufficiently important to warrant a separate section later in this chapter.

Tools must be integrated. They must permit participation in a full range of quality activities, from process examination to solution implementation. Sometimes, tools that are powerful parts of a complete quality capability are rendered useless because they are not integrated with other tools, but instead are used alone. A common example is statistical process control (SPC). One of our clients applied SPC with great vigor on the production floor. Workers scurried about measuring everything they could see. The Pareto charts and histograms were beautiful. But no one knew what to do next! Data had been collected, but without the skills to act on the data, to find the causes of problems, the quality activity became a relatively meaningless exercise of data gathering.

Over time, we have established a set of tools which, when taught and applied properly, meet these criteria. Much of this book will be devoted to the detailed description of their content and usage. For now, we will just list the contents of the quality toolbox.

> **Process observation and data-gathering tools** enable people to identify that a problem exists, and to evaluate its scope. Such tools include the typical parts of SPC and data gathering, such as tallying, Pareto, histograms, and control charts.
>
> **Flowcharting** remains the most effective way to visualize and then understand any work process and the steps that constitute it. Flowcharting is essential for the proper analysis of a process, especially in the company's service activities.

Problem-solving skills include a thorough capability to identify, describe, analyze, and find the most probable cause of a problem.

Process analysis skills, especially useful in service jobs, enable workers to recognize customers, suppliers, and needs. Employees are able to fully analyze the extent to which their work processes meet their customers' needs and their needs, and to determine what to do when those needs are not met.

Decision making is a structured process that leads the way to the best solution for a discovered problem cause.

Implementation skills are needed because the best recommendation cannot always succeed if a complete plan of action is not generated. The plan should recognize possible disruptive events, and incorporate steps to avoid, eliminate, or minimize them.

Team-leading skills facilitate the proper orchestration of an effective team's efforts. The ability to lead a team in the application of its individual members' skills to achieve a desired result is critical.

Team participation skills are similar to team-leading skills in that they provide to each team member the capability to recognize and more fully draw on the strengths of other members, despite their often differing social styles.

Presentation skills are needed because the hoped-for end result of team activity is a coherent and well-documented recommendation, presented to management for its consideration and approval. Often, workers have not had significant experience in this activity, and can negate much good work by a poor presentation.

Consistency is the last refuge of the unimaginative.
—Oscar Wilde

Flexibility for Varying Department Needs

To date, much of this country's quality efforts have been in manufacturing areas. This is probably because quality issues often seem simpler in manufacturing. The nature of the problems are more obvious. Specifications are met or not. Waste can almost always be counted, weighed, or in some other way measured. Assembly time can be determined. The number of reworks are identified. And customer complaints are logged.

Early, as well as current, quality activities addressed these kinds of measures in production environments. Quality awareness training was brought to the shop floor. Some measurement tools, often SPC, were introduced. And occasionally, some corrective tools, such as problem-solving techniques, were included.

All manufacturing organizations have certain things in common. They all produce a discrete product usually having well-defined specifications or other norms, such as time and cost of assembly. Problems with the product are readily identified, either by management, workers, a quality assurance group, or a combination of these and others. Workers are often put into teams and pointed toward a problem by management. When the team has successfully identified the source of the problem, it reports its findings to whatever quality process structure the company has implemented, often some sort of quality project review committee. Then some form of action is then taken.

Recently, serious attention has been paid to the service organizations in our economy. (By the way, no company is totally manufacturing, and few are totally service. Accounting, marketing, personnel, and other departments are examples of service organizations almost always found in manufacturing companies; whereas records management, report generation, and other activities can be considered examples of the manufacturing arms of service companies.) This attention to service organizations comes none too early, since 1989 data show that nonmanufacturing parts of the economy have not matched the significant productivity gains of manufacturing (see Figure 3.1).

Early attempts to deal with productivity, or quality, in the service areas exported tried-and-true methods from the production floor. SPC and other data-gathering tools were introduced. Sometimes problem solving was included. And almost always there was a general feeling by management

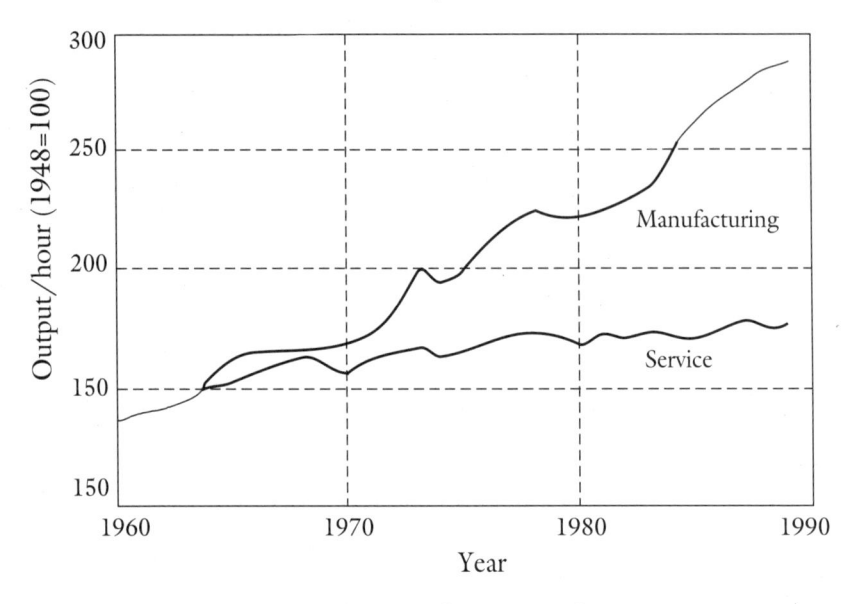

Figure 3.1. Productivity in the manufacturing and service sectors.

and employees that in one way or another, all this quality stuff just didn't seem to fit. There seemed to be a difference between manufacturing and nonmanufacturing groups, at least in the application of quality principles.

Some time ago, when we were less aware of the fundamental differences between manufacturing and nonmanufacturing organizations in their utilization of quality processes, we had agreed to conduct a tailored quality process for a company in our area. The participant group consisted of several interrelated departments, each of which was a service organization, in that none manufactured a discreet product. In all our work with manufacturing organizations, we had developed, as an early part of the process, the selection of quality teams that would undergo training as a group. Each team was assigned a real company problem to work on during the workshop. In many cases, the most probable cause of the problem was identified before the training was concluded.

We asked the management of the service organizations for some real problems of their workplace, problems on which the newly formed quality teams could work. (Real problems have a specific definition, which will be discussed in chapter 7.) After almost a day of thinking about real problems, though, we were unable to define one sensible team problem that could be used! No one was prepared to assume that problems didn't exist, but we could not define them, except as vague generalities such as, this part of the business could be better, or I'm sure we could improve this.

While discussing this turn of events with our client managers, and then agreeing to do the workshop without having first assigned problems to the trainees, the reason for the difficulty in identifying problems became apparent. Manufacturing organizations have clear, well-defined norms or specifications. The failure of a product to meet those specifications is readily determined by measurement. Thus the problems of manufacturing are easily identified and listed.

Nonmanufacturing is often different, however. Specifications or norms are frequently absent, having never been clearly determined. Sometimes, people are doing a job with no idea if they are doing it as well as it could be done, simply because there is no standard of measure. Often, the standards of measure that might be established are done so in a completely arbitrary way, and may be too lax or too stringent. There is nothing solid against which to compare the current productivity of the jobs in such a service organization. How could the person responsible for accounts payable in a medium-size company know whether the current standard of, say, 48 hours to process a check is terrific, average, or abysmally slow? Perhaps comparison with accounts payable statistics from similar companies would help. But within the structure and policies of the person's own company, which themselves govern how easily he or she can perform the accounts payable function, the person couldn't know. He or she would have to guess.

The basic difference between quality efforts in manufacturing and nonmanufacturing organizations is this: Manufacturing organizations identify their problem areas by a process of *comparison of discrete products against standard norms*. Once identified, the problems can be solved. Nonmanufacturing organizations identify their problem areas by a process of *analyzing the work they do, to find where customer needs are not being met or could be met more efficiently and effectively*. Once the work is truly understood and analyzed, tough service norms can and should be established and used.

Productivity improvements come from solving the problems that exist in an organization. Since different kinds of organizations identify their problems differently, each must have tools appropriate to its needs. Application of SPC and/or data-gathering techniques to the nonmanufacturing organization usually results in the feelings we mentioned before—"all this quality stuff just doesn't seem to fit." Use of process analysis in production environments can work, especially in the interactions between production and the rest of the company. The actual production process, however, is rarely subjected to frequent and untested changes. Flexibility in the quality process ensures that the varying needs of each organization in the company are met.

> *The individual's whole experience is built upon the plan of his language.*
>
> —Henri Delacroix

A Common Language

Successful teams plan and coordinate their activities using a common language. Sometimes the language is understood only by the team itself. For example, the football quarterback who joins the huddle with the instructions "32 slant right on 2" is conveying the next play to the team in a special language that they understand. Baseball coaches use a sign language of touching the brim of their hat, brushing their pants, and other motions to call for stolen bases, hit and run, and so on. Wall Street brokers use a seemingly frantic form of sign language to buy and sell stocks. The skipper of a sailboat might yell "Cleat the jib sheet!" If you're the crew, and only your actions will prevent capsizing, you better know that the skipper wants you to tie off the rope leading to the sail up front!

Without languages common to their members, these teams could not achieve their goals. They would be forced to rely on what each individual thinks is best. The result would be at best uncoordinated; at worst, divisive. The same is true with quality teams. They need to speak a common language to ensure that each individual understands the direction of the team, and can participate in the activities needed to achieve the team's goals.

Interestingly, even with the use of a common language, communication can be elusive. We often do this exercise in our workshops, which you can try as you read this book. We'll give a four-letter word. When you read it, what immediately comes to mind?

The word is *post*.

What did you think of? Was it fence post? Post office? Emily Post? Or was it any of dozens of other word associations that we have heard over the years. Usually, a workshop of 20 people will generate at least 12 different responses to the word *post*. All of them are right, of course, since there are no wrong answers.

But think of the implications to communication. The language was perfectly clear. But what was our meaning, our intent of communication? Did we mean post office, but you heard *Saturday Evening Post*? If so, we failed to communicate despite the fact that we used a common language.

Unless great care is taken, the inevitable result of an attempt to communicate is misunderstanding. Each member of a communicating pair has a significant responsibility to ensure that misunderstanding does not result. Speakers must make sure that when they want to say *post office*, they don't say *post*. Listeners, hearing *post*, have the corollary responsibility to probe for meaning.

A common language generates team success in a number of ways.

- A common language gives a team the capability to communicate within itself and logically deal with the issues at hand.
- A common language provides a means for the team to effectively present conclusions and recommendations to senior management. The management group will understand the process that the team went through and can relate the recommendations to the steps of that process.
- A common language generates communication between teams working on different issues, perhaps in different parts of the company. This creates a cross-flow of ideas and strengthens each team. It also allows for the flexibility to restructure teams as new needs arise, using any company employees in the process.

Often, companies do not achieve the full use of a common language among their employees, despite its being so essential to the success of quality efforts. Our experience shows us that there are two typical reasons for this.

First, facility managers or key departmental heads are not only permitted, but often encouraged to select a quality initiative independently and autonomously. "Let's see what they can do on their own" seems to be the justification from above for such a direction. The quality effort becomes some sort of test, with managers being watched to see the sound reasoning and judgment they will demonstrate in selecting a favorite process. Another reason this independence is encouraged is that senior management wrongly believes that different parts of the company need completely different rather than flexible initiatives. The result of multiple activities is predictable. Each department of the company starts to speak the language of the quality process chosen. True, each will understand the importance of quality, and each might agree with each other's respective definitions of quality terms, at least at the fringes. But they can't really talk with each other. Imagine playing a football game effectively when each player comes from a different sport. One is looking for plays called from the football playbook, another is watching for the hand signals of baseball, and a third expects to haul in the jib sheet. Chaos and failure will inevitably result.

Sometimes in such an environment, strong managers make the situation even worse by pitting their gurus or processes against each other. "My guru really knows what's going on around here," one might say, inviting the open derision of the other. Now the differences between groups become even more polarized, and through subtle (or sometimes obvious) signals, people are ordered not to talk with those other departments that don't know what they are doing. Of course, it doesn't really matter, they don't speak the same language anyway!

The second reason we find that companies do not achieve the necessary common language is the failure to train the *entire* work force. The company might embrace a common process of quality, but feels that it is too expensive to train everyone. Most managers that we have met who initially embraced this philosophy later admitted they had made a mistake. The trained cannot talk to the untrained. *Everyone* needs to learn the playbook if the football team is going to have a chance at the Superbowl!

One of Deming's 14 points is to break down barriers between departments. A good way to do that is to get everyone communicating about issues of the company and solutions to the problems. Communications requires a common language. Whatever the process used, make sure everyone knows the language, and that it is common throughout the company.

One other benefit of a common language: We have often heard about (and have mentioned in this book) the importance of company culture. Management will talk about the need to have a quality culture, or a culture without fear, or this kind of culture, or that kind of culture. Often management is not sure what company culture is. Sometimes it feels it must change the culture before any quality activities will work.

The fact is, quality activities are one of the best ways to modify the culture in a company, and make it more consistent. Consider selected definitions of culture from Webster *(Websters II, New Riverside University Dictionary.* Boston, Mass.: Riverside Publication Company, 1984):

> **culture** n. The totality of . . . behavior patterns, arts, beliefs, institutions, and all other products of human work and thought typical of a . . . community at a given time. A style of social and artistic expression peculiar to a class or society. Intellectual . . . activity. The act of developing the social, moral, and intellectual faculties through education.

Common language is the foundation of a common culture. This certainly is true for large cultures. Think of how aggressively France has defended the purity of its language, and in doing so has protected the uniqueness of its culture. Common language can also be the foundation for a smaller culture, such as that of your company. The presence of a common language of quality will provide the additional benefit of instilling, almost automatically, a common culture of quality.

This section can be summarized very readily: *Train everyone in your company to use the same basic quality process.* We will discuss further into the book how this is done while still retaining the flexibility to meet varying needs of different departments.

> *Treat people as if they were what they ought to be and you help them to become what they are capable of being.*
> —Johann W. von Goethe

Involvement of the Problem-Solving Network

We have seen that everyone must become familiar with the common language of quality implemented in the company, so that communications between individuals and teams are facilitated. There are other reasons why it is important to involve everyone in the company.

The largest store of data about how your company actually runs on a day-to-day basis is not found in reports to management, engineering specifications, management itself, or procedural manuals. The largest and most valuable store of data about what really goes on every day—what works well and what does not work well—is locked in the minds of your employees. Why? Your employees are the front-line troops. They see and experience each work process at its source. They are the people who understand the intricacies and idiosyncrasies of the work, and know when it is working well and when it is not.

We refer to your entire employee population as your problem-solving network. All of the data locked in their heads could be used to solve almost any problem that may arise. All that must be done is to somehow release that data, to allow it to be used effectively. That's sometimes harder than it sounds. Let's look at an example.

A foreman named Mark walks up to a worker on an assembly line that manufactures precision aluminum castings for various industrial machines. Mark is holding a casting for a gearbox cover, and he looks angry.

"Hey, John," he shouts over the din of the machinery, "look at what's going on here!"

John, who has worked for this company 17 years, and who is one of the few genuine casting experts on the production floor, has heard it all before. He turns to Mark and waits for him to continue.

"John, this flange is warped. We're never going to be able to grind it to specs. And it's not only this part. We've checked the entire run from the night shift, and most of them are the same way. What's going on here? Are you guys asleep or what?"

"Mark, how would I know what's wrong? You said yourself that most of the problem is with the night shift run. Why don't you ask them?"

"I will, you can be sure of that! But I'm also asking you, because you've been around longer than anyone else around here. I would think you see things, don't you?"

"I don't know why you have that problem. And I really wish you'd go ask the guys who did the work, and let me get back to mine!" And with that Mark turned away, angry with John's attitude and angry about the problem that he couldn't solve.

Let's look at what happened here. Mark certainly has every right to be concerned about the warped flanges. After all, most of a shift's production will have to be redone. Mark also is being reasonable in coming to John, in that the night shift workers have all gone home, and although Mark knows that John wasn't directly responsible, he thinks that John may have some ideas about what went wrong. Perhaps he's hoping to present the night shift crew with the solution, to increase his stature in their eyes.

Mark's language, though, is that of blame assessment. It might well be the common language of the company. He can hardly expect John to respond to that language, since in doing so John would implicate his peers. So John, fearful of being blamed in some way, or of placing blame on his friends, responds in the time-honored way of the American worker confronted by the American foreman. I don't know anything about it! That didn't happen during my shift! That must have happened when I was at lunch! Gee, I guess I wasn't watching that part of the line—I was just doing my job!

And in using a language that John doesn't speak, Mark has not involved John, an essential member of the problem-solving network. He has virtually guaranteed that John will not share the wealth of data about the production process that is in his head, data that could represent a significant start toward solving the problem.

This scenario easily occurs whenever no alternative language, such as problem solving or process analysis, has been taught. What might an alternative conversation, one which uses a problem-solving language, sound like?

"Hey, John, you got a minute?" John looks up and walks over to Mark, wiping his hands on a rag. "The flanges on these pieces are getting warped again. I just don't know why it should be happening, and I need to bounce some ideas off you."

"OK, Mark, what do you have?"

"Well, we're noticing that the problem seems to be more pronounced after we've run at least 100 pieces. Usually that would occur sometime during the night shift, but, of course I don't know yet whether that means anything or not. At any rate, when the warpage starts it just continues to get worse. And another thing, we noticed that . . ."

Soon, John is responding with several possible causes of the problem that are consistent with Mark's observations.

In this example, Mark has spoken to John in a very different language, one of problem solving. (We will discuss this and other languages in later chapters.) John knows this language, and he understands why Mark is speaking it. Not to pin the blame, but to find the most probable cause of the warped flanges. John is not afraid to converse with Mark, and, in fact, can do so very effectively since the language they are speaking is logical, systematic, and common to both of them. The problem is well on its way to being solved. Mark has utilized the special store of data in John's head.

This second scenario cannot happen unless two conditions are met. One, a common language of quality must be implemented in the company. Two, the entire problem-solving network must be trained in the use of the language. Only then will solutions to problems be found quickly and effectively.

If we don't change our direction soon, we are likely to end up where we are going.

—ancient Chinese proverb

A System of Top-Down Management

Quality in all its forms comes primarily from the organization itself, not from the company management, or the quality experts. We have talked about the problem-solving network consisting of everyone in the company. This entire group has all the knowledge typically needed to identify and solve quality problems. We have talked about training everyone, so that full communications can be established and maintained, and so that a new culture of quality can flourish.

Quality comes up from the bottom of an organization. Mobilize, train, motivate, and energize the people of the company, and quality is well on its way. But management of quality must come from the top and percolate down. We have already discussed the essential need to train managers first in whatever process is to be used, to ensure their understanding of it, and to signal employees that their management is serious. We have talked at length about the need for genuine commitment. The role of management must include these steps and more.

Over the past decade, a number of efforts have been made to engage workers in quality activities. Quality circles is a good example. Most quality circles consisted of a group of employees, who received some kind of training and who met periodically to deal with company problems. Usually, some senior or quality person joined the team to support it in its efforts. Many quality circles worked well then, and many continue to do so today. But often, as a totally democratic gesture, the selection of problems was left to the team. As a result, the problems teams addressed caused management to wonder what they were doing, because the problems often did not represent the true issues of the company.

Even in a fully participative company, complete equality of jobs and responsibilities is not a desired end. Managers are still expected to understand the big picture and to support quality teams in a number of ways. We'll talk more about this later, but for now, management's ongoing responsibilities include the following:

- Introduce and constantly communicate the need for quality.
- Set up quality teams in the appropriate way.
- Ensure that training is properly accomplished.
- See to ongoing training needs.
- Determine the problems or processes that need attention.
- Assign problems or processes to quality teams.
- Ensure that teams have time and resources to do their job.
- Review the work of quality teams.
- Decide on quality teams' recommendations. Give feedback.
- Authorize corrective action to be taken by teams.
- Do it all again, over and over.

Knowledge is the only instrument of production that is not subject to diminishing returns.

—J. M. Clark

Effective Training for Adult Learners

Adult learners participate in all the training programs done within a corporate setting. Yet the style used for teaching these learners is often the same as that used in a high school or elementary school. It is a style we are all accustomed to, and on the surface it seems to make sense. There are, however, some significant differences between the adult and child learners, differences that go far beyond the obvious difference in age.

We don't pretend to be formally trained education experts, especially in the subject of adult learning. Our experience, though, has helped us develop some general thoughts about how adult learners differ from children. More important, we have found some simple training rules to recognize those differences, and make them work for us and ultimately the company.

There are three fundamental differences (again, other than age) between the adult learners you are likely to train in your company quality process, and child learners.

Low Risk of Nonparticipation

Since teachers are often peers and sometimes organizational subordinates, the adult learner does not have strong authority figures who demand performance in a classroom environment. Thus strong external motivation to perform may be absent. We choose those words very carefully. There may be other motivators. For example, if a worker's job depends on learning the material, motivation to perform might be extremely high. If the company somehow grades the participant and ties merit raises into classroom performance, there might be some burning of the midnight oil. We've never seen this, but there's no reason it couldn't be done. And, of course, there are always dedicated people whose internal motivation is sufficient to compel them to high performance standards.

Under typical conditions though, the adult learner who attends a company training session recognizes that there is very little risk associated with low or nonparticipation, and that no one is likely to give a final exam and send the grade home on a report card. That individual might attend the course with high internally generated motivation and be fully participative. We estimate about 25 percent of adult workshop attendees are in this group. Alternatively, one might decide that class time is a good opportunity to get some rest; that it is prudent to let everyone else respond and do as little as possible, to blend into the background. We find that these attendees represent another 25 percent of workshops. The remainder are wait and see. Of course, the content and style of the workshop must motivate the participant to choose the first alternative.

High Experience Levels

The second difference between adult and child learners may seem at first glance to be very desirable to teachers. Adults bring into the classroom environment an enormous number of experiences. They know how things are done. They know how to do their jobs. They have a significantly higher skill level in almost everything they do, when compared to children.

Sometimes, those experiences are desirable. They provide a framework into which new learning can be integrated. More about that later. But the same experiences that can prove useful also represent the established way of doing things. They represent the set of procedures, processes, and behaviors to which an individual will likely revert, especially in a pressure situation, unless training in a new technique or behavior is completely assimilated.

Most of us at one time or another have discovered that when driving a car we have arrived at our intended destination without remembering exactly how we got there. Usually the destination is very familiar to us, such as home. In such cases, our brains have relied on subconscious behavior patterns, learned long ago, which get us to our destination without significant conscious thought. The same situation can occur with a work procedure, which has been assimilated so thoroughly that it often operates at a less than conscious level. When that happens, new learning hasn't got a chance. Old habits are resurrected. So adult learning must also recognize the need to overcome the established way of getting things done. Otherwise, a lot of learning will take place, but very little corresponding behavior change.

Illusion of Ineptitude

Finally, here is the third difference between adult and children learners. Unfortunately, many American employees have been conditioned into what we call an illusion of ineptitude. Little respect is given to their inherent abilities and intelligence, often because these characteristics are assumed to exist in proportion to the organizational level the person has achieved. We might hear, "If lower-level people are so smart, why are they lower-level people?" As a result, workers enter a learning experience with some degree of skepticism and doubt whether they will be able to learn anything new. Their attitudes often become offensive: "I'm here, and I can't get out of it, but you can't make me learn anything." The practical result is that they will look for the first opportunity to fail to understand something, and then fold their arms in triumph that their preconceived notion has been proved.

Thus, effective training of adult learners has three needs: (1) the need to convince people that learning is in their best interest; (2) to overcome powerful habits of experience; and (3) to banish the illusion of ineptitude. How might these needs be accomplished with adult learners?

We have developed 10 steps to successful adult learning. They apply regardless of the subject being conveyed, but are especially useful with quality concepts.

1. Demonstrate usefulness of training right away.
2. Make how-to explanations explicit.
3. Show that something works; don't just say it works.
4. Show why techniques are used.
5. Use short sessions, no more than four hours.
6. Use the 25 percent, 25 percent, 50 percent rule of learning.
7. Permit three weekly practices of principles.
8. Balance technical and social skills.
9. Utilize strong pictorial content.
10. Have fun!

Step 1: Demonstrate usefulness of training right away. The participant must immediately experience relevance and usefulness of all topics taught. All experiences in the class environment must suggest to the participant a personal win. The hoped-for reaction is, "I see a good reason to learn this stuff. I think this can help me in my job, or in the things I do at home." Adults will spend little or no time paying attention to information that they deem useless.

Step 2: Make how-to explanations explicit. Avoid empty how to explanations. Trainers typically know the material better than the learners, and consequently, might make a shaky decision. By hurrying the participants through the lesson, a failure to learn occurs. It's like trying to teach golf by saying, "Just hit the ball with the club and get it into that hole in the ground." Not bad, but it does nothing to convey the skill needed to actually hit the ball.

The failure to learn has nothing to do with the actual learner's intelligence, which is typically quite up to the task. Remember that participants are often looking for an opportunity to not understand the material, to justify mental withdrawal from the activity. In fact, in many companies which are trying to move from a quality-hostile environment to a quality-supporting environment, mental withdrawal was the previous expected behavior. ("We don't pay our workers to think.") So, when the going gets tough, old behavior patterns are reestablished automatically.

Step 3: Show that something works; don't just say it works. Teachers in our youth could get away with a reliance on our faith. If they said it would work, it would work! As adults, however, we are much less likely to accept an instructor's assurances that Pareto charts are very useful in your job! Adult learners have to see how that is true.

Step 4: Show why techniques are used. If the idea is pointless in the minds of the participants, they will not use it even if they know how. Participants will not automatically accept and begin to use new ideas until they have a pretty firm idea of why the idea is being used.

Step 5: Use short sessions, no more than four hours. Adult learners have heads filled with all kinds of extraneous thoughts which compete for attention during a class. Of course, schoolchildren have different but equally competitive thoughts too. For adults, the interest and applicability of the material helps retain their attention for about four hours. After four hours, it is very difficult, if not impossible, to keep a group concentrated on the material. People are not used to sitting still for long periods of time, and, even with frequent breakout sessions, four hours seems to be the maximum time for effective learning.

Step 6: Use the 25 percent, 25 percent, 50 percent rule of learning. The sessions should be divided into three fundamental sections, two of which are one-quarter of the time, and the remainder is one-half of the time. For each concept, spend 25 percent introducing it. Then, spend 25 percent applying it to an unfamiliar case. For example, if the subject group consists of accountants, the case study might be from production, and vice-versa. The final 50 percent of the time is spent applying the concept to the actual issues of the participant group. As we will see, they usually have a problem assigned to them when they enter the session, and it is to this problem that we spend half our time applying the newly learned concept.

People often wonder why we spend 25 percent of our time applying the newly learned concepts to unfamiliar cases. Why not just spend 75 percent of the class time applying the concept to real company problems, and then we'll get a lot more done? The answer is important, and can be understood with an explanation of adult learning based on our experiences.

We have found that adult learning consists of the integration of knowledge (newly learned concepts) with prior experience (things we know and beliefs we have). We experience such integration many times, and at such times might say "Ah, I see how that new idea can apply to my job!" But such integration is not always an easy step to achieve.

Newly acquired knowledge can be so different, or can be presented in a way that is so different, from our existing experience that the gulf between the two is too broad. For example, we were once teaching selling skills to a group of nuclear engineers, who were consultants to the nuclear power industry. They were not particularly happy to be with me, because they didn't want to become salespeople, but changes in their business mandated it. In an example designed to show how to deal with client objections, we used a videotape of a cinderblock grinder salesperson. Learning was not optimum, because the knowledge (a cinderblock grinder) was too different from the participants' experience (nuclear reactors) to allow them to easily bridge the gulf, integrate the knowledge, and learn. Of course, we also violated other successful adult learning techniques in this case, not the least of which was the failure to show the immediate relevance of a cinderblock grinder salesperson's job to that of a nuclear engineer.

Similarly, newly acquired knowledge can be provided in a form that is too similar to existing experiences. The integration step doesn't occur, because the participant often doesn't immediately see the difference between the knowledge and the experience. They short-circuit. For example, we once were teaching problem solving to a group of automotive repair technicians. They saw themselves, of course, as talented problem-solvers long before the course began. Our mistake was using as a case study the diagnosis of an unknown problem with a car. We found that the participants were able to solve any such problem we were able to devise, using their experience only! Why use these fancy problem-solving techniques when we can solve the problems without them? And, as a result of the poor selection of a case study, learning did not occur. For this reason, we believe that a concept should be introduced and then applied to an unfamiliar case. Prejudices about how to really do the job don't exist, and the integration of knowledge with experience can occur. ("Ah, I think I see how I might apply this idea to my job!")

Step 7: Permit three weekly practices of principles. Adults have a considerable amount of on-the-job experience. They know how to get things done and how to do their jobs. As a result, responses to problematic or stressful job situations are almost automatic. There is no time to stand around wondering how to deal with the problem—it needs fixing now! Consequently, people in stress situations (for example, the boss is on the rampage, or the production line is spewing out off-spec material) react quickly in the only way they can, and that is to utilize well-practiced and comfortable approaches and behaviors.

We've all seen this happen many times. For example, who is not familiar with the supervisor who tends to yell at subordinates when something goes wrong? That supervisor may be sent to interpersonal skills or awareness training (often disparagingly called charm school). He or she might return to the job a new person, presumably fully in touch with the effect of his or her negative behavior on other people, and completely resolved to never let it happen again. Sometimes the resolve is sharpened by the threat of discipline or some equivalent. And it works, until the next time a crisis occurs, when the supervisor's old behaviors reassert themselves.

People in stressful situations will always try to reduce the stress, and to do so they will apply the behaviors, techniques, and other learning that are comfortable and automatic. In the absence of any alternative, they will rely on prior experience. Often, experience is very useful, such as when a veteran of the company can solve a problem that is vexing everyone else. But at other times, experience becomes the method by which the old ways of doing things become entrenched and unchangeable. Unless something can be applied that will overcome experience, the prior ways of doing things will always prevail in an emergency, and long-term, sustained improvement becomes almost impossible.

What can overcome these experiences that cause people to react the old way to problems? New experiences! The key is to provide people with a new set of tools and techniques that are practiced enough to become automatic. When the crisis occurs, the new experiences are applied. These new experiences come from training.

The classroom is a place where new tools and techniques are introduced and practiced. Unfortunately, the classroom environment usually has two distinctions that can result in a failure to assimilate the new material. First, the environment is controlled: Exercises are well defined, and the stress of a real emergency does not exist. It is easy to follow the leader's instructions and do the exercises, but the experience does little to prepare people for the effect of a genuine stressful situation. Second, too little time is typically provided. Many companies with which we work establish training time somewhat grudgingly and certainly control its duration. So we find that the first and most popular way to reduce the time spent in the classroom is to diminish (or sometimes eliminate) the 50 percent of time preferably devoted to practicing with real company issues.

The end result of these classroom distinctions is that people return to the job with a general understanding of the concepts taught, and perhaps a success or two in applying them to a standard case. But when the going gets tough, they revert to what they are most comfortable with, and in such situations a few hours in class cannot overcome years of experience. The training doesn't stick, and while managers continue to say the right things, (we need more training around here), they begin to think something very different (what a colossal waste of time and money).

Wise managers view the classroom training exercise as only a small portion of the learning experience. They recognize that new concepts must be practiced at least three times before people tend to become comfortable with them. As a result, they insist that time be spent on the job practicing the concepts learned in class on real company issues. When crises arise, they stop people who are beginning to respond in the old ways and direct them to apply the principles recently learned. They recognize that only through real practice can old experiences be replaced with new ones. And that only through real practice can those new experiences become strong enough that they will be automatically applied to the next crisis.

Step 8: Balance technical and social skills. We have seen quality teams that have become masters in quality techniques. They have the capability to do almost everything necessary to continually improve the products, services, or organizations they represent. Process analysis, problem identification, and analytical, innovative, and reporting skills are superb. Unfortunately, they don't talk to one another. All their skills reside in the team members individually, and the power and synergy of the team is never harnessed.

Although a group of people can readily learn the same tools and techniques, they certainly never apply them in exactly the same way. Each of us has a preferred style with which we interact socially. Our style determines how we might relate to and contribute within a team. Some of us are controllers and tend to be the most vocal and desirous of immediate action. Others of us are analyzers, more quiet and interested in the data at hand. These and other styles, and their value and potential disruptions to teams, will be discussed in a later chapter.

The presence of different styles and the interpersonal barriers that can arise from failing to recognize them can negate a significant amount of technical training on quality issues. If people cannot effectively relate to one another, they cannot effectively apply technical skills to the quality issues facing them, except as individuals. And individuals are not as effective as teams in dealing with quality issues. So all quality training should be an appropriate mixture of technical skills (how to do) and social skills (how to relate, especially in teams). The combination of the two provides the most bang for the buck.

Step 9: Utilize strong pictorial content. Over the past several years, many computer software manufacturers have steadily improved programs that are user friendly. Often, these programs use pictures to convey ideas. For example, some word processing programs have a picture of a file cabinet on the screen to convey the idea of document storage. Moving the cursor to that picture and clicking the mouse button opens the file cabinet. People easily learn the concept of finding documents in such a program because simple pictures allow them to easily relate to a concept already mastered (a file cabinet, in this case).

Similarly, the use of pictures in quality training has significant value. Pictures summarize abstract concepts and permit people to refer to something familiar to reconstruct the concept or later utilize it.

Step 10: Have fun! Little needs to be explained about this step, except that adult learners will not tolerate dry, repetitious, and boring instruction.

We introduced this section on adult learning by suggesting that adults differed from children learners in three fundamental ways.

1. They tend to have fewer external means to provide motivation, such as teachers and parents. Thus they may not automatically demonstrate a desire to learn something new. They will ask, what's in it for them?
2. They have a greater number of frequently practiced experiences which provide a time-honored set of methods for dealing with situations of many types. Thus they may not readily see a need to learn something new.
3. Their attitudes about learning are often the result of company practices which viewed people as just workers and no more, producing a vague illusion of ineptitude. Thus, many adult learners feel that they can't learn something new.

The ten steps to successful adult learning deal with each of these concerns. They produce a desire to learn by demonstrating immediate usefulness to the learner in a fun and not onerous or lengthy way. They instill a need to learn by ensuring that through practice, new techniques are mastered enough to be seen as superior to the old ways of getting things done. And they overcome the illusion of ineptitude through full explanations, visual techniques, and plenty of practice.

> *Even if you're on the right track, you'll get run over if you just sit there.*
>
> —Will Rogers

Quick Results . . . Not a Quick Fix

American companies tend to be on a constant search for the quick and immediate fix to their problems. Some experts have surmised that constant bombardment by television shows which neatly wrap up problems in a 30- or 60-minute segment have conditioned us to this view of life. Whatever the reason, which is beyond the scope of this book or our experiences, it does remain true that the provider of the quick fix in our companies is usually viewed as the innovative hero. At the other end of the spectrum is the employee or team who steadily implements small but measurable improvements to its process and/or product. Often such employees or groups are labeled as plodders.

We like action, and we are galvanized by the vision of the leader who, damning all torpedoes, charges the enemy (quality problems) and deals them a swift mortal blow (implements something, who cares what, as long as it looks good).

Companies can become very disappointed in their quest for the quick fix, because it usually is only a pipe dream. The quick fix assumes, first of all, that one or perhaps a few simple solutions are all that is required. That is, of course, not true. Genuine quality results from the continual improvement of product and processes. The quick fix is also a pipe dream for another reason. It relies on luck, not a systematic process of investigation and analysis of the problems facing the company. It relies on the flash of insight that often does not happen. So, disappointment results.

Flirtation with the quick fix has become a sufficient impediment to good quality processes that most quality practitioners have, at one time or another specifically warned against pinning all hopes on it. We are counselled to apply solid principles of quality in a steady, consistent way, and that doing so will generate continual improvement. This is true, but it often becomes the justification for poor or absent results in a quality process. Companies have often said to us, "We haven't seen a lot of results yet, but we've only been at this for six months."

Spurning the idea of a quick fix, and instead, implementing a steady and consistent process of quality, does not mean that quick results cannot be obtained. Quite the contrary, a good quality process should begin to show results right away. Measurable improvements in the business and its products and services should result during the first training session if the teams are properly constituted and the training material well selected, developed, and presented. Failure to achieve such results is a failure of the process being used and is not a failure of the idea that steady progress with a consistent approach leads to the most effective long-term benefit.

Quick results are also important in that they nurture and sustain senior management's belief that the process it has embarked upon is the right one.

By perseverance the snail reached the ark.
—Charles Haddon Spurgeon

A Process that Becomes Yours

Companies often find that an outside consultant's services in the design and implementation of a total quality approach are very helpful. Often companies may lack satisfactory internal resources or may simply believe that new perspectives are needed.

We do not believe, however, that it is in any company's best interest to become consultant-dependent. The role of a consultant should be to assist the company in establishing a quality process that is right for it and tailored to its specific needs, to ensure that the company becomes capable of sustaining it, and then to get out. This idea results in a few simple rules that we think should apply to any quality effort.

- The process used should be your process. Your name should be on it, and it should be written with your culture and environment in mind. If you use one of the established quality gurus, don't fall into the trap of calling yourself a Crosby or Deming company. Your employees will question your commitment to something that is invented by and carries the name of someone else.
- Use your people as trainers. Train them, or have your consultant train them, very early in the process. They best understand the concerns of the rest of your work force and can relate to the shared experiences that make up your company's culture. Using your people as trainers will also demonstrate your high level of commitment for an effective and sustained quality effort.
- Change the process if results don't meet early expectations. Show your flexibility in responding to feedback about your efforts, especially if the feedback is coming from the workers. They will, given the chance, show you the way to achieve consistently superior quality.

The only man who can change his mind is the man who's got one.
—Edward Noyes Westcott

The Elements of Superior Quality
- A good start
- Usable tools of quality
- Flexibility for varying department needs
- A common language
- Involvement of the problem-solving network
- A system of top-down management
- Effective training for adult learners
- Quick results . . . not a quick fix
- A process that becomes yours

These nine ideas will ensure the effective implementation of quality into your company. They may seem difficult at first. But they are much easier than doing only part of the quality job because it seems easier, only to be required to start the process all over again, usually with a more demoralized employee group.

Now, let's take a closer look at the tools of quality.

Part II
Quality Implemented... The Tools of Breakthrough Quality Improvement

4 Quality Awareness and Management

*The Carpenter is not the Best
Who makes More Chips than all the Rest.*

—Arthur Guiterman

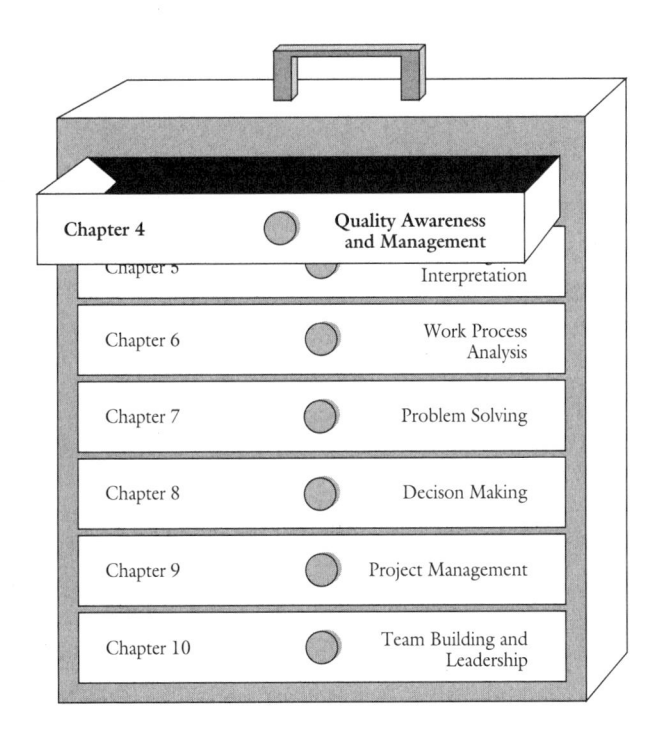

Chapter 4	○	**Quality Awareness and Management**
Chapter 5	○	Interpretation
Chapter 6	○	Work Process Analysis
Chapter 7	○	Problem Solving
Chapter 8	○	Decison Making
Chapter 9	○	Project Management
Chapter 10	○	Team Building and Leadership

Let's begin to explore the quality toolbox, starting with the first drawer, quality awareness and management. As the name of this chapter suggests, the tools in this drawer are quality awareness, which helps employees understand the purpose and importance of quality, and quality management systems, which provide the means to sustain the quality activities. In addition, the drawer contains the skills that management must apply to ensure that quality activities continue to grow in effectiveness. As an example, this entire book might be a useful tool for the first drawer.

If better is possible, good is not enough.

—Pat Croce

Quality Awareness

Quality awareness is rarely thought of as a tool to be used in the improvement of work processes. Unlike problem solving, Pareto charts, or control charts, quality awareness by itself does not generate continual improvement. We include quality awareness in our toolbox, however, because when properly taught and reinforced, quality awareness becomes essential to the proper use of all the other tools.

When building a house, carpenters must understand the purpose and master the use of a variety of tools, such as hammers, saws, squares, and so on. But to use these tools to their maximum effectiveness, carpenters must also understand the purpose of the building—they must be able to visualize (using imagination or a blueprint) the finished product. They must know whether it is to be a home or a barn, where the doors and windows are to be, and which direction the front of the structure should face.

In a similar way, workers cannot use their quality tools to their full potential without a vision of the purpose of their use. Workers need to understand the direction the company is taking, and why. Ongoing meetings with management, as we discussed earlier, remain essential to achieve and sustain this ongoing understanding. But what ultimately ties it all together? What provides the glue to bind the direction of the company to the efforts of individuals or quality teams? It is a sound awareness of quality, and its importance and purpose.

Traditional Versus New Views of Quality

Some interesting changes have occurred over the past several years in the view of quality, and the awareness that managers and employees have of its importance. Figure 4.1 lists some of these changes, the traditional view being that which has prevailed over much of our past and which is being supplanted by the new view.

We find that many traditional quality views are alive and doing very well in American companies. Most prevalent are the ideas that quality is primarily a

In the traditional view, quality is	In the new view, quality is
The production manager's job	Everybody's job
Controlled and audited	Built into the process
Some acceptable level	Perfection; no defects
A fixed target	A moving target
An increased cost which decreases production	Lowered cost which increases production
General and theoretical	Measureable and specific
Produced by machines	Produced by people
Negotiable; a want	Nonnegotiable; a must

Figure 4.1. Traditional versus new views of quality.

production-related activity; that it is solely the job of management and/or engineers; and that it is produced by machines, not people. Another compelling—but in our view, wrong—argument is that a zero defect goal is a mistake, because since it is impossible to achieve, asking people to achieve it can only demotivate them.

Believers in the new quality views create effective and sustained quality processes in their companies. They create believers among their employees through ongoing communication efforts. And like the carpenters in our example, the employees of the company have the necessary framework within which to apply their quality tools. They understand that their overall objectives are lower cost, higher productivity, and complete perfection in meeting customer expectations.

Employees realize why they are asked to apply such skills as problem solving, decision making, and project management. They recognize why team-strengthening capabilities are so important to the realization of their overall goals, because they'll realize how important the team itself is to those goals. And they will enter into a new relationship with management—one of mutual trust and working together—to attain and maintain continual improvement in the workplace.

Process Knowledge

The capability to understand what a work process is, and how it fits into the overall scheme of a company's operations, is another integral part of quality awareness.

Often, employees see only the job they are doing and have little or no understanding of its relationship to the company's total activities. This means more than understanding similar jobs, such as those jobs immediately before and after on the production line. It means understanding in a fundamental way how all the work processes contribute to the company's objectives, what they are trying to accomplish, why they are important, and why ongoing modification and improvement to them are essential.

Such an understanding provides support and reasons for all the quality activities in which employees are involved. It also dispels a typical response of workers when they see constant change. Can't the management group figure out what they are doing, put it in place, and just let it alone for awhile? The workers will see an overall purpose for the constant change.

Quality Awareness and Management 89

We use a device in seminars and with client companies that helps show employees and their management the overall role of any business, its relationship with its external customers, and why ongoing change is necessary. This device is shown in Figures 4.2 through 4.6.

Figure 4.2 depicts a typical business cycle any company undergoes. This cycle should not be confused with the more cynically stated (but still true) American business cycle described in chapter 2. Since it is a cycle, we could begin its explanation anywhere, but let's begin in the with the "strategies, mission" box. This is where a new business might spend a lot of effort prior to start-up. What is our purpose? What service or product do we intend to provide to our customers? Answers to these kinds of questions enable the company to establish a satisfactory set of tactical plans.

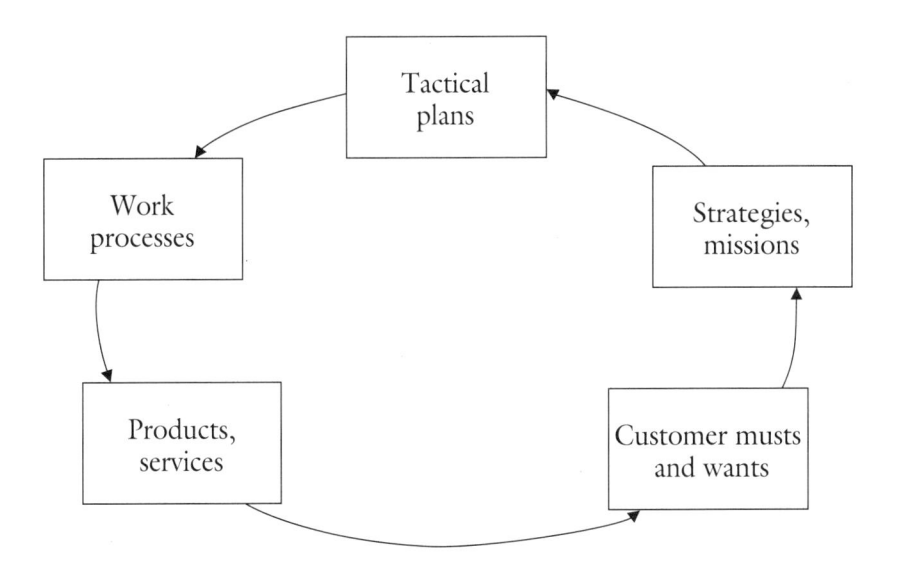

Figure 4.2. The business cycle.

Tactical plans include decisions about facilities, numbers of employees, required skills of employees, annual budgets, research and development issues, advertising plans, public relations activities, and other things necessary to begin to translate the strategy of the business into the final products or services.

Work processes, or employees' daily activities, are designed to enable the company to achieve its tactical plans. If the plan is to manufacture tires, then some appropriate work processes must be established. Proper tire-making equipment must be purchased and installed, and the right people (in skills and numbers) must be hired and trained to operate it.

The resulting products and services hopefully meet the needs of the external customer. They always would in an ideal world because the company would have fully considered customer needs in the formulation of its strategies, mission, tactics, and work processes. But in the real world, customer needs are often not fully met by a company marketing a new product or service. The company usually has to struggle to improve its products. Nor are customer needs fixed—they will continually change. That's why we show a cycle. The unending effort is to identify new or changed customer musts and wants so that the strategies, tactics, and work processes can be modified to continue to meet or to better meet those customer needs.

Consider the first manufacturer of microwave ovens for consumer use. Customer needs were difficult to meet with the first efforts, probably because customers had no idea what their needs might be. But after the first ovens were used in homes for awhile, the now microwave-educated consumers became very aware of needs not met. Needs for more internal space, better timers, revolving carousels, and so on were identified. Microwave manufacturers who paid close attention to these developing consumer needs, and incorporated them by changing their strategies, tactics, work processes, and, ultimately, their products, became successful.

What about the changing needs of customers? When we are doing a good job, and all indications suggest that we are meeting our customers' needs fully, it becomes easy to forget that customer needs are not static: they tend to change for a number of possible reasons. Think of banking back in the 1960s. We had to go to the bank to make deposits. Banks tried to meet our needs by staying open on Friday nights or Saturdays. But we didn't expect 24-hour service: no one considered such hours reasonable. Enter automatic teller machines (ATMs) in the 1970s. Banking became a 24-hour possibility. Money became much more easily available at any time. What if ATMs suddenly reverted to the banking hours of the

1960s? Most customers would, of course, be significantly inconvenienced if not outraged. Over the ensuing years their expectations of banks and their needs, have changed. Banks' strategies, tactics, and work processes are very different as a result.

Customers' relationships with businesses are also cyclic, as shown in Figure 4.3. New or returning customers receive products and/or services and have some degree (low, average, or high) of satisfaction with them. High satisfaction means that the customers' musts and wants were largely met, which determines whether the customers will return.

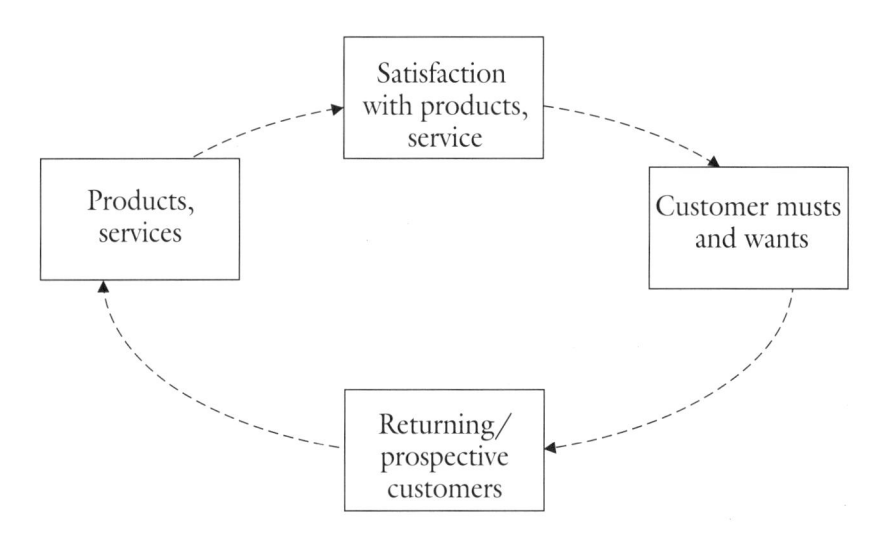

Figure 4.3. The customer cycle.

These two cycles, one of business and the other of the customer, are integrated in that each contains two items that are identical: products and services, and customer musts and wants. Looking at how these actually integrate gives some new insights into three types of business success: the prospering business, the business running on luck, and the business doomed to failure.

Figure 4.4 shows the integration of both cycles in the prospering business. The business recognizes new and modified customer musts and wants, which results in improved products and services through modifications in strategies, tactics, and work processes. The customers return, and undoubtedly bring friends, because their changing needs are being satisfied by ever-improving products and services. Simply put, they are fully satisfied with the results of the interaction with the business.

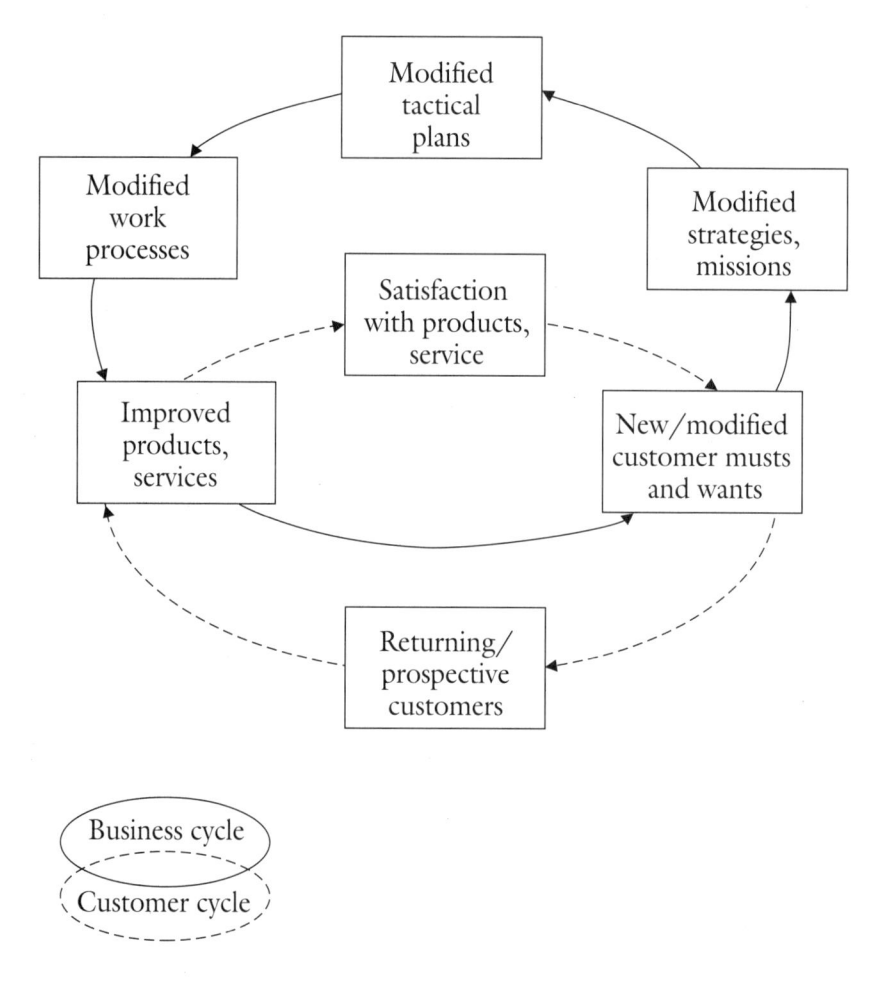

Figure 4.4. The customer-business cycle of the prospering business.

Quality Awareness and Management   93

Figure 4.5 depicts the business running on luck. In this case, customer musts and wants are assumed or ignored by the business. We've been doing things this way successfully for a long time! As a result, nothing changes significantly; not strategy, tactics, work processes, and most importantly, the products or services. As long as the customer needs, as assumed by the company, reasonably match the actual customer needs, the customer will return. But we have seen that customer needs change. Perhaps a

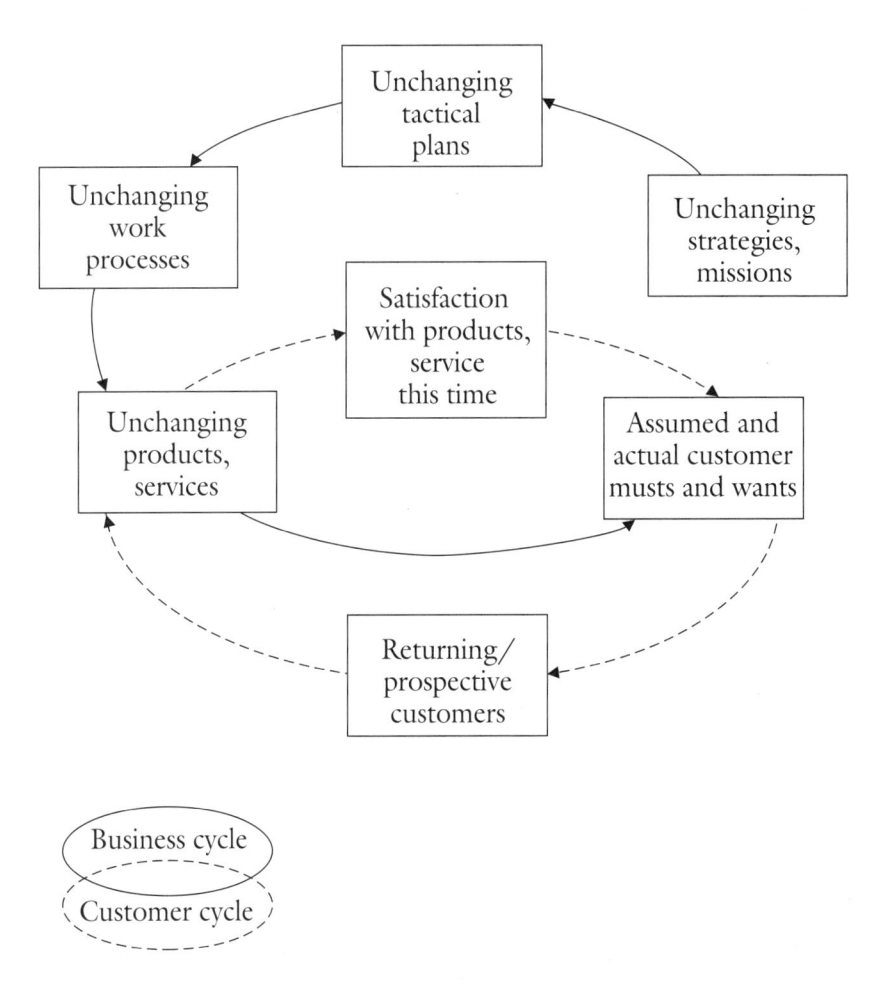

Figure 4.5. The customer-business cycle of the business running on luck.

competitor has produced a better product or service, or figured out how to provide the same product at a lower cost. This business is running on luck because it has no control over the satisfaction of its customers. It must rely on the "cooperation" of its competitors.

Finally, we can look at Figure 4.6, the business doomed to failure. In this case, the customer needs assumed by the business no longer match

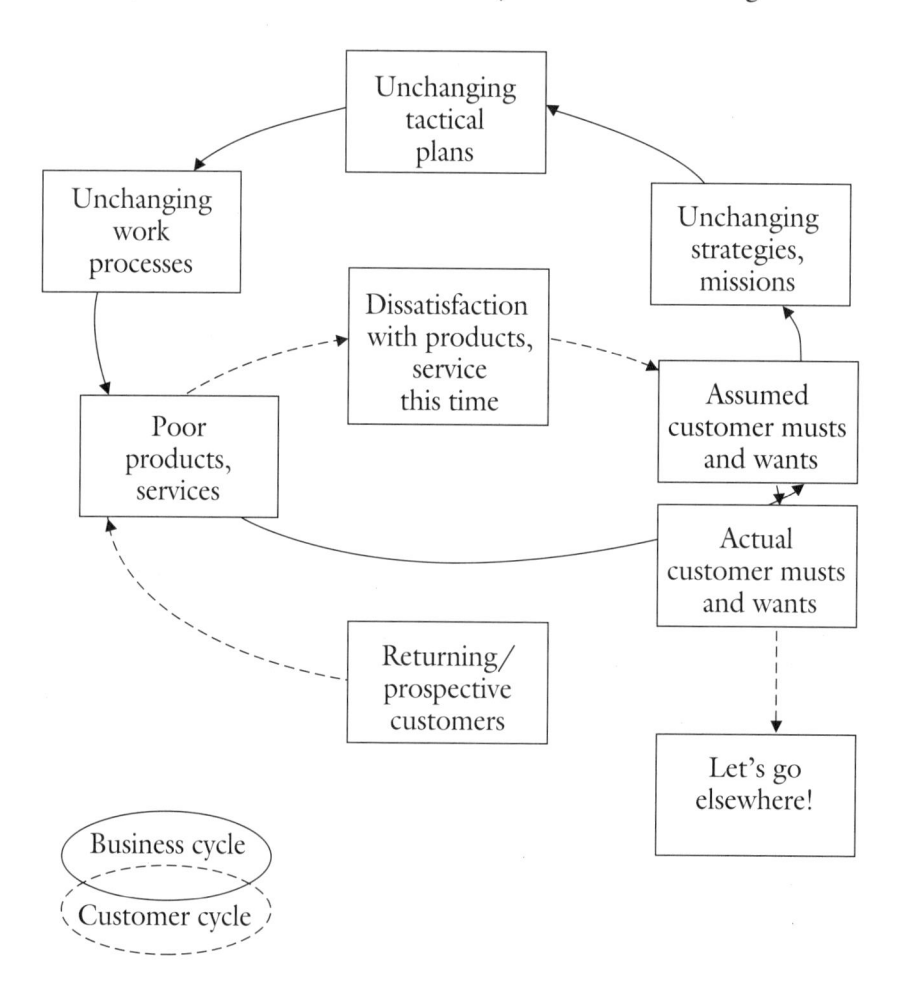

Figure 4.6. The customer-business cycle of the business doomed to failure.

the actual customer needs. Products and services are deemed poor by the customer because they are dissatisfied with them. And they will never return!

Thus we have an ongoing customer-business cycle. Continual changes in the needs of customers must be addressed, and that requirement reaches from the boardroom to the production floor—the boardroom through recognition that company strategy and tactics must match the new needs of customers, and the production floor through the efforts to continually modify work processes in response to those new needs.

The knowledge of the ongoing operation of this cycle, firmly entrenched in each employee, gives meaning to the continual application of quality tools, and helps to ensure that changing customer needs are met well into the future.

Only mediocrities rise to the top in a system that won't tolerate wavemaking.

—Laurence J. Peter

Quality Management Systems

Three good friends, Connie, Clare, and Carole, were enjoying a sunny day at a local lake. They had rented a small rowboat, and dropped anchor about 100 yards off the shore. Suddenly Connie snapped her fingers and said, "I forgot the soda I was going to have with my lunch." And she stepped out of the boat, walked across the water to shore, retrieved her soda, walked back, and stepped in the boat without getting more than the soles of her shoes wet.

Carole didn't seem to take notice, but Clare couldn't believe her eyes! In fact, she was so sure she was hallucinating that she decided to say nothing.

A while later, Carole looked in her lunch basket. "Do you believe this? I brought everything but my sandwich! I'll be right back." And she too stepped over the side, walked to shore, and came back with her sandwich. Connie took no notice, but now Clare was doubly amazed.

"Well," she thought, "if they can do it, so can I!" She turned to the others and said, "This sun is really starting to get hot! I'm going to shore to get a hat!"

With all the faith she could muster, she stood up, stepped over the side, and dropped like a stone into water well over her head. Sputtering to the surface, yelling for help, she finally got her hands on the edge of the boat, where Connie and Carole were anxiously waiting to help her back in.

"Say," said Carole to Connie, "we ought to tell her where the rocks are!"

Management's Ongoing Role in Quality

Knowing where the rocks are is very necessary to the success of a company. Sometimes, as for the friends in the rowboat, the rocks are an aid. Sometimes, they are an obstacle. One of management's jobs is to identify the rocks, and then array its resources to use them if they will help, or, if they are barriers, to break them up.

Some quality processes are designed as totally egalitarian exercises. Democracy reigns, and employees are given full control over the problems on which they work. This was often the case, for example, with earlier quality circles. One result of complete democracy can be that the wrong problems are being worked on, problems that are not critical to the near-term and future success of the company. We have seen, for example, a quality team wrestling with its problem of whether to paint the rest rooms. When this happens, it is usually an indication that management has, in its effort to show how enlightened it is toward its work force, completely abdicated its proper and essential role. Management usually doesn't think so, but it is so anxious to achieve total employee involvement in the process that it adopts a complete hands-off approach.

Later, when such teams return with recommendations to paint the rest rooms, management begins to question its own sanity in allowing work time to be spent on what it sees as frivolous activities. At best, the results are given token attention, and rarely are followed up. At worst, management ultimately decides that employee participation in quality is a waste of time, because "workers clearly don't know what's important to work on!"

That's partly right. Workers are usually not in a position to figure out the really important issues of the company. Their job is to help solve the problems—utilize or break the rocks once they are pointed out to them. And it is management's job to do the pointing.

A Quality Council

A forum consisting of the appropriate members of management must be established to guide the quality efforts. Such a forum might be called a quality council, or any other name that denotes its general purpose. The council often consists of a senior person, or facility head, who has overall responsibility for a key area of the company, and several of his or her direct reports. A quality professional is almost always included. Again, the exact structure is less important than the role such a group plays. Structure your own quality council in the manner which best fits your organization's and company's culture. But be sure that the mandate of the group includes four broad areas of responsibility.

- Selection of problems or processes to be analyzed by teams
- Establishment and training of quality teams and assignment of problems or processes
- Review of, and decision on, teams recommendations
- Ongoing reapplication of the first three areas

Figure 4.7 shows a detailed description of the typical role of a quality council.

Manufacturing and Nonmanufacturing Councils

A review of Figure 4.7 indicates that a quality council assigns quality teams problems or processes to analyze. You'll remember in chapter 3 we discussed some of the fundamental differences between manufacturing and nonmanufacturing activities. The responsibility of the quality council differs somewhat depending on the kind of activity addressed.

Manufacturing groups tend to identify problems more easily since they usually have a discrete product with clear specifications. The product meets the specifications or it doesn't. Little room is left for subjectiveness or speculation.

Nonmanufacturing groups, however, provide service or some other work often, though not always, without the benefit of clear specifications. Specifications may exist, but, in our experience, they are developed primarily as indicators of what someone thinks is right or reasonable for the work. Worse, the specifications are historically established: they simply formalize in writing the way the job has always been done. Historically established specifications are, of course, almost always met. The resulting sense of well-being can make efforts of improvement seem unimportant. Whether the nonmanufacturing specifications are set arbitrarily or historically, some analysis of the work itself is usually needed before one can determine whether the specification is a good one.

Problem and process selection
Select problems for which solutions are, in management's opinion, most likely to generate maximum benefits. Or, select for analysis, processes that have no *apparent* problems, but which management believes can and should be improved.

Establish and train quality teams
Select employees for quality teams based on the problems and processeses chosen. Appropriate employees are those *most familiar* with the problem and/or process selected.

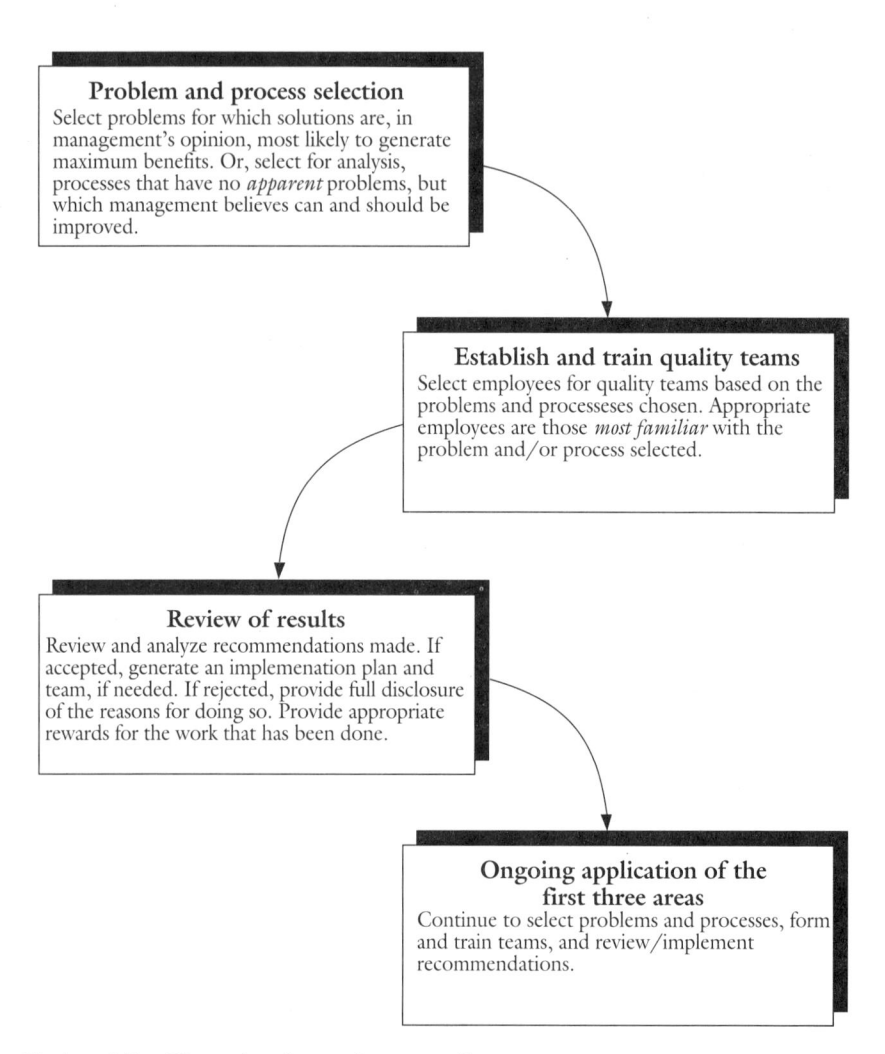

Review of results
Review and analyze recommendations made. If accepted, generate an implementation plan and team, if needed. If rejected, provide full disclosure of the reasons for doing so. Provide appropriate rewards for the work that has been done.

Ongoing application of the first three areas
Continue to select problems and processes, form and train teams, and review/implement recommendations.

Figure 4.7. The role of a quality council.

Quality councils have slightly different jobs, then, depending on whether they oversee the work of quality teams from a manufacturing or nonmanufacturing area. In both cases, the overall purpose of the council is to see to it that problems are solved—problems that prevent the organization from being the best it can be. But the difference between manufacturing oriented quality councils and nonmanufacturing-oriented quality councils is this: In the former case, the council identifies and assigns *problems* to quality teams. In the latter case, the quality council identifies and assigns *processes* to the quality teams.

How this works is shown in Figures 4.8 and 4.9. The manufacturing-oriented council compares the production output with the existing product specification and readily identifies deviations or problems. After deciding on the priority of the problems, if there are several, the council assigns a properly constituted quality team to solve the problem. More often than not, the

---

1. One or more high-priority problems, usually related to the manufactured product, are selected for analysis.

2. For each problem, a quality team is assembled from employees whose jobs and/or experience relate to the problem. Such a team is often horizontally arrayed, that is, consisting of members of different departments, such as operations, maintenance, engineering, and so on.

3. Each team receives proper training (if it has not already done so), meets to analyze the problem, and determines its probable root cause.

4. Depending on the cause and type of proposed action, the team either corrects the problem or recommends appropriate action to the quality council.

5. The quality council authorizes implementation of the proposed action.

6. The team may continue to meet periodically to analyze new problems and to identify process-improvement methods. Alternatively, the quality council may form new teams more properly constituted to address new problems.

Figure 4.8. The manufacturing quality council process.

1. One or more high-priority work processes are selected for analysis.

2. For each process, a quality team is assembled from employees whose jobs and/or experience relate to the process. Such a team is often, though not always, vertically arrayed, that is, consisting of members of the same department.

3. Each team receives proper training (if it has not already done so), meets to analyze the process, and determines areas of unmet customer needs.

4. Depending on the cause of the unmet need, the team will correct the problem through process modification, renegotiate the need, or apply problem solving to the unknown causes of the unmet need. Significant changes result in a recommendation of appropriate action to the quality council.

5. The quality council authorizes implementation of the proposed action.

6. The team may continue to meet regularly to further identify problems and new ways to improve the process. Alternatively, the quality council may form new teams more properly constituted to address other parts of the work processes.

Figure 4.9. The nonmanufacturing quality council.

quality teams put together by this council are structured horizontally. That is, the members come from several organizations, all of which are associated with the problem. For example, the team might consist of representatives from operations, engineering, quality assurance, maintenance, and so on.

The nonmanufacturing-oriented council reviews the various work processes that its members preside over, and although it may be able to compare the output or performance of each to some preestablished standard, it does not readily know whether the standards are stretching the workers, or allowing them to glide along. Therefore, unlike the manufacturing council, this group decides on the process that it wants analyzed, and establishes one or more quality teams to do so. The analysis identifies the problems, which in this case are deviations from customer needs, the causes of which are unknown. Once the problems are identified, nonmanufacturing quality teams look very much like manufacturing quality teams: they both have the same set of tools for solving their respective problems.

Two Important Points

In summary, there are two important points that should be made. The first is to reemphasize the importance of assigning processes to be analyzed. Although many nonmanufacturing organizations have established standards, these often mirror the performance that was achieved when the standard was set. Without critical analysis of the process, there is no way to know how to improve the standards being applied, or to what extent. Consequently, service organizations can easily fall into the trap of everything is OK around here! We're meeting our standards!

The second important point is to remember that although we believe there are differences between the way quality teams work in manufacturing and nonmanufacturing organizations, the differences can and should be subtle. For example, it might be true that manufacturing operators have little opportunity to make significant on-the-spot modifications to the production process. (Note, we are not saying adjustments.) But there are plenty of opportunities to analyze and recommend improvements to the service part of the production process: the timing of shifts, the method by which maintenance is scheduled, or the training of operators. These are all examples of production activities that lend themselves to analysis of the process.

At the same time, many service organizations have easily and accurately measured standards of performance, and can identify problems directly from them. Customer complaints, returned documents, and time spent with a customer all represent examples of issues that can be turned into a problem statement and, as we would do with manufacturing teams, be directly assigned to a quality team.

5 Data Gathering and Interpretation

The Universe is full of magical things patiently waiting for our wits to grow sharper.

—Eden Phillpotts

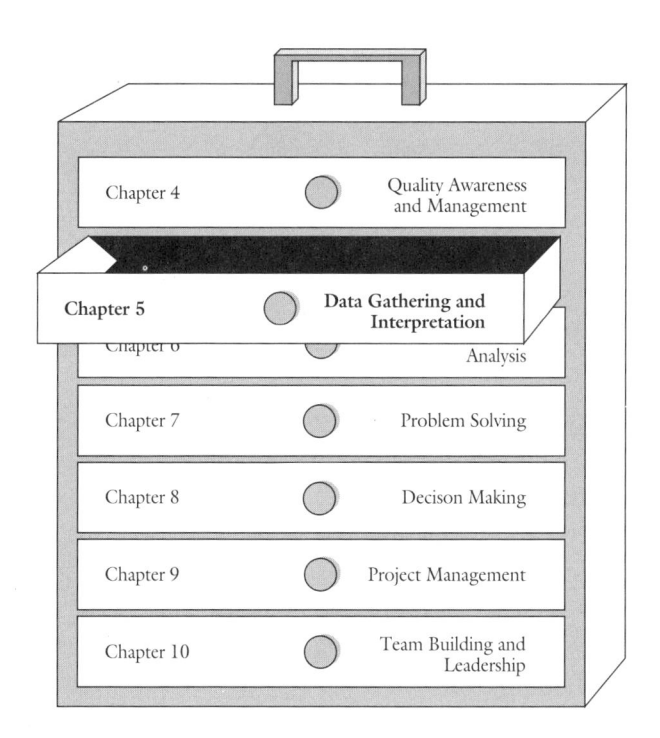

This book is not a definitive text on the subjects of data gathering and interpretation methods. There are many such texts available to quality practitioners at all levels, from the basic to the very advanced.

Our intent is to demonstrate what we believe to be the proper level of statistical and data-gathering methods provided to all employees. Too few details make the techniques useless and fail to harness the power of the problem-solving network. Too many details can immediately turn off most employees, rendering the techniques just as useless. For example, complex statistical methods often confuse employees, and consequently, they have no desire to learn and then use them. There is a place for these techniques, especially the seven "new" techniques,* in many companies. But the most important people in the company—the problem-solving network—need a set of simple tools that they can readily apply. The techniques we describe provide the proper tools. All but one of the seven basic tools are included: check sheets, Pareto charts, histograms, scatter diagrams, control charts, and cause and effect diagrams. The seventh, flowcharting, is an integral part of work process analysis, and is covered in chapter 6.

> *I always find that statistics are hard to swallow and impossible to digest. The only one I can ever remember is that if all the people who go to sleep in church were laid end to end they would be a lot more comfortable.*
> —Martha Wheaton Taft

Check Sheets

Ongoing quality improvement requires clear and useful information about processes and their problems. The absence of such information is often what prevents effective problem solving.

Note that we use the word *information*, not data. Many organizations are consumed with the collection of data, much of which is simply an interesting compilation of facts. Information contains data, of course, but goes beyond by answering questions that are relevant to the problems at hand. Information, then, is the right data captured and shown in such a way that it

---

*The seven new techniques are often described as relational diagrams, KJ method, systematic diagram method, matrix method, matrix data analysis method, PDPC method, and arrow diagram method.

can be properly interpreted. Check sheets are a convenient way to capture and show data.

There are several types of check sheets. In general, they are simple devices designed to collect data in a way that information can be gleaned from the form itself. They provide a way to visually show important patterns in a process. Check sheets are easily learned and used by workers at all levels.

Figure 5.1 shows a commonly used kind of check sheet. This version looks very much like a trend chart, since it shows a variable's trend of change. Some variable, such as temperature or production rate, is plotted against another variable, commonly time. The effect of the one variable on the other is clearly shown. In Figure 5.1 the worker is quickly alerted that an increase in temperature occurred, and that the process seems to be stabilizing at the new temperature.

The most commonly used check sheet is shown in Figure 5.2. Notice the marble production worker's clipboard in each case. Does the nature of the problem stand out readily? When facts are collected merely as data, they

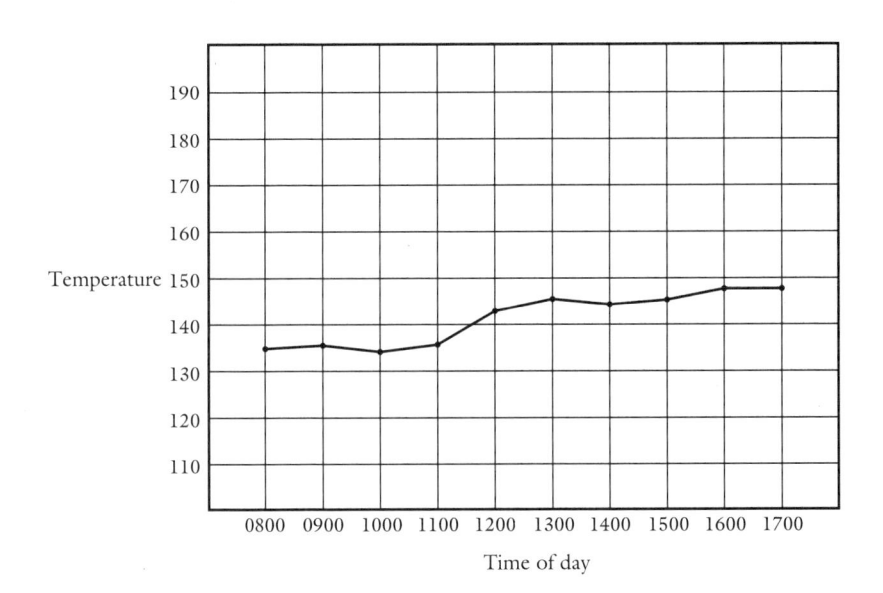

Figure 5.1. A check sheet.

do not easily yield information that can help solve problems. Conversion of the data on the clipboards to a check sheet or more appropriately the collection of marble production data onto a check sheet in the first place allows the major problems areas to stand out.

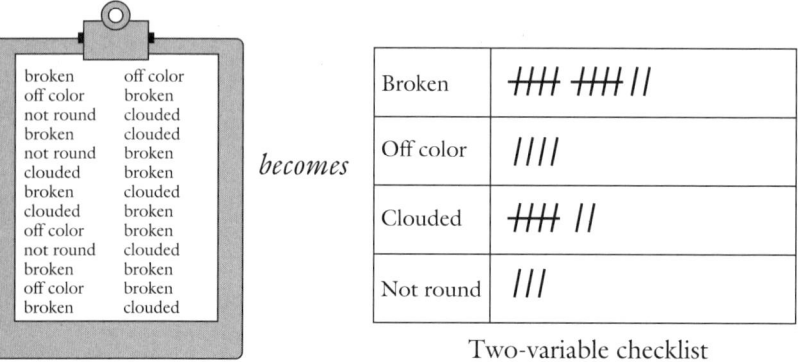

Broken													
Off color					
Clouded								
Not round				

Two-variable checklist
(marble defects and their number)

	Red	Green	Blue	Yellow
Broken	||||	||	|||	|||
Off color			|||		
Clouded			|||||	||
Not round			|||	

Three-variable checklist
(marble defects, their color, and their number)

Figure 5.2. Multiple-variable check sheets.

The top example of Figure 5.2 is a two-variable check sheet. Defect type is one variable, and the number of defects of each type is the other. The random data of the clipboard becomes information, showing that broken marbles is a problem worth the most attention, with clouded marbles being second in importance. The bottom example of Figure 5.2 is a three-variable check sheet. The same variables of defect type and number of defects of each type exist. The additional variable is marble color. The data of the clipboard still do not visually show very much: they are not yet usable information. But the same data shown on the check sheet now enable the production worker to quickly see that the problem of marble breakage is not unique to any of the colors, but that blue marbles are experiencing the largest share of defects of all types. If each color of marble was being produced on a different line, for example, the production worker might look for abnormalities on the blue line.

Rules for Collecting Data

Data become useful information only when they are collected with foresight and with the application of some simple rules. Collection is a work process itself, and can be performed well or haphazardly. The rules of data collection are

1. Fully understand the information needs of the particular situation. Ask some probing questions about what needs to be answered, and then decide on the appropriate data to provide the desired information.
2. Design simple data-collection devices that reduce the chance of error.
3. When necessary, prepare complete instructions for the use of data-collection devices, which alert the worker about when to collect, duration of the collection activity, and so on. This minimizes disruption of the process. Train the data collectors if necessary.
4. Test the forms after they have been in use for a while, and audit the results to ensure that valid collection techniques continue to be used.

It isn't that they can't see the solution. It is that they can't see the problem.

—G. K. Chesterton

Pareto Charts

If a check sheet was turned on its side and the marks fell to the bottom, the result could easily be converted to a bar graph representation of the observed problems. Then, if the highest bar was placed to the left, with successively shorter bars following in sequence, a Pareto chart would result. Figure 5.3 is an example.

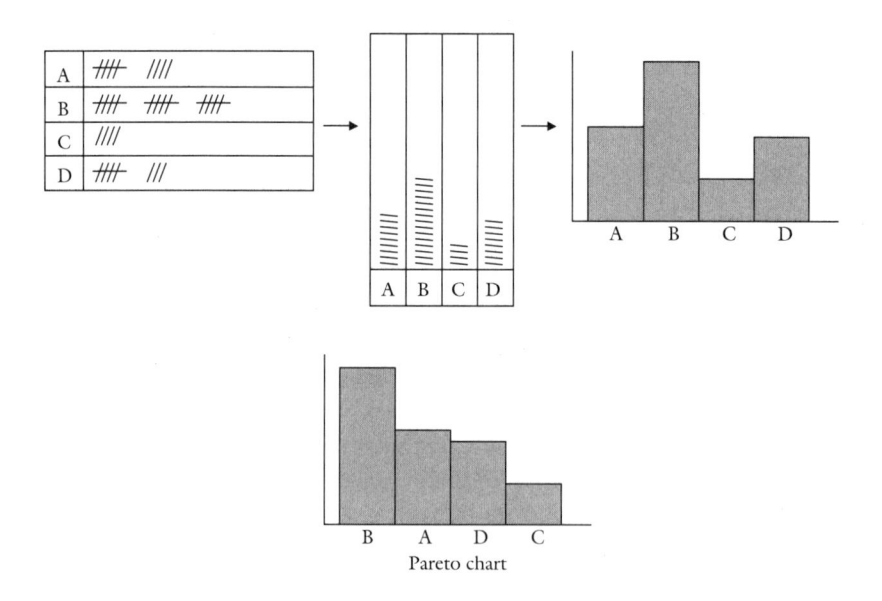

Figure 5.3. Check sheet to Pareto chart.

The Pareto principle was first defined in a quality sense by Joseph Juran in 1950. He described it as a "maldistribution of quality losses." Vilfredo Pareto, by the way, was a 19th century Italian who first stated that most wealth is owned by relatively few people, another form of maldistribution.

The Pareto principle states that most effects come from a few causes. Often heard is the 80/20 rule, which states that 80 percent of the problems come from 20 percent of the machines, materials, workers, and so on.

A Pareto chart is a special vertical bar graph that shows the relative importance of problems in a process. This information helps employees decide what is important to work on first.

Let's continue to follow the production difficulties of the marble manufacturing company. In Figure 5.2 we saw the benefit of check sheets in visually depicting data about marble defects. If, as shown in Figure 5.3, the check sheet results were transformed into a Pareto chart, the result would be diagrams as shown in Figure 5.4.

The top diagram is a Pareto of the top check sheet of Figure 5.2. In this simple example, the check sheet clearly indicated the most prevalent problem as broken marbles. The Pareto demonstrates the same conclusion. With more complex sets of data, the Pareto is extremely useful in showing the relative seriousness of problems. The marble manufacturing company is best served by working on broken marbles first. Assuming they do so aggressively, and reduce broken marbles by 70 percent, for example, the Pareto chart would now look like Figure 5.5. Then, attention is appropriately diverted to the problem of cloudy marbles, which is now most prevalent.

Figure 5.4b shows the Pareto of the data in the lower check sheet of Figure 5.2. Clearly, the production line making blue marbles has an inordinate share of the problems and deserves immediate attention.

So far, these are very simple but powerful applications of Pareto charts. In many ways, they simply show the check sheet conclusions in another way. But there are more effective ways to use Pareto charts.

For example, looking at problems by marble color alone tells the whole story if each marble costs the same to manufacture. But suppose we dig a little deeper and discover that because of the cost of different color glasses, the cost to manufacture each color varies considerably.

Color	Cost/marble
Blue	$ 0.12
Yellow	$ 0.35
Red	$ 0.11
Green	$ 0.18

Applying these costs per marble to the data in Figure 5.4b gives us Figure 5.4c, which quickly shows that although the blue marble line has

110   Breakthrough Quality Improvement

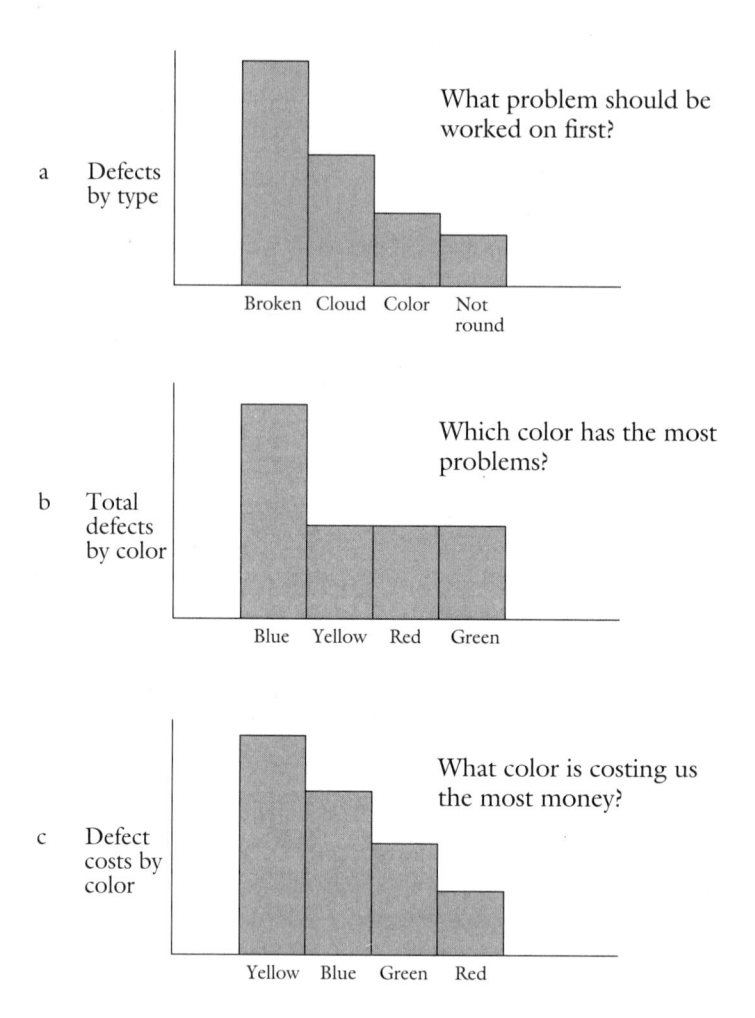

a   Defects by type

[Bar chart: Broken, Cloud, Color, Not round]

What problem should be worked on first?

b   Total defects by color

[Bar chart: Blue, Yellow, Red, Green]

Which color has the most problems?

c   Defect costs by color

[Bar chart: Yellow, Blue, Green, Red]

What color is costing us the most money?

Figure 5.4.   Pareto charts.

the most number of problems, the relatively fewer problems on the yellow marble line are costing the company more money. This simple application of a Pareto chart helps the workers in our marble factory target the most leveraging problem.

Data Gathering and Interpretation

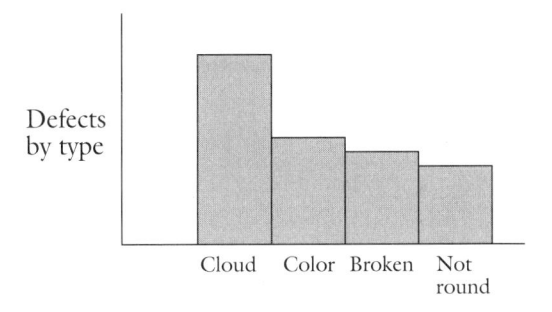

[Bar chart labeled "Defects by type" with bars for Cloud, Color, Broken, Not round in decreasing order]

Figure 5.5. Pareto chart after reducing broken marbles by 70 percent.

In general, Pareto charts compare measures on the vertical axis (time, cost, number of defects, impact to the company) to categories on the horizontal axis (products, production lines, divisions, workers, organizations, equipment, cost centers).

> *Aristotle could have avoided the mistake of thinking that women have fewer teeth than men by the simple device of asking Mrs. Aristotle to open her mouth.*
> —Bertrand Russell

Histograms

Histograms are another way of showing data pictorially, enabling the user to see patterns that are not obvious in tabular data. Histograms have a different purpose—they show the distribution of, and variations in, a set of data.

The values in a set of presumably identical data almost always show some variation. Think of these examples.

- Number of phone calls received per day
- Number of cars in freight trains
- Number of apples on apple trees
- Number of passengers on 727s

In each case, some variation will be found. If enough apple trees of about the same size are counted, however, we would find that a pattern will result. Very few trees would have no apples (unless they are dead, or if we mistakenly counted fruit on a cherry tree). No one would expect an extraordinary number of apples, like one million, either. Some number of apples, say between 475 and 484, would predominate. Fewer, but still many trees, would have 465 to 474 apples, or 485 to 494 apples. Fewer still would have less than 465 or more than 494.

This is an example of random distribution around some average number of apples. We are all familiar with the idea of random distribution, and the bell-shaped curve that results. For our apple grove, the bell-shaped curve might look something like Figure 5.6.

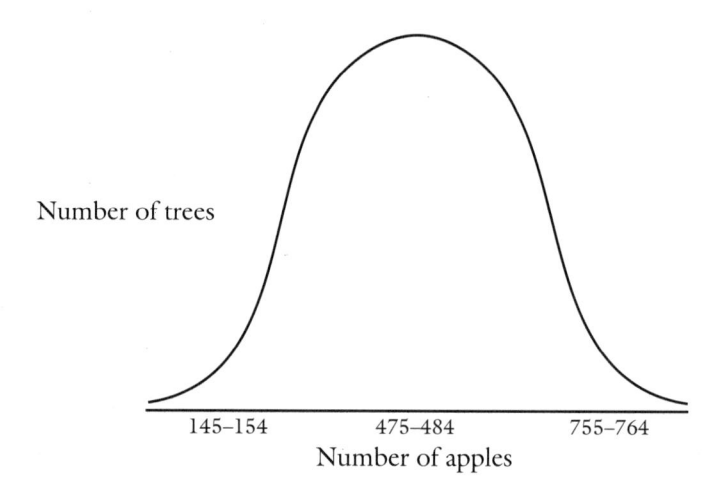

Figure 5.6. Distribution of number of apples on apple trees.

The idea of random distribution around some average is commonly shown by quality professionals with a device such as that shown in Figure 5.7. Balls are released from a hopper and encounter several pins (shown as black dots) that cause them to bounce back and forth as they fall (similar to an old-fashioned pinball machine). All the balls start from the center, and most have about the same number of random bounces left as they do right, and enter the center row. Some, though, bounce toward an outside row. The result is a bell-shaped distribution.

More important to production workers is the distribution of some product variable that is not simply random, but the result of variation in the manufacturing process. In the case of our marble manufacturer, a variable of interest might be the marble diameters. There may be an upper and lower

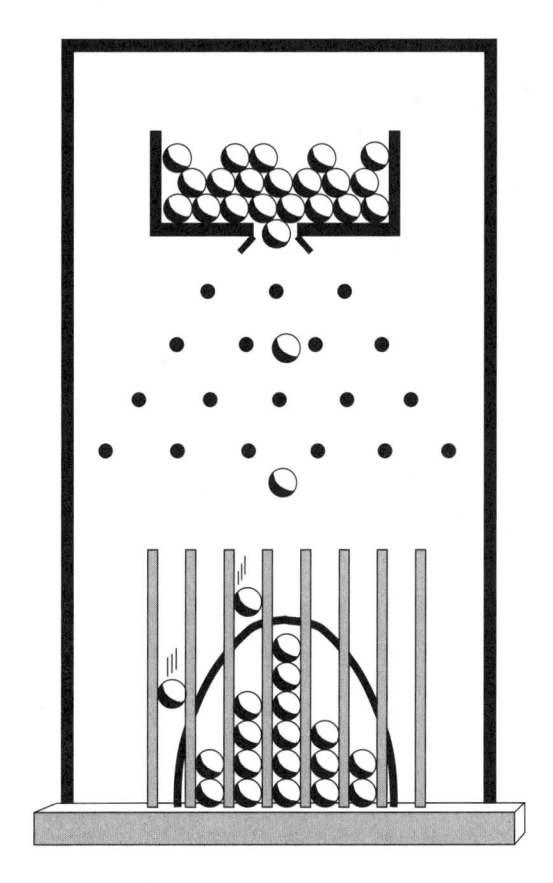

A typical way to demonstrate the formation of histograms

Figure 5.7. Random distribution into a bell-shaped curve.

limit, beyond which the marble is not useful for certain purposes, such as a Parcheesi game.

Figure 5.8 shows a histogram of marble sizes, with the data coming from a check sheet. Most marbles are at or near one-half inch in diameter, but many are smaller or larger. Notice that the check sheet, when held sideways, approximates the shape of the histogram.

Histograms are useful in several ways. First, they can provide information at a glance about the distribution spread, or width of the bell. In the case of our marble manufacturer in Figure 5.8, the spread of marble sizes might be deemed too large, and efforts would then begin the identify the cause of the variation with the intent to correct it. Histograms are also useful in problem solving by showing the pattern of the variation, or shape of the bell. (Sometimes it might not look like a bell at all.) While bell shapes are the common pattern for a process, they are by no means the only one. And in some cases, another pattern is appropriate.

Figures 5.9a through d shows four of the many histogram patterns that can be useful to employee problem-solvers. The two-peak pattern, having a distinct valley between two peaks, is generally the result of two bell-shaped distributions, and indicates that two processes are operating where only one was expected. The problem-solver's first step is to better understand the processes involved, with the goal of being able to measure each separately.

Figure 5.9b shows a plateau distribution. If it exists at all, the peak is very small. One interpretation is similar to the two-peak pattern, except that here many bell shapes and therefore processes are at work. Flowcharting to separate them can help. At the extreme, this pattern can also indicate that everyone in the organization is doing things his or her own way, in the absence of any standardized procedures and/or training.

The alternating distribution is shown in Figure 5.9c. It is characterized by recurring high and low values. Usually, an alternating distribution demonstrates poor data collection, or perhaps some sort of bias in the way data were rounded off. The problem-solver in this case should carefully examine the methods by which data are collected and used.

The fourth pattern of Figure 5.9 is skewed, so called because of its asymmetric shape, with one side tailing off gently and the other sharply. Skewed patterns are common in some processes that have natural limits that the process operates near. For example, suppose the histogram showed

Data Gathering and Interpretation

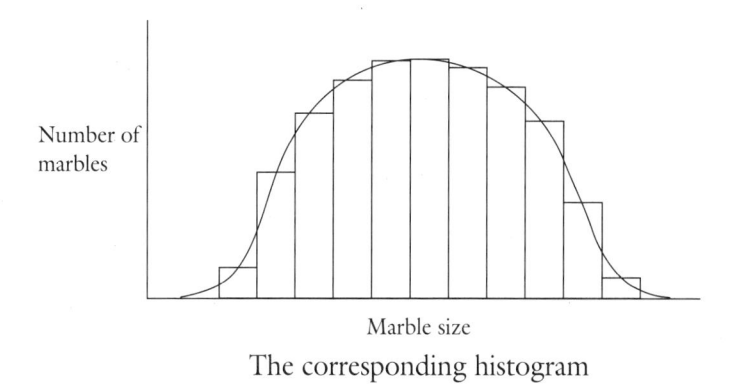

Size range (in.)	Number of marbles
.484–.486	ℍℍ ℍℍ ℍℍ //
.487–.489	ℍℍ ℍℍ ℍℍ ℍℍ ℍℍ ℍℍ ℍℍ ℍℍ ℍℍ ℍℍ ℍℍ ℍℍ ℍℍ ////
.490–.492	ℍℍ ℍℍ
.493–.495	ℍℍ ℍℍ ℍℍ ℍℍ ℍℍ ℍℍ ℍℍ ℍℍ ℍℍ ℍℍ ℍℍ ℍℍ /// ℍℍ ℍℍ ℍℍ ℍℍ ℍℍ ℍℍ ℍℍ ℍℍ ℍℍ ℍℍ ℍℍ ℍℍ
.496–.498	ℍℍ ℍℍ ℍℍ ℍℍ ℍℍ ℍℍ ℍℍ ℍℍ ℍℍ ℍℍ ℍℍ ℍℍ ℍℍ // ℍℍ ℍℍ ℍℍ ℍℍ ℍℍ ℍℍ ℍℍ ℍℍ ℍℍ ℍℍ ℍℍ ℍℍ ℍℍ
.499–.501	ℍℍ ℍℍ
.502–.504	ℍℍ ℍℍ ℍℍ ℍℍ ℍℍ ℍℍ ℍℍ ℍℍ ℍℍ ℍℍ ℍℍ ℍℍ / ℍℍ ℍℍ ℍℍ ℍℍ ℍℍ ℍℍ ℍℍ ℍℍ ℍℍ ℍℍ ℍℍ ℍℍ
.505–.507	ℍℍ ////
.508–.510	ℍℍ ℍℍ ℍℍ ℍℍ ℍℍ ℍℍ ℍℍ ℍℍ ℍℍ ℍℍ ℍℍ ℍℍ ℍℍ ℍℍ ℍℍ ℍℍ ℍℍ ℍℍ
.511–.513	ℍℍ ℍℍ ℍℍ ℍℍ ℍℍ ℍℍ ℍℍ ℍℍ ℍℍ ℍℍ ℍℍ /
.514–.516	ℍℍ /// ℍℍ

The corresponding histogram

Figure 5.8. A histogram.

116 Breakthrough Quality Improvement

Two-peak pattern
a

Plateau pattern
b

Alternating pattern
c

Skewed pattern
d

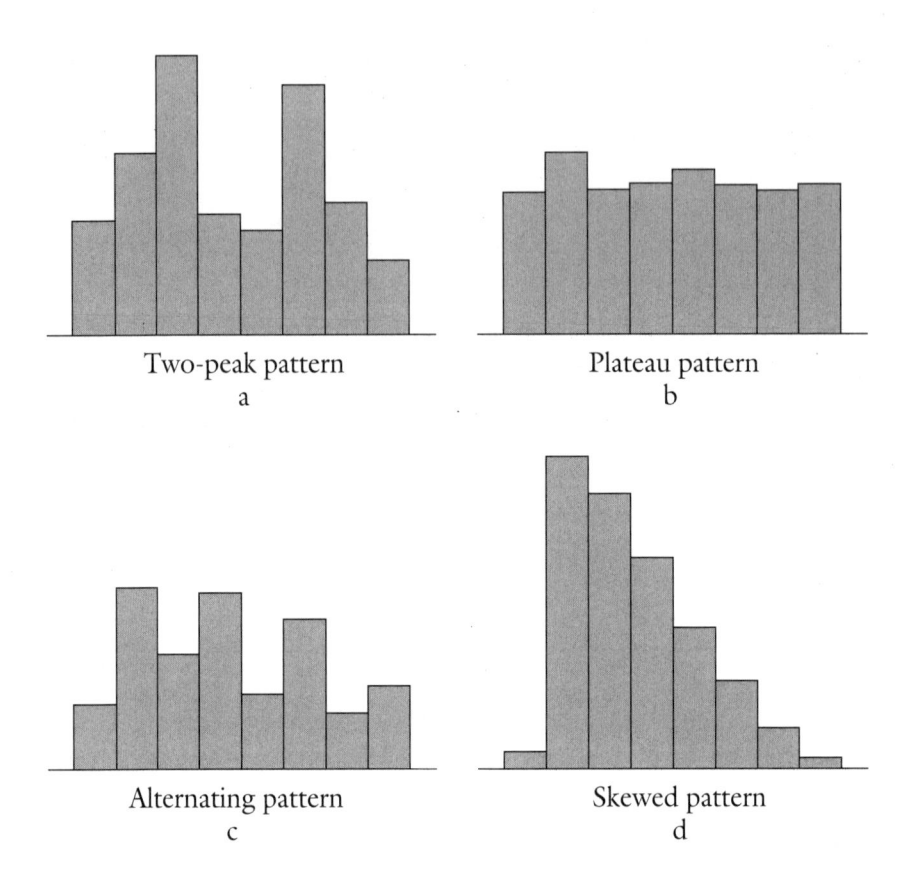

Figure 5.9. Histogram patterns.

passengers in a 727. If the airline is fortunate enough to operate its flights at near capacity, then the ultimate capacity of a 727 would be a limit, and there cannot be any data points which exceed it. Another example is a histogram showing complaints in a customer service department over many equal time periods. Zero is a natural limit, and if the department is a good one, it will typically operate at or near this limit. The problem-solver should carefully examine the gently tailing end of the histogram though, since there are often significant cost saving measures that can be taken there.

A beautiful theory, murdered by a gang of brutal facts.
—Thomas Huxley

Scatter Diagrams

Scatter diagrams are so named because they often resemble the pattern made by a shotgun blast. They are typically used to show what happens to one variable when another variable changes, to test a supposition that the two variables are somehow related.

Imagine the conclusion a worker might draw after plotting just a few of the points that show the relationship of variable a to variable b, such as shown in Figure 5.10. He or she might logically decide that no relationship at all exists, but in fact, Figure 5.10 contains the same points that will be shown in the middle example of Figure 5.11, just fewer of them. Perseverance in data collection, though, can result in a very different conclusion.

The top diagram of Figure 5.11 shows a relationship between the two variables, because one tends to increase as does the other, despite the scatter. This is referred to as a positive relationship. Any relationship between two variables does not prove that one causes the other. But, if the problem solver is looking for ways to achieve a high value of a (perhaps, for example, a represents surface smoothness), he or she will want to try to do so by increasing b. Of course, if a is undesirable, then b needs to be decreased.

The middle diagram of Figure 5.11 also shows a relationship between a and b. This time one variable decreases while the other increases, and the

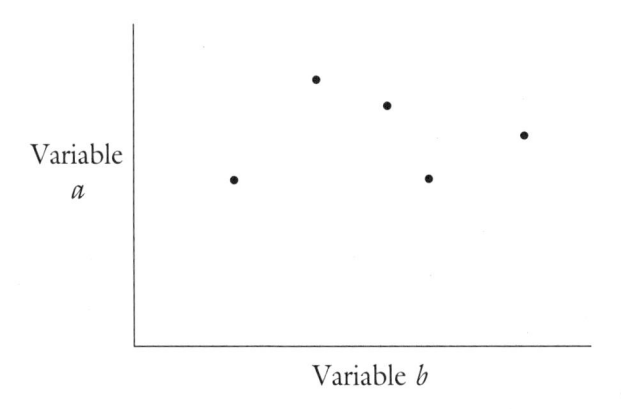

Figure 5.10. An incomplete scatter diagram.

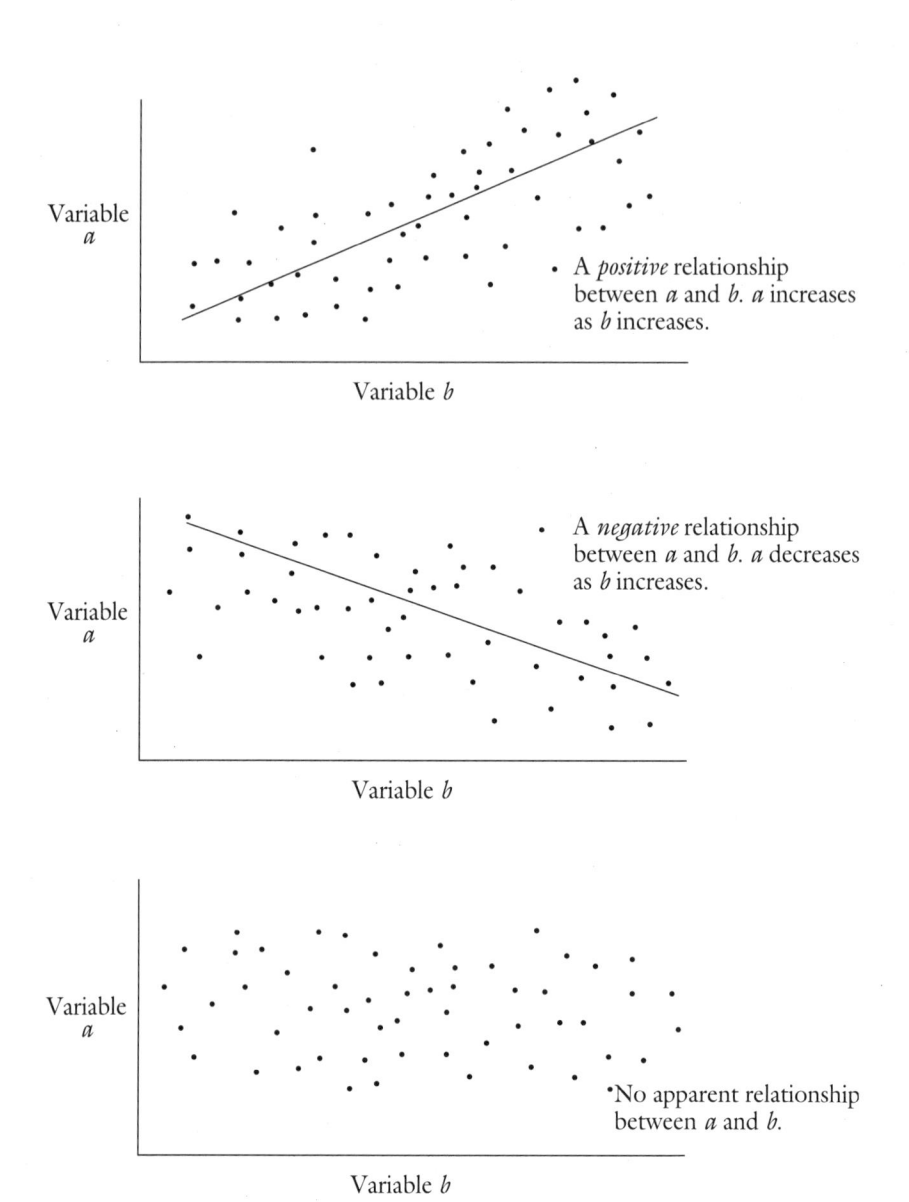

Figure 5.11. Scatter diagrams.

pattern is called a negative relationship. If the problem-solver wants less of *a* (supposing it is rejected product), *b* needs to be increased. Again, the opposite is true if *a* is desirable.

The extent to which the cluster of data points is tight, that is, has less scatter or resembles more of a straight line, gives the problem-solver a clue about how strong the relationship between the two variables is.

Sometimes no relationship exists between the two variables being measured, as shown in the bottom diagram of Figure 5.11. If certain that sufficient data have been collected to make that conclusion, the problem-solver would stop adjusting *b* in an effort to influence *a*.

One look is worth a hundred reports.

—Japanese proverb

Control Charts

A comprehensive review of control charts requires an excursion into standard deviations and a somewhat higher than usual level of mathematics. That is beyond the scope of this book. It is also beyond the interest of most of your problem-solving network, who ought to understand how to use control charts and their basic purpose, but who typically are not the people who create them. The interested reader will find many good texts on the subject. We will restrict this section to a discussion of the intent and purposes of control charts.

As quality consciousness increases in a company, and as product designs get more complex, one common result is a tightening of tolerances on the materials produced. Tight tolerances are a major competitive advantage. Diligent workers, who because of the quality activities in the company understand the desire for tighter tolerances, are naturally interested in adjusting their machinery to meet them. Unfortunately, such constant adjustment can actually make the situation worse!

Consider a schematic of a simple demonstration commonly done by W. Edwards Deming, shown in Figure 5.12. The intent of our process is to drop a ball onto the page of this book so that it rests on the desired target, marked *T*, representing the ideal specification. Your hand, poised over the page with the ball, is the machine, and its relative location over the page is the current state of its adjustment. As you move your hand to aim your drop of the ball, you further adjust your machine.

Your first approach is to adjust your machine so that it is directly over target T. But when you drop the ball, it rolls to a final resting place X, which is not within the tight tolerances that you expect. Observing this, you move your hand on the assumption that the same deviation occurring again will result in the ball resting the proper target T. But the second drop of the ball onto Y results in a roll toward Z, no closer to and possibly even further from T.

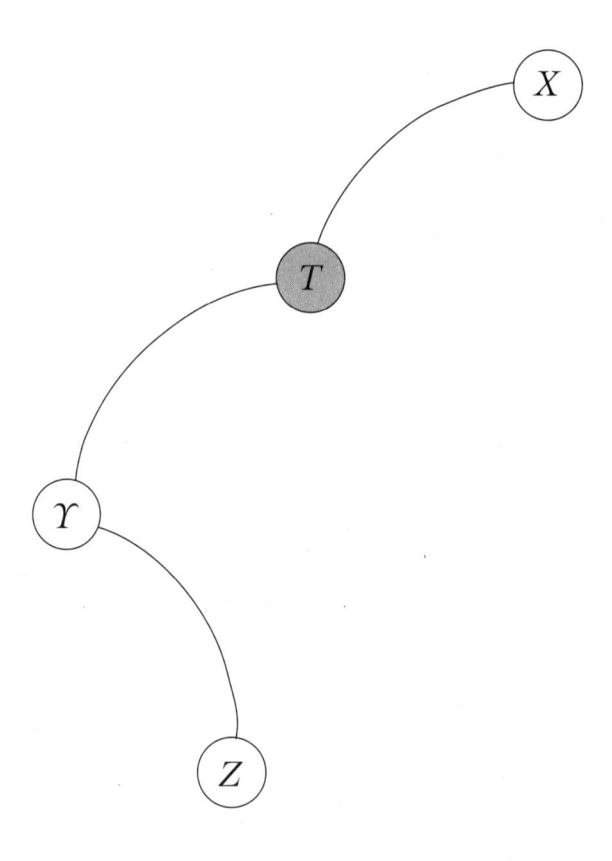

Figure 5.12. W. Edwards Deming's demonstration.

Additional attempts to adjust the machine will result in the ball moving further from the desired target. What is happening here? If the original process was obeying a stable distribution around T (as might be evidenced by a histogram that, with repeated measurements, remains about the same), then each successive drop might move in any direction and distance from T that is within that distribution. If the process is stable, constant attempts to adjust it based on individual data points only make the situation worse.

We might decide the stable distribution is too wide, and the ball is going too far away from T on individual drops, but that is a different problem. In that case, the process must be examined for ways to reduce the distribution spread (make the page perfectly level, for example).

Control charts are devices that tell production workers when the distribution of products is stable or has changed. Control charts, then, tell when it is appropriate to adjust the process and when it is appropriate to leave it alone.

Control charts measure the average of some quality characteristic of identical product groups. Using standard deviations allows the quality engineer to calculate the desired upper and lower limits for the quality characteristic. Any average of a new product group that falls outside of either limit shows that the product distribution has changed, and is unstable. The process is then deemed out of control.

Let's look back at the marble manufacturer's histogram shown in Figure 5.8, and assume it represents an acceptable distribution of marble sizes. Of course, any quality practitioner would continually strive to generate a very narrow distribution if it would help the company's profitability. The histogram looks like Figure 5.13, with the horizontal axis showing marble sizes and the vertical axis showing the amount of each size manufactured in a stable operation.

Several positions have been noted along the horizontal axis because they are of interest to the quality-minded marble manufacturer. Hopefully, the largest number of marbles in the distribution represents the desirable, or specified, diameter. In this example that is the case, and the specified diameter, or norm, is shown by a vertical line through the center. Further, there are some diameters at either end of the distribution that are sufficiently outside of the norm so as to be called out of specifications. Using statistical standard deviations, these outside diameter limits are usually set in such a

122   Breakthrough Quality Improvement

Number
of marbles

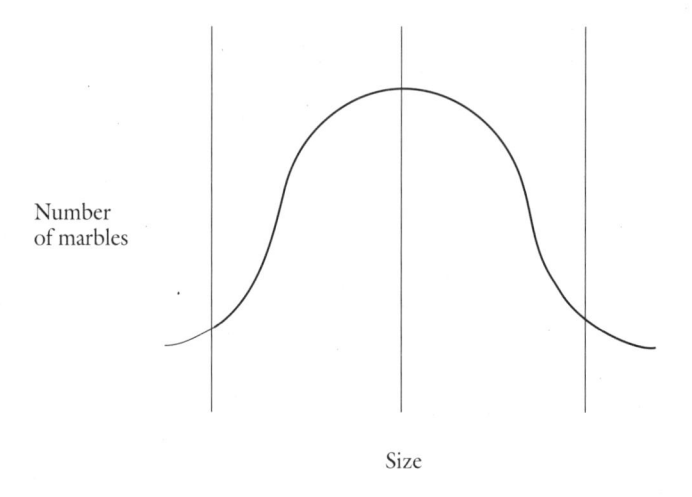

Size

Figure 5.13.   A histogram.

way that 99.74 percent of all marble diameters are within them. (This somewhat odd percentage is achieved when the outside limits are set at something called plus and minus three standard deviations.)

If the drawing of the marble histogram, along with the norm line through the center and the lines at the outside limits, is placed on its side, we have the beginning of a control chart (see Figure 5.14).

Now the vertical axis shows the marble diameters (or any other quality variable), but the horizontal axis now shows time. That is, the emerging control chart allows the marble manufacturer to follow, over a period of time, the actual marble diameters being produced, and to determine whether the distribution is changing. The two diameters that represent the largest and smallest desired size are termed the upper and lower control limits.

Now, if every single marble was measured, some would fall outside of these control limits—statistically, 0.26 percent of all marbles produced. And the diligent worker might adjust the machine when such an event happens, with the undesirable results that have already been demonstrated. But if subgroups of four or more marbles were each measured, and the average diameter of these subgroups plotted over time, the resultant line would

Size

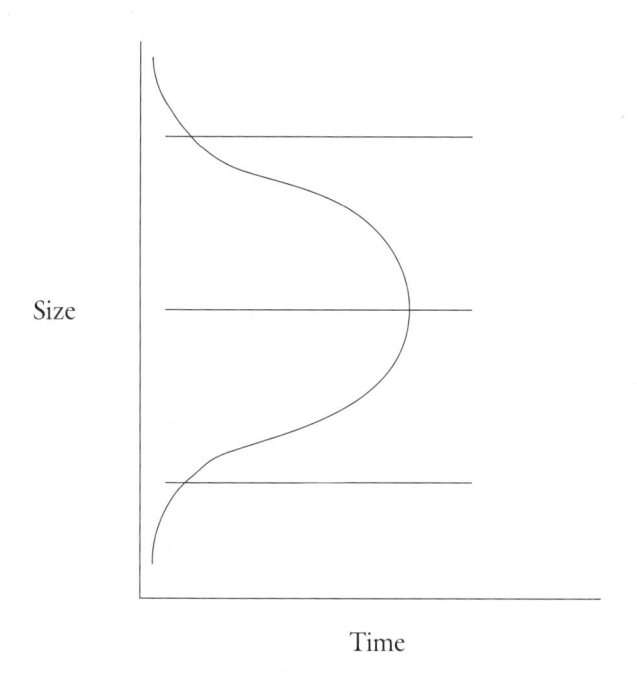

Time

Figure 5.14. Emerging control chart.

remain within the control limits if the distribution remains unchanged. The process would not be adjusted.

Figure 5.15a demonstrates this situation. Subgroups of four or more marbles are measured and the averages for the subgroups are plotted over time. If the distribution remains unchanged, the plot will remain within the control limits and no changes are necessary.

If for some reason, however, the distribution does change, because of some equipment malfunction, for example, the situation becomes that of Figure 5.15b. The average size of the subgroups follows the new, changed distribution. As a result, many of these averages now fall outside of the control limits. Now the process is out of control, and adjustment is warranted.

Of course, there are no actual histograms lying on their sides on an actual chart of this kind. The operator of the process sees a control chart such as Figure 5.15c.

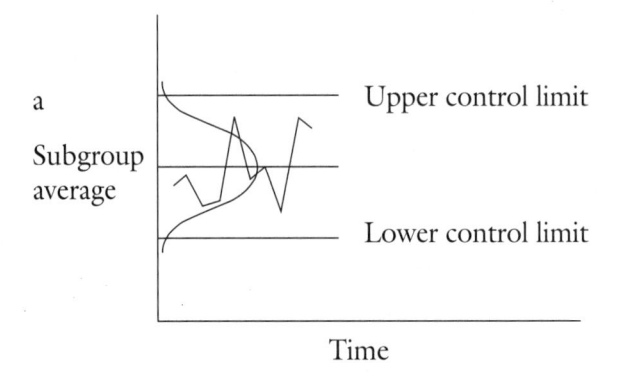

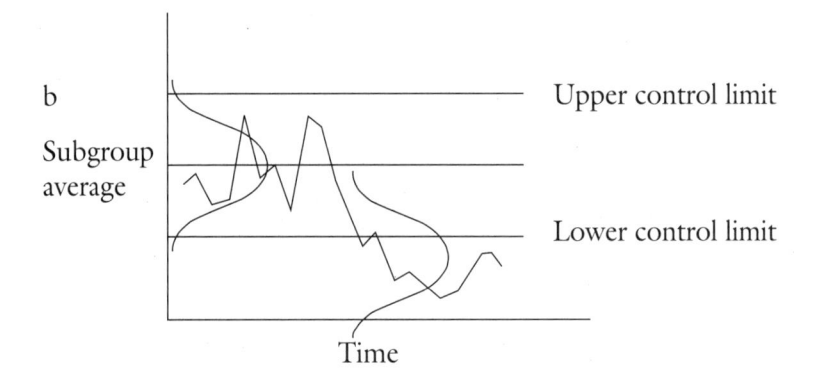

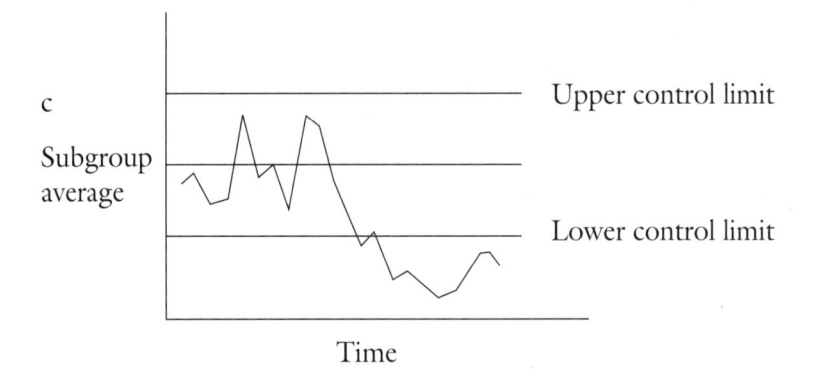

Figure 5.15. Basic control charts.

Figure 5.16 shows the two typical types of control charts. The top chart plots selected quality characteristic averages of product subgroups. For example, a bakery worker might take periodic samples of six cookies each and weigh them. Here the quality characteristic is the cookie weight. The average weight of the subgroup of six cookies must fall within the control limits that were earlier established for the process to be considered in control. Control charts based on the averages of some quality characteristic, determined through periodic sampling of product subgroups, are called *X-bar charts*, and are designated by the symbol $\overline{X}$.

The bottom graph of Figure 5.16 is similar, except that in this case workers are tracking the range of values found in each product subgroup. In our cookie bakery, the worker would average the weights to determine the first control chart, and then would plot the range between the highest and lowest subgroup weight for this second control chart. Both are required to fully understand whether the distribution is stable or not. Control charts that follow the range of the quality characteristic being measured are called *R charts*. Together, these two charts are commonly referred to as $\overline{X}$–R charts.

The real danger is not that computers will begin to think like men, but that men will begin to think like computers.
—Sydney J. Harris

Cause-and-Effect Diagrams

Cause-and-effect diagrams are one of the seven tools of quality, and have significant application if understood fully and used properly. Sometimes they are called fishbone diagrams because of the tendency of complex ones to resemble a fish skeleton.

Cause-and-effect diagrams are designed to continually obtain more information about a process and its outputs. They relate causes and effects. The most common form of a cause and effect diagram is shown in Figure 5.17. The top drawing depicts the main potential causes for the effect being studied: in this case, a 10 percent increase in product returns. We say *potential* cause on the assumption that within one or perhaps more of these is the *actual* cause. These main potential causes might be related to manufacturing,

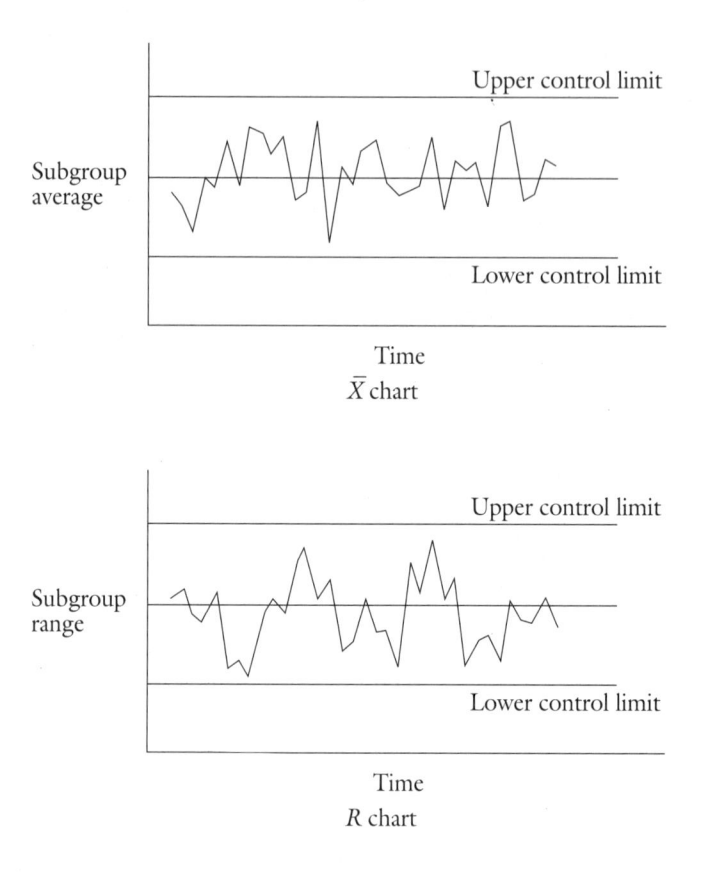

Figure 5.16. $\overline{X}$ and R control charts.

shipping, inspection, installation, or packing. Any other main potential cause that the quality practitioner might imagine could also be included.

As starting points, many problem-solvers look at categories of causes; for example, the four Ms—methods, manpower, materials, and machines, or the four Ps—policies, procedures, people, and plant. Of course, any cause category that is effective in solving the problem can be used.

A cause-and-effect diagram is hierarchical, somewhat like an organization chart. Each main potential cause has numerous potential subcauses that may influence its contribution to the effect. The bottom drawing of Figure 5.17 demonstrates the potential subcauses of the main potential cause shipping. In this example, the quality practitioner has determined that shipping equipment (perhaps the conveyor system), handling procedures, personnel training, and the carrier being used all contribute to shipping as a main potential cause of the problem. In turn, each of these potential subcauses has a number of contributing causes. For example, the carrier might be influenced by the contract with the company, experience with shipping this type of product, and so on.

Cause-and-effect diagrams are most effective when employed by a quality team and a skillful facilitator, because they stimulate effective brainstorming.

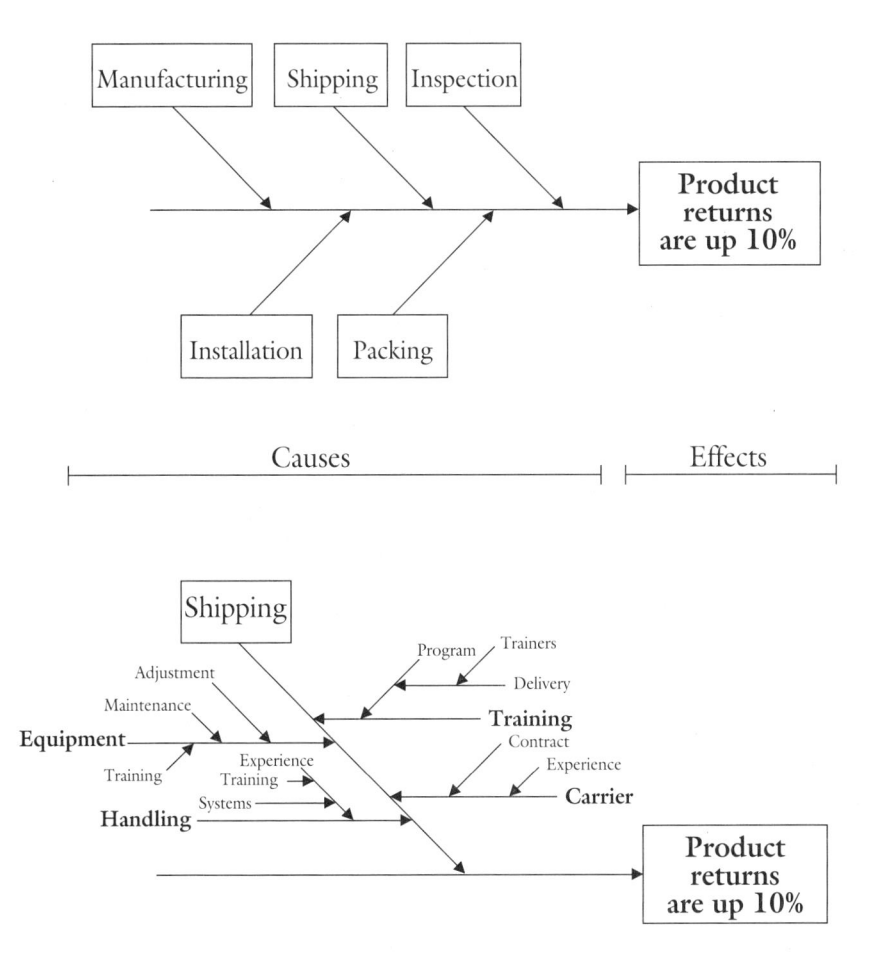

Figure 5.17. Cause-and-effect diagrams.

Team members can visualize potential causes that might relate to the effect being studied, and can add more as they brainstorm the issue. Some cause and effect diagrams grow over weeks or even months, and some we have seen cover an entire wall!

As a tool to organize information about processes and to understand them, cause and effect diagrams can be very valuable. Care must be taken, however, to ensure that the actual cause of the effect (or problem) is not determined simply by acclamation of the team members (the most popular cause), but that its selection is, in fact, based upon some rationale.

6 Work Process Analysis

The fatal tendency of mankind to leave off thinking about a thing when it is no longer doubtful, is the cause of half their errors.
—John Stuart Mill

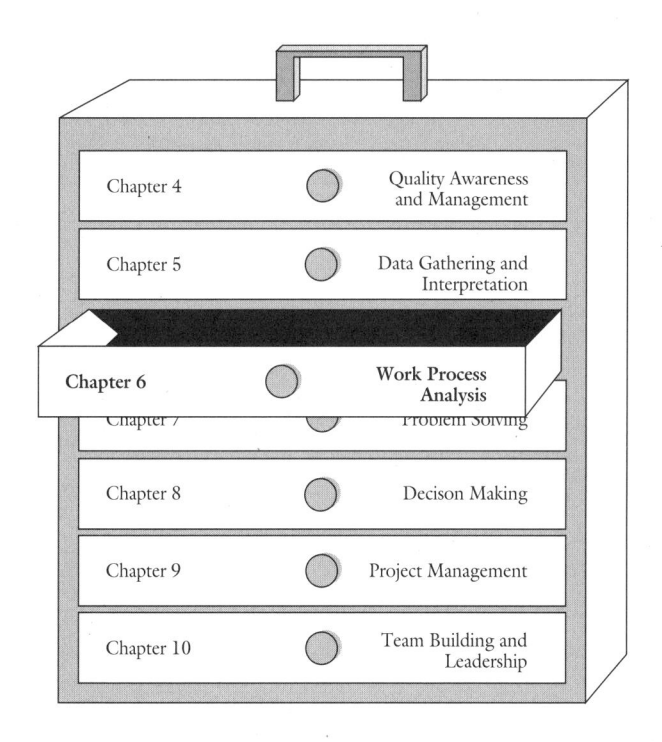

Chapter 4	Quality Awareness and Management
Chapter 5	Data Gathering and Interpretation
Chapter 6	Work Process Analysis
Chapter 7	Problem Solving
Chapter 8	Decison Making
Chapter 9	Project Management
Chapter 10	Team Building and Leadership

Work process analysis is a technique that is applied to a company's nonmanufacturing activities, such as accounting, personnel, research, or preventive maintenance planning. These activities differ from production of a discrete product in several key ways.

- The desired quality characteristics, or norms, of the group's output are often unclear, perhaps because they have never been established, or perhaps because they are inherently difficult to measure. Problems do not "announce" themselves as they do on a production line, and are often unrecognized as such.
- Frequently, there are many suppliers to, and customers of, the group. Respective inputs and outputs are somewhat intangible; for example, they may include ideas and information. The group's specific expectations of its suppliers, and the needs of its customers may not be carefully documented. Indeed, we have found that in many cases the nonmanufacturing organization cannot even identify all of its suppliers and customers!
- Unless someone in authority demands it, there is usually no effort to improve the operation, especially when everything seems to be working OK. After all, why rock the boat? (Look again at the quote that introduced this section!) When things get particularly bad, demand for improvement is usually forthcoming. But the group has no well-understood means to achieve it, except through trial and error, luck, or the individual effort of a forceful team member.

Nonmanufacturing organizations need a way to fully identify their suppliers and customers and their respective needs. They also need a way to continually identify ways to improve the productivity of their activities. Work process analysis helps organizations do both.

The obscure we see eventually. The completely apparent takes longer.
—Edward R. Murrow

The Steps of Work Process Analysis
Work process analysis consists of two primary sections, process description and process evaluation. Process description includes the three steps:

throughput analysis, customer analysis, and supplier analysis. Its purpose is to ensure full understanding of the process (the throughput), including what is done and how it is done. Specific inputs needed from suppliers, and outputs provided to customers, must also be fully understood.

Process evaluation has five steps: self-evaluation as a processor, self-evaluation as a customer, self-evaluation as a supplier, customers' evaluation of a processor, and processor evaluation of suppliers. Its purpose is to continually look for, identify, and implement ways to get the job done more effectively and efficiently.

Each of these steps will be fully described in this chapter. But first, we will look at one of the integral elements of work process analysis, the skill of flowcharting.

To understand is hard. Once one understands, action is easy.
—Sun Yat Sen

Flowcharting

A flowchart is a picture of a process. It shows the inputs to and outputs from the work activity, and the steps taken to add value—which is the purpose of the work. Flowcharts provide greater understanding of the process.

A full understanding of how a process works is critical to the ability to control it, and then to improve it. Understanding leads to the ability to better define problems with the process and its important elements. Without a full understanding, employees tend to use hit-or-miss methods: Let's try this and see what happens.

The Elements of a Flowchart

Flowcharts are usually, though not always, constructed as a series of boxes and other simple structures. They depict the steps of a process, its suppliers and their inputs, and its customers and outputs. A very simple flowchart form was shown in Figure 1.3 on page 14.

This diagram is, of course, not very useful for process diagnosis; it is far too simple. Significant benefits can be derived, however, from more rigorous detailing of all inputs, outputs, operations performed, and decisions made.

Engineers, quality professionals, and others use several complex diagrammatic forms to develop flowcharts. Again, we believe the elegance of the format is less important than the completeness and accuracy of the data captured. The problem-solving network of your company can make perfectly adequate flowcharts by using simple boxes to show inputs, actions and outputs, and diamonds to show decisions that must be made. Figure 6.1 illustrates the simple case of paying a bill by check. Of course, more or less detail could be shown, depending on the needs of whomever is analyzing this process.

Flowcharting at the Right Altitude

The right level of detail is essential to achieving the maximum benefit from a flowchart. That does not mean that every conceivable step must always be shown. Sometimes, a broader view of the process is the best. We have found it useful to think of examining a process from several altitudes, as if the viewer was looking down from an airplane.

Consider a flowchart of the dairy business in the United States. Although we are not farmers, and do not profess great knowledge of this business, a flowchart of this country's dairy activities from a very high altitude might look something like Figure 6.2. From this perspective, we might see an entire farming area as one box. Broad distribution routes are readily apparent. We would see overall inputs, such as feed and empty containers; throughputs, including dairy farmers and their activities; and outputs, including packaged milk finding its way to the ultimate retail consumers. This level of detail could be very useful to people who are interested in the big picture, or who are teaching a course in dairy macroeconomics. But, of course, it would be of little value to the dairy farmer, because the smallest level of detail is a large group of farms. The farmer cannot get any information from this altitude regarding operations of his or her farm operations, and thus cannot use this flowchart to improve operations.

As our airplane loses altitude, more detail becomes apparent, and the big picture of the nation's dairy farm system is lost over the horizon, as shown in Figure 6.3. More farms come into view, and some information about how they interact can be seen. For example, the way that milk is collected from individual farms and is brought to a central bottling and distribution area would enable regional dairy managers to better understand their areas of responsibility.

Work Process Analysis **133**

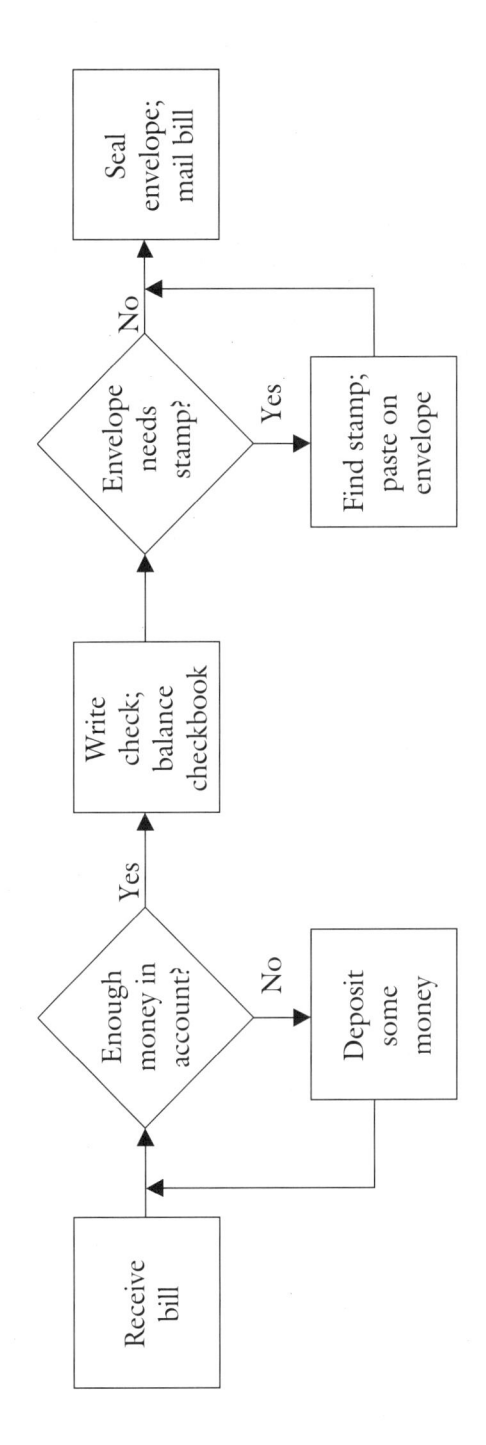

Figure 6.1. A flowchart of paying a bill by check.

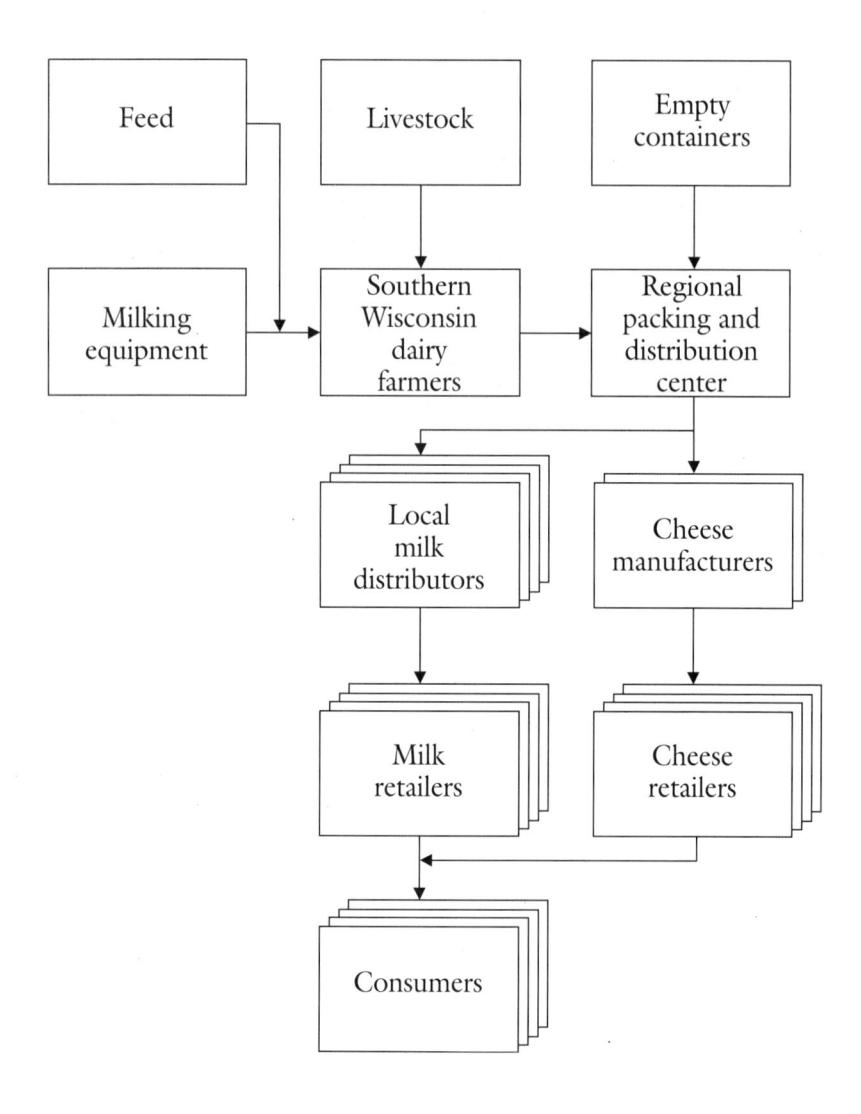

Figure 6.2. Dairy operations flowchart from high altitudes.

Work Process Analysis 135

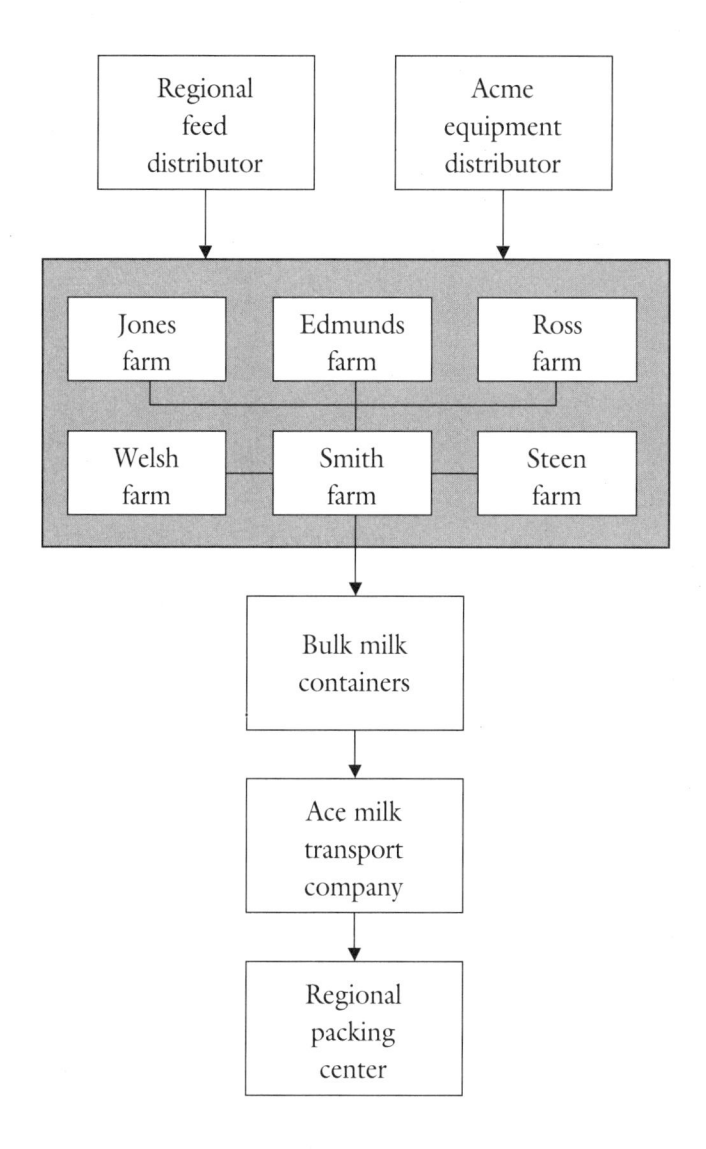

```
    ┌──────────────┐      ┌──────────────┐
    │   Regional   │      │     Acme     │
    │     feed     │      │   equipment  │
    │  distributor │      │  distributor │
    └──────┬───────┘      └──────┬───────┘
           │                     │
           ▼                     ▼
  ┌──────────────────────────────────────────┐
  │  ┌────────┐   ┌─────────┐   ┌────────┐   │
  │  │ Jones  │   │ Edmunds │   │  Ross  │   │
  │  │  farm  │   │  farm   │   │  farm  │   │
  │  └────────┘   └─────────┘   └────────┘   │
  │                                          │
  │  ┌────────┐   ┌─────────┐   ┌────────┐   │
  │  │ Welsh  │   │  Smith  │   │  Steen │   │
  │  │  farm  │   │  farm   │   │  farm  │   │
  │  └────────┘   └────┬────┘   └────────┘   │
  └───────────────────┼──────────────────────┘
                      ▼
              ┌───────────────┐
              │   Bulk milk   │
              │   containers  │
              └───────┬───────┘
                      ▼
              ┌───────────────┐
              │   Ace milk    │
              │   transport   │
              │    company    │
              └───────┬───────┘
                      ▼
              ┌───────────────┐
              │   Regional    │
              │    packing    │
              │    center     │
              └───────────────┘
```

Figure 6.3. Dairy operations flowchart from middle altitude.

The individual farmer is most interested in the view from ground level. What is happening on this farm? This view is of little interest to the macroeconomist and regional dairy manager. But, as shown by Figure 6.4, the farmer can now identify the bottlenecks and other problems that need to be corrected. This level of flowchart is of most benefit to the individual dairy farmer.

Flowcharts, then, should show a level of detail that is most important to the users, whether they are workers or company presidents. Chief executives are rarely interested in the details. There is no time for that, and after all, that's what delegation is all about! Conversely, although we believe every employee should be aware of the big picture, it is of rare use in diagnosing and correcting specific workplace problems.

When the high altitude flowchart picks up a problem it cannot pinpoint (for example, low milk volumes from a certain farm group), the airplane can swoop down for a better look at a lower altitude.

The Use of Flowcharting
Successful flowcharting exercises result when some useful rules are applied.

1. Construct the chart using a group of people who, together, have complete knowledge of the process. Usually, the group consists of appropriate workers in the process, customers, and suppliers. Sometimes, supervisors add a unique perspective. Strong facilitation can be especially beneficial. A facilitator ensures that the entire group participates and that the right questions are asked.
2. Show the entire flowchart at all times. This often means taping large sheets of paper to the wall. Constant visual display allows each participant to review, add to, and challenge past work. This is important because flowcharts are rarely, if ever, created perfectly in a smooth sequence.
3. Question, question, question! Continue to answer the questions what, where, how, and who. Look for decisions that must be made. Sometimes, the group decides to pull the airplane up to a higher altitude, because unnecessary details accumulates. (For example, one group developed a flowchart depicting how to start a

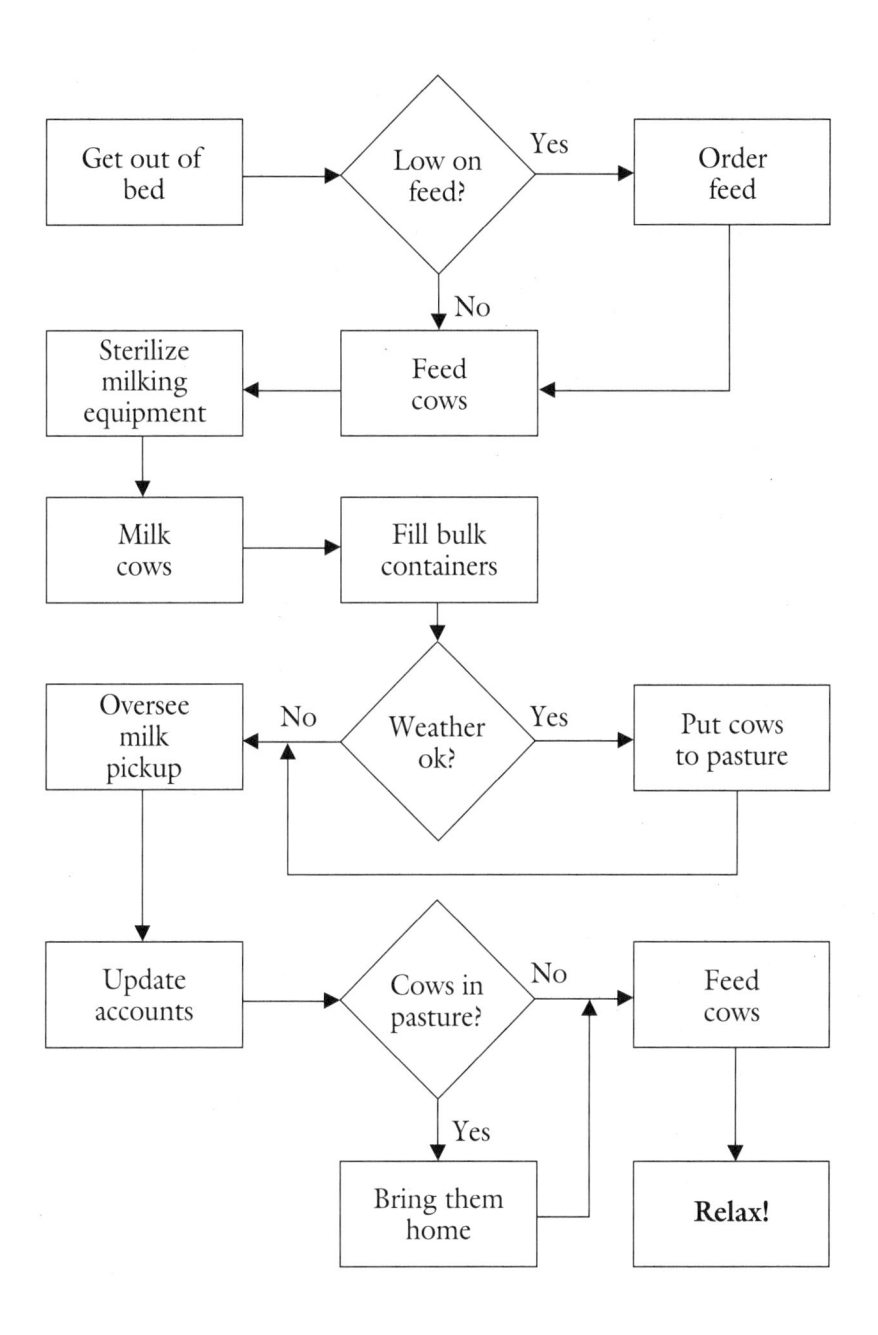

Figure 6.4. Dairy operations flowchart from ground level.

car. Having shown that the car must be walked to, they added the step "stop at the door." They soon decided that this was absurd!) If insufficient understanding results from a lack of detail, lower the altitude from which the process is viewed.

The Benefits of Flowcharting

Work process improvements are often identified in the flowcharting session. We once had an employee group from an automobile dealership flowcharting their various areas of responsibility. One responsibility of the salespeople was to order new cars, and, on delivery, to send them to the service department for preparation. Both sales and service flowcharts showed these steps. But the service department complained that the new cars would just appear, often at inconvenient times. They had no prior knowledge of the order or delivery dates. A simple addition to the sales flowchart (notification to service when a car was ordered, including model type and expected delivery date) solved the problem. The service department was then able to schedule its time more effectively.

This kind of benefit comes from better understanding the process and how it impacts others; this is the primary purpose of flowcharting. Other, less easily measurable, benefits can also be achieved in the area of employee enthusiasm. When employees better understand their roles and feel a part of the decision-making process, they will almost always support the quality efforts across the company, with predictable results. We like to term this company ownership. When employees treat their work process as if it was their own company, improvements will readily follow.

Now let's return to the steps of work process analysis.

We must ask where we are and whither we are tending.
—Abraham Lincoln

Process Description

The first half of work process analysis is process description, consisting of the three steps throughput analysis, supplier analysis, and customer analysis. The purpose of these steps is simple: to gain a complete understanding of what is and should be going on in the process.

Throughput Analysis

Throughput analysis deals with the job itself, which creates the throughput—turning inputs into more valuable outputs. In broad terms, four steps are completed.

1. **Throughput identification.** What is the name of the process (such as accounts payable, customer service, and so on)? What are the beginning and ending points that represent the boundaries of the process? Who is the owner of the process; that is, the individual or group who is accountable for its performance?
2. **Throughput purpose.** Why does the process exist? What is its mission? The purpose of an accounting department might be to provide customers with invoices for the goods and services we provide. This statement does not include modifiers, such as "within three working days." These customer needs will be identified later. Purpose, by the way, is *not* a recitation of employee's daily activities. These may be completely inappropriate. For example, if an employee spends most of the day staring out the window, that activity is certainly not the purpose of the job!
3. **Throughput description.** What are all the tasks, activities, decision points, inputs, and outputs that appropriately belong within the established boundaries? This step commonly employs flowcharting, which has been discussed.
4. **Throughput check.** What overlapping or otherwise seemingly useless activities have been identified? What problems, bottlenecks, or weak links become apparent? And most importantly (as with the auto dealership we described previously), what can we do right now to correct things?

The first three steps lead to a comprehensive understanding of the process itself. The fourth step is a quick checking step, to make sure that tasks, inputs, and outputs are useful.

Customer Analysis

Throughput analysis begins to consider customers in that it identifies work process outputs. Customer analysis goes several steps further, however, to ensure that what the process is trying to achieve is desired by and useful to the customer, and that the customers' viewpoints are being considered. Customer analysis includes five steps.

1. **Customer identification.** Who are all of the customers to whom the process provides outputs? They may be external, such as the retail buyer, or internal, such as the manager of the work unit. Most people are surprised at the number of customers they have when they delve into their work process.
2. **Customer ranking.** All customers are, in an ideal world, equally important. The real world, however, provides most people with a limited amount of time to perform work. Thus priorities must be established. In most companies, the external customer is most important. If time is better spent with an external customer's needs, the importance of an internal customer, for whom the output of the process is a mere convenience, might have a lower priority. Ranking helps ensure that the greatest amount of productivity is achieved by each unit of work.
3. **Customer needs.** The most important element of customer analysis is the determination of their needs. Remember that customer needs can be considered *musts*, things that have got to be satisfied and which can be measured, or *wants*, things that are desirable but not mandatory. Wants, however, must be weighted, and the most heavily weighted should be considered very important. The best way for the group analyzing the process to obtain this information is also the most obvious: ask the customer!
4. **Needs measurements.** All customer-identified musts should be measurable. The standard of measurement should be established and agreeable with the customer. For boss-subordinate pairs, most people recognize this as the performance contract by which the subordinate's performance will be judged. But workers within a process must understand the measurement criteria for all customers' musts.
5. **Future needs.** Conversations with customers provide a perfect opportunity to probe into the future. What needs does the customer anticipate? By when? How can the process be adjusted to ensure that these needs are fulfilled?

Supplier Analysis

Supplier analysis is very similar to customer analysis. Throughput analysis begins to consider suppliers in that it identifies inputs to the work process. Supplier analysis helps ensure that what suppliers are providing is desired by and useful to the work process, and that the workers' viewpoints are being considered. Supplier analysis also includes five steps:

1. **Supplier identification.** Who are all of the suppliers who provide inputs to this process? They may be external, such as the raw material supplier, or internal, such as the production maintenance group. As was true with customers, most people are surprised at the number of suppliers they have when they delve into their work process.
2. **Supplier ranking.** Again, in the real world, priorities must be established. In this case, though, internal and external suppliers may be ranked equally. The situation must be analyzed before any decision is made.
3. **Supplier needs.** Needs assessment is also the most important element of supplier analysis. What needs of its suppliers, expressed as musts and wants, does this process have? To complete the analogy with customer analysis, the most obvious way to make sure that all suppliers understand the needs of the process is to convey those needs to them!
4. **Needs measurements.** As with customer analysis, any musts of the work process that are identified to a supplier should be measurable. The standard of measurement should be established and agreeable with the supplier.
5. **Future needs.** Finally, conversations with suppliers provide a perfect opportunity to probe into the future. What needs of the process are expected to change, and how might that affect suppliers? This enables the supplier to consider how his or her activities can be adjusted to ensure that your future needs are fulfilled.

These various steps complete the rigorous job of process description, the first half of work process analysis. The process and its needs, as well as the needs of its customers, should now be thoroughly understood. A review of Figure 6.5 should put these steps into perspective.

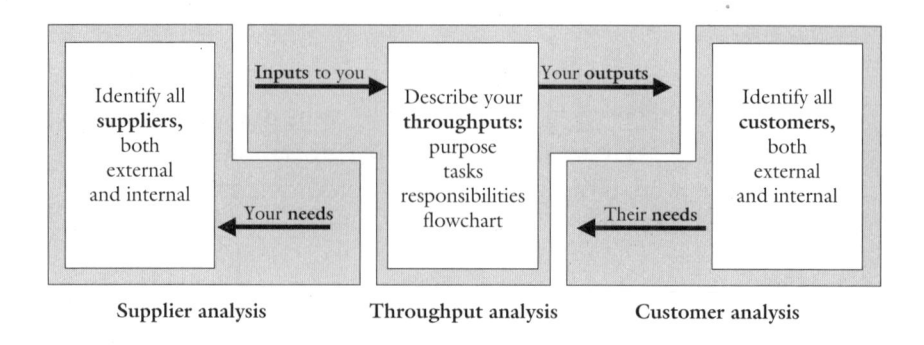

Supplier analysis	Throughput analysis	Customer analysis
Identify all suppliers, both external and internal	Describe your throughputs: purpose tasks responsibilities flowchart	Identify all customers, both external and internal

Inputs to you → ; Your outputs → ; ← Your needs ; ← Their needs

Figure 6.5. Process description.

The Key Questions

Having done all the work of process description, most work units find a number of quick fixes to make, correcting bottlenecks and eliminating obsolete methods. In addition, a much greater understanding of customers' and suppliers' needs is gained. Often, people regard this information as the primary output of process description, and feel that it is now time to proceed to the second half of work process analysis, which is process evaluation, finding ways to continually improve the process. But it is not time to do so until two critical questions are asked, answered, and acted upon, if necessary. These two questions, which are the backbone of work process analysis, are

1. Are *all* of the musts and the highly weighted wants of each customer of this work process fully met?
2. Are *all* of the musts and the highly weighted wants of this work process fully met by each of its suppliers?

If the answer to either of these key questions is no, then the time for process evaluation, or continual improvement methods, has not yet been reached. To consider continual improvement at this point is analogous to the farmer who paints the barn (continual improvement) while the animals are escaping (basic needs unmet).

The unmet needs of customers and the work process must be met first. To do so, one of three things is done.

1. Fix the cause of the unmet need, if it is known.
2. Renegotiate the unmet need if it cannot be achieved or is unreasonable.
3. Use problem solving (chapter 7) if the cause of the unmet need is not known.

The art of progress is to preserve order amid change and to preserve change amid order.
—Alfred North Whitehead

Process Evaluation

Having met all the needs of its customers, and assured that all of its needs are met by its suppliers, the process can be considered stable. Many groups stop here, especially when there is no incentive to continually improve the process. But quality improvement should never stop. Stable processes contain a wealth of potential improvements. All the group needs to do is look in a systematic way.

Process evaluation takes a look at how the stable process is working, and finds ongoing ways to improve it. There are two major evaluation themes, self-evaluation and supplier/customer evaluation. Figure 6.6 shows this other half of work process analysis.

Self-Evaluation in Three Roles

In chapter 1, the triple role of each work process operator was discussed. Any processor is simultaneously a supplier (providing expected materials or information to some customer) and a customer (receiving some materials or information from a supplier). Thus, any work process and its operators must evaluate themselves in each of their three roles: processor, supplier, and customer.

There is no detailed procedure for achieving this three-part evaluation. There are only three questions. But the persistent inquiry by workers who understand their process, their expectations of their suppliers, and their customers' needs will continually improve the process. The three questions and the evaluation steps they support are as follows:

1. **Self-evaluation as a processor.** Based on the ongoing evaluation of all aspects of this work process, how can we find ways to meet or exceed the outputs expected by our customers in less time, at lower cost, using fewer resources, and with less waste?
2. **Self-evaluation as a supplier (to customers).** Based on the ongoing evaluation of all aspects of the outputs of this work process and of our customers' needs, what changes or improvements to our outputs can we suggest that will permit us to continue to meet or exceed customers' expectations, in less time, at lower cost, using fewer resources, and with less waste?
3. **Self-evaluation as a customer (of suppliers).** Based on the ongoing evaluation of all aspects of the inputs to this work process and our needs from our suppliers, what changes or improvements to our inputs can we suggest that will permit us to continue to meet or exceed our customers' expectations, in less time, at lower cost, using fewer resources, and with less waste?

Customer and Supplier Ratings

Finally, the work group should periodically reevaluate how it is doing in the eyes of its customers and how its suppliers are doing in its eyes. This happens, of course, during the first part of work process analysis, the process description step. But needs change. It is prudent to revisit these issues at some appropriate interval. Ask your customers three questions:

1. On a scale of 1 to 5, with 1 meaning *never* and 5 meaning *always*, how would you rate the degree to which we meet your expectations?
2. What comments can you provide to us concerning cost or productivity deficiencies that you have observed?
3. How might we *ideally* satisfy your needs? If you could create the ideal situation, what would it be? What do you wish was different?

Significant data can be gleaned by a group courageous enough to ask these questions. And the customers will be delighted by the opportunity to respond.

In the same manner, each work group can rate its suppliers, by providing feedback on these three questions. Hopefully, a company would use this process fully, and each group would request customer ratings of it (which

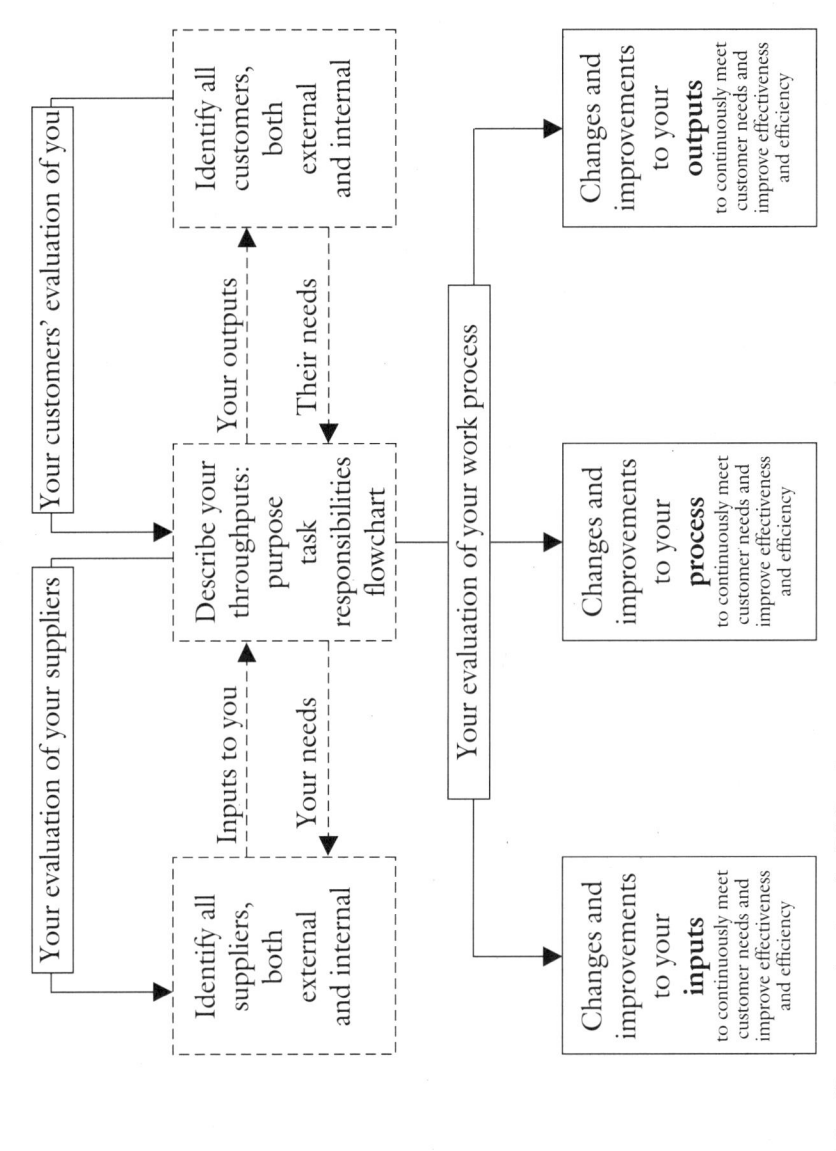

Figure 6.6. Process evaluation (solid lines).

the group's suppliers would then provide), thus negating the need to force answers down the throats of unconvinced suppliers. If that is not the case, some prework with the suppliers will help them understand the mutual benefit that can be derived from this periodic exercise.

It is not enough to be busy . . . the questions is: what are we busy about?
—Henry David Thoreau

Work Process Analysis

Work process analysis is the means for nonmanufacturing groups, or the nonmanufacturing activities of production organizations, to first ensure that all needs are met (that the process is stable), and then to find ways to continually improve the process. This is not a one-time effort to be completed during some seminar. Rather, these analyses must become part of the company's operation. As has been said before in this book, quality cannot be effective if it is the project of the month.

To become ongoing, a nonmanufacturing quality council (Figure 4.9 on page 100) would assign initial groups to processes that it deems worthy of analysis. Training would be provided to the teams formed. After reviewing each team's results, the nonmanufacturing quality council would assign another process to the same or newly formed and trained team. The council might use Pareto charts, for example, when assigning work processes that appear to have the largest potential for improvement. The system continues, and improvements are steadily gained.

Earlier in this chapter, two key questions were identified, which help an organization determine whether its processes are stable. Paraphrased, these questions were: Are my customers' needs fully met? and Are my needs fully met? There are several actions that an organization may choose when the answer to either of these is no. When the cause of the unmet need in unknown, though, the best course of action is problem solving. So let's look at it next.

7 Problem Solving

The message from the moon that we have flashed to the far corners of this planet is that no problem need any longer be considered insoluble.
—Norman Cousins

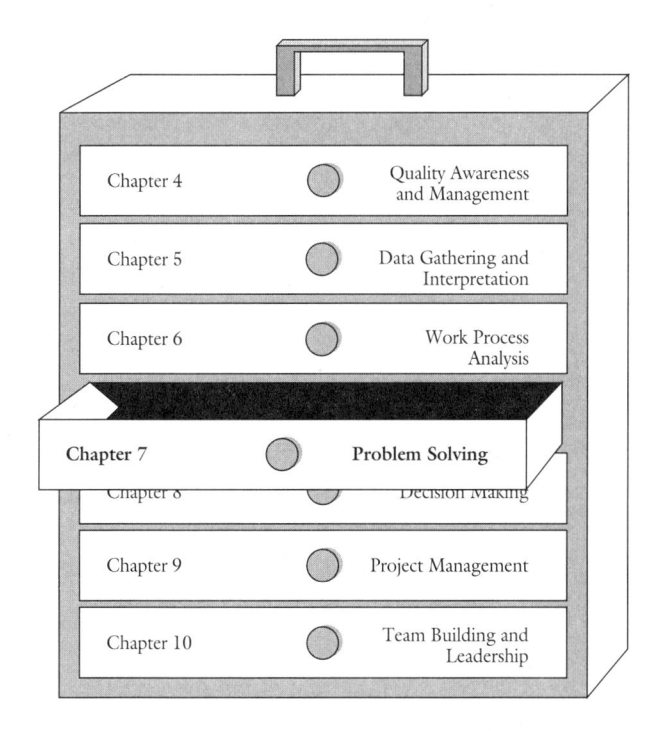

Chapter 4	○	Quality Awareness and Management
Chapter 5	○	Data Gathering and Interpretation
Chapter 6	○	Work Process Analysis
Chapter 7	○	**Problem Solving**
Chapter 8	○	Decision Making
Chapter 9	○	Project Management
Chapter 10	○	Team Building and Leadership

Problem solving is fast becoming vogue in many companies. After a period of strong growth during and especially after World War II, the process of systematic analysis of problems became less popular. But now, everybody professes to using some sort of problem-solving technique. After all, what is the key role of a manager, if not to solve problems? We hear this question time and time again. We don't subscribe to the idea that problem solving is a manager's only role, nor even necessarily the most important one. But it is a very important factor in modern business, as problems become more complex and harder to solve.

Many who try to apply problem solving find that the results are not what they might have hoped them to be. Problems are interminably studied, but actions don't seem to result. A proposed cause of a problem is brought forth, only to have its proponent attacked by adherents of other theories of why the problem exists. These experiences often result in a rejection of formal problem-solving methods, or in the incorporation of a belief that such processes rightly belong only in the engineering department, or with some Ph.D. think tank!

Others view problem solving differently. They think it is their job. It would seem, listening to these people, that problem solving is perhaps some genetic instinct that is passed on through generations of management; that perhaps promotion to management automatically bestows upon the promoted the capability to solve problems.

When we present problem solving to groups, we often ask participants to raise their hand if they ever received formal problem-solving instruction in school. We've never seen a hand rise to that question. Occasionally, someone will have been exposed to formal problem solving through course work offered by an employer, but even these people are few and far between, unless we are working with a company that has actively pursued problem solving in the past. Yet so many people assume that problem solving is a skill that is automatic and does not require any formal training. Our purpose in this section is twofold: to show that systematic problem solving is anything but automatic and to show the right way to do it.

To solve a problem it is necessary to think. It is necessary to think even to decide what facts to collect.

—Robert Maynard Hutchins

Requirements of Good Problem Solving

Good problem solving, like anything else we have talked about in this book, comes from the application of a few fundamental steps. Failure to follow these steps almost certainly reduces the problem-solving effort to one of guesswork or of relying on the most powerful person in the group. That person is the one whose solution to the problem is most likely to be accepted and implemented, whether it is the correct one or not!

The fundamental steps of good problem solving are

- A clear and specific *recognition* that an actual problem exists. Many problem-solving teams become frustrated with their efforts because they are trying to find the solution to an issue that is not a problem at all! More about this later.
- A stepwise *process* of moving from recognition of a real problem to agreement on a probable cause. Not only does such a process speed up the problem-solving activity (by eliminating all the false directions an unguided team might take), but it also helps ensure that the correct cause is found. Most of this chapter is devoted to an explanation of this process.
- Identification of the *root cause* of the problem. Many problem-solving techniques work fairly well until this point. They identify a probable cause, but not the probable root cause. As we shall see, there are several layers of cause of almost any problem, but only one root cause at the bottom layer. Failure to find the root cause, and to understand that it is the root cause, generates significant amounts of confusion, dissension, and frustration in problem-solving teams, because non-root causes are only a more detailed statement of the problem! Again, more later.
- *Integration* of the problem-solving method with a solid decision-making process. Root causes often have multiple ways by which they can be eliminated. Without the ability to properly select among these choices, the problem-solving team is again reduced to guesswork and might negate all of the sophistication applied to the problem-solving effort. An analogous situation might be the repair technician who applies very high tech electronic sensing and measuring apparatus to determine the cause of a computer malfunction, only to then take out a hammer and hacksaw to fix the problem.

I kept six honest serving men, they taught me all I knew; their names were What and Why and When and How and Where and Who.
— Rudyard Kipling

The Process Steps of Effective Problem Solving

There are six steps used in the process of effective problem solving. They move the problem-solver, either individually or as a team, from the recognition that the issue at hand is, in fact, appropriately dealt with using formal problem solving, to the result, which is agreement on a probable root cause of the problem. The six steps of problem solving are

- Problem recognition
- Organization of relevant data about the problem
- Research of changes that occurred
- Identification of possible causes
- Reduction to probable cause
- Testing for root cause

Step 1 Problem Recognition

In the very exact terminology of problem solving, the meaning of the word problem is very precise. In fact, the exactness of the definition aids an organization, in that it introduces a common language. This can help ensure that all members of a team or the organization understand the issue, know what the issue is, and discern how they are going to deal with it.

A problem always has three common elements.

1. A problem is always a *specific and measurable defect* related to a *specific object*. Although we use the phrases *object* and *defect* in this definition, you should add any words which are comfortable, and which expand the meaning of the definition to its fullest. For example, you might prefer to say that *something* (our car, the product we are manufacturing, our job, the report due yesterday, and so on) is not the way we want it to be.
2. A problem exists only when the cause of the defect is *not known*. People who learn formal problem solving often have difficulty with this rule at first, because it goes against common usage of the word

problem. For example, if the family teenager announces that he or she just got another traffic citation for failing to stop the family car at a stop sign, we'd all decide that we have a problem with this kid! But not in our terminology. The cause of the citation is known; the kid ran the stop sign. (Yes, purists might argue, but we don't know the cause of the inattention! Was it a love interest? an upcoming test? a brain tumor? We'll resist the temptation to get silly about this!)

The teenager's family does not have a problem in our terminology. What they do have is a decision to make. Should the teenager be grounded? If so, for how long? Should he or she instead be sent back to driving school? Made to work off the fine? And so on.

3. Finally, after an issue meets the first two tests, it can be called a problem only if it can be deemed important enough to be solved. If it is not, then it might be reduced to the category *irritant*, or *prefer not* (as in, I'd prefer not to have this happening here). Some early quality circles lost the support of their management groups because they dealt with issues that were not considered very important; they were not, in fact, problems!

Let's look at an example of problem recognition using a situation with which we are all familiar. After a hard day at the office, your spouse and you decide to unwind with a hearty steak dinner at a local restaurant. You have had a cocktail, ordered, and are just being served the steak.

Scene 1: You cut off a piece of steak, taste it, put down your fork and knife, and call for the server. "This steak is burned!"

Review the three requirements of a problem, and see whether you think the restaurant owner has a problem here. The object is the steak, and the defect is that it is burned. Of course, if you were actually facing the burned steak, you'd darn well feel that the owner did have a problem, but in fact he doesn't. The cause of a burned steak is apparent, both to you and the restaurant owner. It was cooked too long. The owner does have a number of decisions to make. Should he give you another steak or a free meal? Should he fire the cook? Meanwhile, you're faced with some decisions, too.

Should you eat it anyway? Perhaps ask for another, cooked right this time? Would walking out be too dramatic?

> Scene 2: You cut off a piece of steak, taste it, put down your fork and knife, and call for the server. "This steak is tough!"

In this case, a real problem does exist, but more for the restaurant owner than for you. After all, even though you don't know why the steak is tough, you probably don't care why. You are thinking about what you want the owner to do, or what you want to do; perhaps one of those choices that you thought of in scene 1. The owner, though, better worry about why his steaks are tough. The cause is not known. It might be that the meat comes from tough old cows. Or, the chef might have managed to somehow toughen it during the cooking. (After all, if she can burn it all the time, who knows what else she's capable of.) It might be that the steak knives need sharpening. Or even that your teeth are not up to the task! (In which case, the restaurant owner has found a probable root cause unlikely to be solved by him!)

> Scene 3: You cut off a piece of steak, taste it, put down your fork and knife, and call for the server. "This steak does not taste good!"

This issue has most of the characteristics of scene 2. Cause is not known, and it sure is important to both the customer and the restaurant owner. But it also shows a common mistake in problem recognition. The object, your steak, is clear. Less clear is a specific and measurable defect. Poor taste is a very subjective thing, and without any further clarity about why the steak does not seem to taste good, there is little that the restaurant owner can do to rectify the problem (unless he tastes your steak and discovers for himself that the dishwasher spilled soap on it). What would the owner do in a case like this? Either ask you what exactly seems wrong with the steak, or if there is a no-questions-asked quality policy, quietly take it back into the kitchen and taste it. Either way, the intent is to determine the specific and measurable defect.

> Scene 4: You cut off a piece of steak, taste it, put down your fork and knife, and start to call for the server. Instead, you

decide the steak will be OK, because you don't feel like waiting another 20 minutes.

If the issue is not important enough to warrant the extra time it would take to fix it, then it is not a problem. Teams and organizations should never apply their valuable time and energy to issues that are deemed problems, but which are not corrected when the team finds out how to do so, because it would be too much trouble. Decide on the importance of the issue beforehand, and if it warrants action, if it is important, and if it meets all of the other elements of the description of a problem, then it is a problem.

There is an important point to consider with scene 4. If the customer decides to say nothing about the steak this time, but makes a mental note to never return to the restaurant, the owner indeed has a problem. The issue does meet all three tests of a problem. But the owner has to know of the defect before it can be corrected. That's why the step of checking the extent to which you are meeting your customers' needs was stressed in chapter 5. Those of us who frequent restaurants see this in action all the time. Servers ask us, "How do like your meal? Is there anything else I can get you?"

All of us have heard people doing problem recognition, and we have often engaged in it ourselves. In a meeting, these activities are characterized by statements such as: "We've got a problem with the timeliness of this report!" or "Our customer doesn't like the way this flange fits!" or "I'm dissatisfied with the progress we've made on this design!" Typically, all of these statements readily identify an object of some kind and a defect associated with it. If the object and defect are specific, and the cause of each of the dissatisfaction is unknown, and if it is important to the company, then a problem exists.

Step 2   Organization of Relevant Data About the Problem

Whenever someone identifies a problem, and everyone agrees that the issue does, in fact, meet the criteria of a problem, further details are needed. Frequently, information is gained through questioning by the problem-solving individual or group. It might be determined that the problem began last Thursday, or that it exists only in the Pittsburgh plant. The exact nature of the problem can be defined, such as voltage output is only 93 percent of design.

The data that are collected about the problem fall into four categories.

- **What** is the problem? Specifically, can the exact nature of the problem be clearly defined? Have both the object and the defect been specified? Is the defect measurable?
- **Where** is the problem? Where is it located on the object? Where is it occurring geographically?
- **When** does the problem occur, or when did it begin? Is it cyclic? Is there a pattern?
- **How much** of a problem is there? If the what questions are thought of as pertaining to *one* object, these questions tell *how many* of those objects are demonstrating the problem.

Answers to these four question types clearly define the nature of the problem. It should no longer be a vague generalization of some performance that is not as it should be, but rather a precise statement of specific and measurable object and defect.

These questions, however, do not complete the step. Four more types of questions must be asked, which are similar to those just mentioned, but concentrate instead on the similar areas that are not experiencing problems. These questions are

- **What** related object could have this problem but does not? Similarly, what related defect could this object have but does not? If it is noted that the positive posts of the automobile batteries are loose, it is equally important to note that the negative posts of the batteries are not loose.
- **Where** could the problem be found but is not? So often, problem-solvers concentrate on a problem that has been uncovered in the Pittsburgh plant, and do not realize that an identical process in the Cleveland plant is fine. Or, they will recognize that accounts payable is falling behind its stated objectives, but not recognize that a reasonably similar process is being used by accounts receivable, and they are achieving far more than expected.
- **When** could the problem have occurred but did not? It is not enough to note that the problem is occurring in 1991. The problem-solver needs to recognize that this problem was not happening in 1990.
- **How** much of a problem could there be but is not? If every fifth widget fails to meet standards, say so. But also say that four of five do meet standards.

Many people that we have worked with are uncomfortable when they start to ask this second series of questions. They don't immediately seem important. The reason for them does become clear as the process unfolds. This series of is and is not questions can be said to put boundaries around the problem or establish the universe of the problem.

One simple example of using is and is not data is that of a tennis shoe manufacturer, who has plants in Seattle, New York, Miami, and Los Angeles. Retail outlets have reported that the soles of a certain model of shoe are coming unglued. Some quick research into the relevant data indicated that the problem was reported by retail stores west of the Mississippi River (where it *is*), but not by stores east of the Mississippi (where it is *not*). Since only the Seattle and Los Angeles plants send shoes to these distributors, the problem would seem to be at one of those plants.

Further research showed that the problem was seen with shoes that were manufactured eight weeks ago (when it *is*), but not before (when it is *not*). The Los Angeles plan was on strike at that time, and the manufacturing operation was shut down. The problem *universe* would seem to be in Seattle.

Asked properly then, these questions allow the problem-solver to clearly say, "This over here is my problem, and that over there is not. Only a possible cause that logically would produce a problem over here, and not over there, is my probable cause." Then he or she can go on to find events that can explain the deviation observed.

Step 3   Research of Changes that Occurred

Good problem-solvers all work under a simple premise: a deviation must be related to some kind of a change that has occurred.

This premise is not always true, as will be shown when diagnostic problem solving is discussed, but it is usually the case. All the problem-solver has to do is find out what has changed. He or she does so by looking back at the answers to the eight groups of questions that were compiled in step 2 of problem solving.

If the problem began last Thursday, what happened then? If it is seen only at the Pittsburgh plant, what is different about that plant, especially something that changed about the time the problem was observed? Almost always, one or more differences and changes can be found that relates to what, where, when, and/or how much the problem is. (It may seem that we use the words *difference* and *change* indiscriminately.)

In our example with the tennis shoe manufacturer, the problem-solvers who are worried about loose shoe soles ought to start thinking about what differences and changes can be found at the Seattle plant commencing about eight weeks ago. In a simple sense, the problem-solver can construct a sentence in which the difference is the noun, and the change is the verb, such as *training was eliminated*. The noun, *training*, is that which is now different. The change, or verb, is that it has been eliminated.

Thus, the differences and changes must be related to the nature of the problem, not the nonproblem. A simple way to remember this is with an example. If the problem began in March of 1990, differences and changes that took place in 1987 (part of the nonproblem universe) are not likely to have been the cause of the problem.

Step 4   Identification of Possible Causes

Problem-solving models do not solve problems; people do, by using models like these to sequence their thinking. But few of us could solve a problem of leaking hydrogen in a space shuttle, for example, whatever the problem-solving model. We would need to know something about space shuttles. Once differences and changes that relate to the problem's data have been found, the problem-solver must use some of his or her experience and knowledge about the system, and make some judgments.

Considering the nature of the problem itself, which is now well defined, and the differences and changes that have been found, what might be a cause of the problem? Usually, each difference and change produces a supposed cause. A case study that we have used can help explain this step.

A company that we will call ABC Technologies has recruited newly graduated engineers for many years and has always met its acceptance targets. This year, however, acceptances were 20 percent lower than would have been expected from the numbers of offers made. ABC Technologies has an issue that qualifies as a problem.

In studying the problem, much information was determined about its nature and that of the relevant nonproblem, which is step 2 of our model. For example, the problem was found at all U.S. locations, but not at any European sites. Several schools had low acceptance rates, but not all. Some eight or nine other descriptors of the problem and nonproblem areas were identified.

One key factor of the problem and nonproblem area was time; it was this year. So, differences and changes that happened this year were identified. Several were found, such as the elimination of interview training for hiring managers, a downturn in the industry in which ABC Technologies competes, and a newly instituted company goal to aggressively identify candidates from the top 10 percent of their class for its jobs.

A supposed cause was then identified for each difference and change. Since interview training for hiring managers was eliminated, the related cause might be that the hiring managers did a less than acceptable job of selling the company to the candidates and as a result fewer accepted the offers that were made. Similarly, ABC Technologies' industry suffered an economic downturn. Consequently, perhaps candidates saw fewer growth opportunities in the industry as compared to others. Finally, the company established aggressive goals to identify candidates from the top 10 percent of their class for its jobs. Thus, perhaps ABC Technologies targeted a group of people who had an unusually high number of very good offers from other companies.

Step 5 Reduction to Probable Cause

At this point, the problem-solver may have many supposed causes of the problem, and must resist the temptation to pick one based on common sense or gut feeling. Each of the supposed causes must be tested for fit with the problem description, which resulted from step 2 of the model. Some of the supposed causes will be discarded because they would not logically cause the problem. Others might fit, but only if assumptions are made. Hopefully, only one, the probable cause, will best fit the data.

Let's look at the supposed causes of ABC Technologies' problem. Perhaps the hiring managers did a less than acceptable job of selling the company to the candidates, and as a result fewer accepted the offers that were made. From step 2 we are reminded that this year was the only time the problem was seen. But note that the training of hiring managers was often not done in the past. Thus, this supposed cause is illogical. Perhaps candidates saw fewer growth opportunities in the industry as compared to others. Yes, but the problem was not observed in Europe, where we could expect candidates to be equally concerned about growth potential. Supposed causes that do not fit that distinction between the problem and nonproblem area are likewise illogical. Perhaps ABC Technologies targeted a group of people who had an unusually high number of good offers from other companies. This is troubling, since the problems were seen in some schools but not in others. An assumption can be made, though. If the schools that generated fewer than expected acceptances were those at which the most offers were made to candidates in the top 10 percent of their class, this could be the fit we have been looking for. A few words on the nature of assumptions is in order.

In the real world, and especially with nonmanufacturing problems such as this one, causes rarely can be found without making some assumptions. Some would say that the most probable cause is the one that fits all of the data of step 2 with the fewest assumptions needed. That's true, as far as it goes. But a more significant and useful value of assumptions is that they enable the problem-solving team to identify the one specific piece of data needed to nail down the problem solution. In the case of ABC Technologies, the clear thing to do is look at offer statistics for candidates in the top 10 percent of their class and how they vary between schools where the problem was seen and schools where the problem was not seen. Assumptions focus the problem-solving team's data-gathering efforts into the few areas that will produce immediate results.

In this step, one most probable cause is the desired result. Sometimes that does not happen. There may be several supposed causes that survive the test of step 5. In that case, one of two things is usually happening. The original problem could have been a multiple problem, which, as its name implies, has multiple causes. It must be broken into its component parts to be solved successfully. (More on multiple problems later.) Another reason that several supposed causes can survive this step is that insufficient data were collected in step 2. The data that will make all but one of the supposed causes illogical has not yet been found.

At other times, no supposed cause survives the test of step 5. Usually when that happens the problem-solver must go back to step 3 to find the as yet unidentified difference and change that has caused the problem.

Step 6 Testing for Root Cause
The probable cause that is identified by steps 1 through 5 may or may not be the root cause, which is defined as the primary source of the problem. Until the root cause is identified, problem-solving teams often find that they

know much about the problem at hand, but have no clear idea of what to do about it. Teams must learn how to identify the root cause.

In one of our experiences, a problem-solving team consisting of district service managers of a major automobile manufacturer was established. These managers had a number of responsibilities, among them counselling independent dealerships in the business of automotive service and repair. The problem was that service business, and thus revenues, were down 15 percent from expected levels. In the course of using the process, data were collected, changes and differences noted, and a number of possible causes developed. Among them were: fewer cars are sold, cars are being manufactured better with less need for repair, the economy is bad and people are deferring service, and independent service organizations, such as the many types of quick lube organizations, are gaining a greater share of the business.

Only one possible cause, the greater share of business by independents, fits all of the data developed in step 2 and was deemed to be the most probable cause. Several team members were satisfied with their efforts and considered the exercise complete. But others realized that this probable cause presented an unacceptable number of questions. Should prices be lowered? Should more advertising be done? Should there be night raids on the independents? This realization led to two important distinctions about root cause.

1. **A probable cause that is not the root cause is simply a more detailed statement of the problem.** The original problem was that business was down, and this had a large array of possible causes. These were reduced (by eliminating lower sales, for example) to the probable cause of independents taking more business. But that can be restated as a problem. Independents are taking our business away. The cause is still unknown. So the problem-solving effort must continue to identify the root cause of losing business to these enterprises.
2. **The root cause suggests a specific course of action.** In this example, the root cause was determined to be a lack of advertising to convince owners that factory-trained technicians were the best choice for their car repair and maintenance. This presents a clear course of action: advertise. There are a number of ways to advertise,

which must be judged using a decision-making process (chapter 8). They include, for example, television, radio, newspaper, flyers, and customer education at the time of sale.

A problem well stated is a problem half-solved.
—Charles F. Kettering

Other Problem-Solving Issues
If only all problems were straightforward! Unfortunately, there are variations of problems that must be considered. We will look at three of them.

Diagnostic Problem Solving
Imagine driving to work one day, and your car suddenly dies. A quick check of gas level and battery cables suggests no obvious reason for the engine to quit, so a problem is born. Later that day, the technician to whom you had the car towed calls to report that the fuel pump broke. After authorizing the repair, you review this problem and the problem-solving method.

Difficulties arise with step 3. What was the specific difference and change that created this problem? You drive the same route every day, in the same way. Nothing unusual happened to the fuel pump. The cause of the problem is that the fuel pump just gave up the ghost. It could have done so at any time.

This is the nature of diagnostic problems. The problem-solver's premise—that a deviation must be related to some kind of a change that has occurred—does not apply. The problem just happens. In these cases, the problem-solver dispenses with step 3. He or she collects data about the problem (for example, whether the carburetor was getting fuel) and jumps to step 4, which is the generation of possible causes. In this case, they may include out of gas, restricted fuel line, and broken fuel pump. It is then an easy step to figure out which is the correct cause.

The Multiple Problem
Earlier in this chapter, the danger of addressing several problems under the disguise of a single problem was mentioned. Several probable causes may result, or the probable cause is identified only after many unusual

assumptions. It is sometimes difficult to recognize multiple problems when they occur. A very simple technique we use is to ask the question why when a problem statement is generated. Often, this little question focuses the problem-solver on a single issue of the observed problem. Sometimes, it serves to solve the problem in that the most probable cause is seen.

Some people say that all nonmanufacturing problems are multiple problems. In the case of ABC Technologies and its recruiting difficulties, they said all of the possible causes may have had some effect. That may be true, but failure to believe that one, and only one, most probable root cause is likely to exist for any problem generally results in a large number of unsolved problems!

The Day-One Problem

"Say, Jim," calls Nancy. "Now that you've gotten some experience using the copying machine, and have learned problem-solving techniques, I'd like you to work on a problem that we've been having."

"OK, Nancy, what's the problem?"

"This machine is supposed to generate 30 copies a minute, but the best it has ever been able to achieve is 20. I have no idea what's wrong."

"Uh, has it ever gotten 30 copies a minute?"

"Well, actually no. But I'm sure you'll figure out what's wrong!"

Jim has been confronted with a day-one problem, that is, a deviation from the norm or expected that has always occurred with this object. Assuming that 30 copies a minute is feasible, which is the first thing Jim ought to determine, there is no difference and change to which the deviation can be attributed.

Jim needs to find other such machines that do make 30 copies a minute, and figure out what is different and changed about this machine when compared to these others. In this way, he can begin to generate a most probable root cause of the problem.

It is an old maxim of mine that when you have excluded the impossible, whatever remains, however improbable, must be the truth.

—Sir Arthur Conan Doyle

The Importance of a Process

A process for problem solving is important, especially for a quality team. Without a process, the team meetings might result in solutions, but generally only after a considerable amount of wasted time. Examine this conversation of a quality team not using a problem-solving technique.

"Folks, we have a serious problem with these computer reports!" The problem is recognized.

"We need to throw out that new computer system and get our old one back!" Here is a proposed action, which is not even part of the problem-solving process.

"Heck, we started seeing this problem long before the new system went on line." This is organization of relevant data about the problem, followed by some research of changes that occurred.

"We still don't seem to have any difficulties at the beginning of the month!" Again, some organization of relevant data about the problem.

"If the new system is at fault, the problem should have started when it was installed." Someone is starting to identify the probable cause.

"That doesn't change the fact that we have a serious problem!" Here they are back at problem recognition.

"Well, I remain convinced that we need to change back to our old system. Let's meet again next week to figure out where we're going." The same proposed action is mentioned, again.

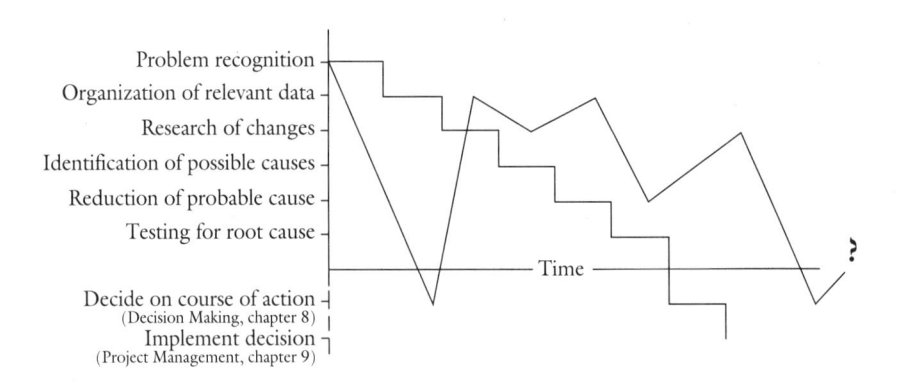

Figure 7.1. Scattered thinking.

Sound familiar? The facts may be very different, but most groups have many meetings like this. The conversation is all over the map, and results are not achieved. If a stenographer was taking notes of the meeting, and each statement was assigned to a step of the problem-solving method, as is noted, the result could be shown graphically as in Figure 7.1.

We call this scattered thinking. It gets very little done. Supposed decisions are made very early in the process, and are almost always discarded because there is no data to support them. By the way, in Figure 7.1 the stepped line is the graph of the meeting as it should occur. An appropriate amount of time is spent on each step of the process, and the most probable root cause is identified correctly and with maximum efficiency. Then, an appropriate course of action can be identified, and the team can quickly decide among any alternatives, perhaps by using a decision-making technique.

8 Decision Making

There is no stigma attached to recognizing a bad decision in time to install a better one.

—Laurence J. Peter

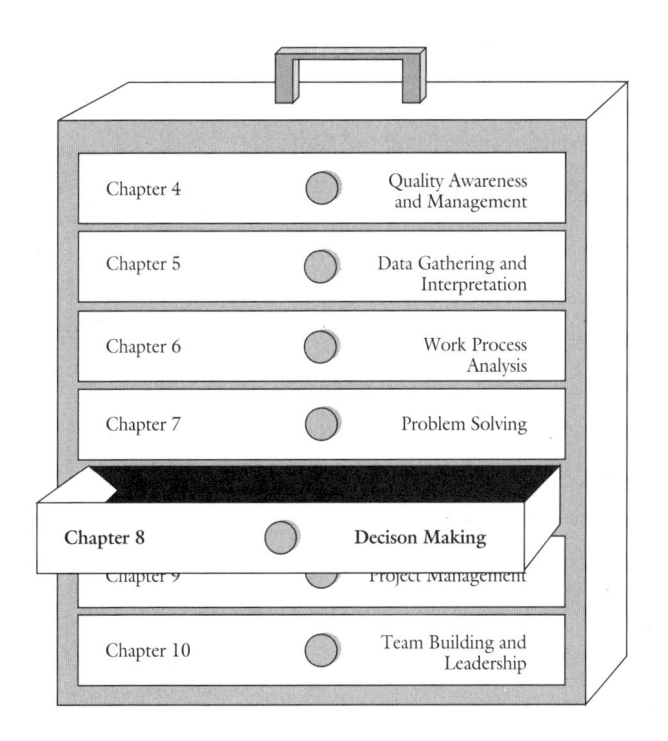

Once the root cause of a problem has been found, a quality team begins the process of selecting the best course of action that, when implemented, will eliminate the cause. Of course, decisions are also made without first engaging in problem solving: sometimes the team knows what it wants to accomplish and needs only to select the best way to do it.

Like problem solving, the process of decision making is one of *structured thinking*. It is not something particularly new, nor is it difficult. In one way or another, we use it every day, usually without thinking about the steps. The importance of the process is to bring the structure to the conscious level and to understand it and apply it in the most effective and efficient way possible.

Knowing what needs to be accomplished is the key to any good decision-making effort. Some time spent at the beginning to define the *characteristics* of a successful choice is invaluable: it permits the evaluation of alternative courses of action against those characteristics. To begin a review of decision making, it may be useful to first look at a few of the types of decision-making models that have been developed.

Not to decide is to decide.

—Harvey Cox

Types of Decision-Making Processes

Several models of decision making exist, and each can be useful for certain types of decisions. A few of the more common ones will be described in this section, and the remainder of the chapter will concentrate on the details of one of them.

- **Coin flip or hunch model.** Not really a model, per se, this method of decision making is unfortunately used too often in situations where a more reasoned approach is needed. It can, however, be the method of choice when the alternatives are very similar, the decision-maker has a lot of experience in similar areas, and the consequences or risks of error are considered low.
- **The balance sheet model.** This is one of the simplest and most easily used models. The decision-maker lists all reasonable alternatives on one side of a sheet of paper. Two columns, marked *Pros* and *Cons*, are created. The decision-maker lists as many pros and cons as he or she can think of

Decision Making   167

for each alternative. When the list is judged complete, the single well-organized picture of the situation helps identify the best alternative.
- **Decision tree model.** Further insight might be required, especially if the decision involves options within options. Then a decision tree can be useful by clearly showing all of the options. For example, if you were considering a vacation, and were sure of neither the means of transportation nor the destination, a decision tree might look something like Figure 8.1.

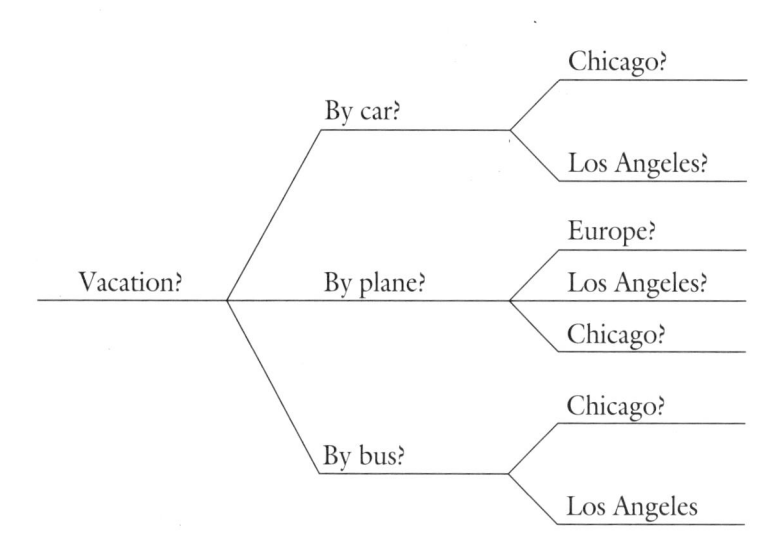

```
                        Chicago?
            By car?
                        Los Angeles?

                        Europe?
Vacation?   By plane?   Los Angeles?
                        Chicago?

                        Chicago?
            By bus?
                        Los Angeles
```

Figure 8.1. Decision tree.

Each reasonable option, such as, you could not travel to Europe from the United States by either car or bus, is considered. Then, other considerations of cost, time, and convenience can be used to compare each.
- **The point-scoring model.** If all other methods fail to provide a satisfactory choice, the decision-maker can resort to the most thorough of the methods, point scoring. In these types of models, each alternative choice is scored to show the extent to which it satisfies predetermined criteria of the successful decision. Since each of the other models we

have described are relatively easy to understand and use, the remainder of this chapter will detail a complete point-scoring method of decision making.

To a greater or lesser extent, each of these decision-making techniques have two things in common. They first try to identify the characteristics of the final choice that must be satisfied, and then they compare all options to see which best meets those characteristics.

> *It is well to open one's mind but only as a preliminary to closing it . . . for the supreme act of judgment and selection.*
> —Irving Babbitt

The Decision-Making Process

The decision-making process that we have found to be most useful for quality teams and individuals has six steps. Each will be described in detail. The steps are

1. Determine the purpose of the decision
2. Establish criteria to be satisfied
3. Consider the solution after next
4. Collect the full range of alternatives
5. Investigate each alternative for fit
6. Evaluate the choice for strategic fit and risks

The Purpose of the Decision

Sometimes the root cause of a problem seems to suggest such a clear course of action that no other options are considered. If, for example, the director of marketing decides that the root cause of low sales is a poorly written product brochure, the likely course of action is the rewriting of the product brochure. But suppose the director of marketing stops for a moment to consider the ultimate objective that needs to be satisfied—to convince potential customers that this is the best product for them to buy. Are there different and perhaps more effective ways to get this ultimate objective accomplished?

Decisions have a *hierarchy*, or several levels. Suppose that your Ford Taurus station wagon, which you use to get to and from work, is for some reason destroyed or stolen. Here are the various levels of decision that can be made.

Level 1: Choose another Ford Taurus station wagon to use to get to work.
Choice options: Color, accessories, new or used.

Level 2: Choose another station wagon (or Ford of any type) to use to get to work.
Choice options: Any make of station wagon (or any model of Ford), *plus* all of the options in level 1.

Level 3: Choose another car to use to get to work.
Choice options: Any make of car, *plus* all of the options in level 2.

Level 4: Choose a way to get to work.
Choice options: Bus, car pool, bicycle, hitchhike, walk, *plus* all of the options in level 3.

Notice that each successive level of the hierarchy expands the number of choices available.

Our job in this first step of decision making is to make sure that the right level of decision is considered. Should we select from among several cars, or should we select from among several ways to get to work? You might end up right where you started—which Ford Taurus station wagon shall I buy? But at least the thinking process helps ensure that the right level of decision is being considered.

Then the intended decision must be written as a *decision statement*, which contains three parts: an *action verb*, signifying what the decision-maker wants to do; an *object* of the verb, or the types of alternatives being considered; and the *intent of the decision*. For example, consider the decision statement, *choose a car to use to get to work*. The action verb is *choose*. The object is *a car*. The intent is *to use to get to work*—the reason we are choosing a car.

Should I fix this old car or not? is not a good decision statement, because it does not incorporate elements of action verb, object, and intent. This example is perhaps better stated as *select a way to restore my personal transportation.* Then *fix the car* becomes one of several alternatives that can be compared against the criteria established for the decision.

The Criteria of the Decision

Before any decision can be made, the characteristics or criteria of the most successful choice must be determined. Each alternative will later be compared against these criteria to see how well it fits them. And in the same manner that was discussed earlier in this book, these criteria are expressed as musts and wants.

Musts are those criteria that the successful alternative choice should satisfy. They are mandatory and nonnegotiable. Any alternative that does not meet each must cannot be selected. *Wants* are criteria that are desirable, or nice to have. The successful alternative does not have to meet each and every want. As before, though, each want is weighted on a scale of 1 to 10; some are much more important to us than others. Alternatives that do not meet important wants, or meet them poorly, are unlikely to be selected.

Care should be taken to ensure that musts do not become mutually exclusive. If, for example, you and your spouse are trying to select a restaurant, you might each select some criteria that must be satisfied. If one of you selects $5 entrees as a must, and the other selects tuxedoed servers and a harpist as must, you are unlikely to find any choice that fulfills this pair of criteria. Use musts with care. Too many can virtually eliminate all alternatives.

Using our commuter example, here are some possible criteria if the first decision level—replace the Taurus station wagon—is selected.

Musts:	Metallic blue	
	Automatic transmission	
	Maximum of 25,000 miles on odometer	
	Air-conditioning	
Wants:	Wire wheel covers	Weight = 4
	22 miles/gallon	Weight = 7
	Power windows	Weight = 9

Notice that each want is weighted; power windows are much more important than wire wheel covers, but not mandatory.

If the fourth decision level—select a way to get to work—is selected, then the criteria might look very different.

    Musts: Costs less than $50 per month
                    Provides convenient nonwork transportation

    Wants: No more than one hour commute   Weight = 8
                    Promotes personal health   Weight = 5

Alternative courses of action here might include walking to work, which may or may not satisfy both musts and both wants.

If level 4 is selected as the decision to be made, and the final choice is to buy a car to get to work, then criteria similar to those shown for level 1 can be established. Then another decision can be made to select the right car.

The Solution After Next

Suppose you awake one morning and notice that it is raining heavily. When you go to the kitchen, you find puddles of water all over the floor: the roof is leaking in several places. Your first thought is that you will have to replace the roof, and you might begin to think about the cost of doing so. But after a minute you remember that you're already planning to build onto the kitchen next spring. During that construction, considerable work will be done on the roof, and the replacement is more effectively and economically done then. Your thinking immediately shifts to ways to live with, or patch, the leaks in the interim. The anticipated construction is the solution after next.

This relatively simple example would not slow any of us down for an instant. The thought process might not even be noticeable. But in business, solutions after next are often missed. In chapter 1, warehouse employees were trying to decide on ways to improve their operation. They expanded their thinking to recognize that the true *purpose* of their job was not to run the warehouse, but to provide goods to retail customers at the point of sale. Additional alternatives were discovered, including the consolidation of existing warehouses into a central distribution area.

Had that decision been made, and implementation of it was expected within, say, a year, no one should propose that a problem in the current warehouses be solved by a course of action that expends a considerable amount of capital. The *solution after next*, the implementation of a central distribution area, does not support significant expenditures on the existing facilities. Like the leaky roof, the right choice would be to find some interim way to deal with the issue or to live with it.

The solution after next is a device that allows the decision-maker to take a moment and look ahead, to see if something is likely or planned to happen that might solve this issue, or to make some present courses of action unnecessary. If such an event is likely to happen, the decision-maker will select a different array of alternatives to consider.

The Range of Alternatives

There comes with each of our core skills modules the point of truth, where the practitioner's experience, skills, and judgment are required. In problem solving, we saw that finding the root cause of a hydrogen leak in a space shuttle required some knowledge of space shuttles. Likewise, in decision making, the selection of a range of alternatives requires some knowledge of those available. All alternatives come in three broad types: corrective, interim, and adaptive.

Corrective alternative courses of action are just what their name implies: they correct (hopefully permanently) the root cause of a problem. For our leaky roof, the corrective alternative course of action is to replace it. For our commuter, it might be to buy that new car.

Interim alternative courses of action are not a permanent fix, but usually some way to mitigate the effects of the problem's root cause for a period of time. Interim alternative courses of action are selected when a solution after next suggests it. The leaky roof's solution after next is the remodeling of the kitchen, so an interim alternative might be to throw a tarpaulin over the roof. (If one of the criteria of the decision is to maintain the well-groomed look of the house, of course, this might not turn out to be the best alternative!) If our commuter realizes that his or her solution after next is retirement in Florida in 10 months, after which he or she may not need a car (or perhaps a convertible!), an interim solution might be to car pool.

Adaptive alternative courses of action are likewise considered when a solution after next is apparent. These alternatives require that the decision-maker live with the problem for a period of time. If the kitchen is wet, go out to eat. For our commuter, the car pool method of transportation might also be considered adaptive.

Many people teach that the time to select the type of action is when the decision making has begun. To the extent that the solution after next might dictate one of the three types of action, that's true. But for important decisions, it is usually in the best interest of the decision-maker to identify several alternatives of each type. Sometimes an interim or adaptive solution is best, even when no solution after next is identified.

The Fit of Each Alternative

Having collected a complete array of alternative courses of action, the next step is to compare each for fit with the criteria established in the second step of the process. The criteria are *musts* and *wants*, the former being mandatory and the latter being desirable, but weighted in importance. The first step is easy. Any alternative course of action that does not meet the musts is discarded. Then a more complex process is used to score the remaining alternatives for their fit against wants.

Each remaining alternative course of action is given a score that shows the degree to which it satisfies the want. Scores are on a scale of 0 to 10, 0 meaning that the alternative does not satisfy the want at all, and 10 showing a perfect fit. Let's look again at the example of our car-buying commuter. The wants and their respective weights were as follows:

	Weight	Ford Taurus	Chevrolet Caprice
Wire wheel covers	4		
22 miles/gallon	7		
Power windows	9		

Two alternatives, a Ford Taurus and a Chevrolet Caprice, are considered. Each car is scored by the extent to which it meets the criteria, with the following results.

	Weight	Ford Taurus Score	Chevrolet Caprice Score
Wire wheel covers	4	0	10
22 miles/gallon	7	6	10
Power windows	9	10	0

The first and third criteria are easy to score. The car either has wire wheel covers or power windows, or it doesn't. So the decision maker scores each car a 0 or a 10 on these. Mileage isn't as straightforward. The Ford gets 22 mpg and seems to fully meet the want. But the Chevrolet gets 25 mpg. (These numbers are for illustrative purposes; they are not factual.) They are not the same. The decision-maker applies some judgment, scores the Chevrolet a 10, and gives the Ford a 6, perhaps realizing that as the car begins to get out of tune, the mileage will drop below 22 mpg.

Whether the mileage score for the Ford is a 6, 5, or 7, by the way, is not very important as long as the relationship between all the alternatives seems correct. In the same way, the actual numbers used to weight the wants back in the second step is less important than the need to have all the wants relatively correct.

The decision-maker now calculates a *weighted score* WS, by multiplying the weight of the want by the score of the alternative.

	Weight	Ford Taurus Score	WS	Chevrolet Caprice Score	WS
Wire wheel covers	4	0	0	10	40
22 miles/gallon	7	6	42	10	70
Power windows	9	10	90	0	0
Total			132		110

By totalling the weighted scores, the best balanced choice among these two alternatives is seen to be the Ford. The strongly weighted want of power windows overshadowed the lower mileage and the lack of wire wheel covers.

Several important points should be made at this time. Don't let a number make your decisions. Apply some judgment and experience, but remember that they are applied when the criteria are established and weighted, and when the alternatives are scored. If that is done right, and the alternative that results isn't to your liking, so be it. But it still must be recognized as the best balanced choice of a course of action.

Second, what should be done if the musts eliminate all or all but one of the alternatives? It may be that the remaining alternative is the only viable choice. More often, though, it means that the musts are too constraining. Review them carefully. Are they musts or strong wants? At the same time, second guess your original choices with caution. Adding or discarding musts to achieve the desired result can result in a return to decision making by hunch!

Strategic Fit and Risks

Congratulations! You have made that tough decision, and now have all the backup material you need to sell it to your management. But lurking in the back of your mind is the realization that no decision is free of risk. What could go wrong? What would be the consequences of an error in this decision? The last step deals with these concerns, by assessing the strategic fit of your choice, and the possible risks associated with it.

Strategic fit is really just another way to check the correctness and completeness of the decision criteria established in the second step. Is the course of action that has been selected compatible with the plans, value systems, policies, and culture of this company? If not, it may be useful to add criteria that cover these needs to the decision model and review all alternatives again.

Considering the possible types of *risk* for any selected course of action requires serious consideration of the kind of things could go wrong. For example, if our commuter selected a very small economy car, he or she might think about it and feel that this choice presents a risk of serious injury or worse in the event of a major accident. Rather than immediately discarding the choice, however, our commuter needs to assess the probability of the risk happening and its seriousness if it does.

Probability and seriousness can be easily estimated using a scale such as this:

Probability		Seriousness
100%	10	Devastating
Very certain	9	Very bad
Probable	8	Severe
Likely	7	Difficult
Very possible	6	Serious
50/50	5	Adverse
Could be	4	Some hurt
Improbable	3	Action required
Unlikely	2	Annoying
Remote	1	Noticable
Impossible	0	None

Our commuter might consider his or her choice of a small car and attendant collision risk and decide that because the drive to work is all on residential streets, the probability of a major collision is low, perhaps a 2, unlikely. He or she continues to recognize that the seriousness of such an accident is high, perhaps an 8, severe.

A risk of a different type might be that the car is rear-wheel drive, and the area gets deep snow a few times a year. Thus the risk is being unable to drive the car in snow. In this case, the probability is high, a 9. But the seriousness is only a 2, annoying, because the bus is always available on bad weather days.

Risk can be measured by using the two numbers that correspond to the probability and the seriousness of the risk. The examples we used are 2:8 and 9:2, respectively. Neither of these should be especially worrisome. As a rule of thumb, choices of action that have risks that measure 5:5, or higher in either number, should be reconsidered. After all, the best decision in the world does not look so good when it backfires on you!

Imagination is more important than knowledge.
—Albert Einstein

Creativity in Decision Making

There is one other aspect of decision making that is very important, yet often overlooked. A good decision is unlikely to be made if good alternatives are not available. We once taught decision making at a small business, where one of the causes of problems was the layout of various buildings on the property. The business had grown over the years, and as it did so, new buildings were added. But there was no good opportunity to plan far enough into the future to ensure that the building layout would support the later evolution of the business. As a result, the layout of certain buildings encumbered work activities.

We had just finished training a new group of decision-makers at this company and set them loose on this problem cause (that is, work activities are encumbered by the building layout). We asked them what should be done about this situation. They pondered and applied their decision-making training industriously. But their answer was unlikely to inspire their management group—tear everything down and start all over!

Sometimes the choice of alternative courses of action just isn't very broad. Even worse, there are times when none of the apparent choices is reasonable. When confronted with such a situation, we must be able to further expand the list of alternative courses of action. This is done through application of techniques of *creativity*.

Many people have a sense of this thing called creativity that is just plain wrong. Creative thinking is not black magic, nor is it an accident. It is not restricted to people with high IQs. It is a technique which, like all the others we teach, can be learned. While the purpose of this book is not to delve deeply into creative thinking, one area of thought may be very useful.

Creative thinking requires a modification of a state of mind that many of us have been carefully trained to have; namely that there is only one right answer to every question. Our schooling tends to reinforce this attitude through our typical testing process, which stresses the one right answer. In fact, a creative person can put a genuine crimp in the education process. One story that comes to mind is that of the physics student at a major university, who had to answer the following question: How would you determine the height of a building using a barometer?

The student pondered a bit, and wrote: Go to the top of the building, and tie the barometer to the end of a long string. Lower the barometer over the side until it touches the ground and note the top of the building on the string. Pull the barometer back up and measure the length of the string.

The student received no credit for the answer, and protested to the professor. "My answer satisfies the question. It determines the height of the building."

The professor countered, "Maybe so, but full credit certifies that you have some understanding of physics, which your answer does not demonstrate." After more discussion, however, the professor decided that for fairness the student could have another chance and was given 10 minutes to answer the question.

After nine of the ten minutes had passed, during which time the student had simply stared at the blank paper, the professor asked, "Are you ready to give up?"

"Oh, not at all," the student responded. "There are so many possible answers that I need to figure out which one will satisfy you best." Then the student scribbled down the answer that was generally expected, having to do with measuring the barometric pressure at top of the building and at ground level.

Afterwards, the professor asked what some of the other possible answers were. "Well," the student said, "I could have gone to the top of the building and dropped the barometer over the edge. By timing the duration of its fall, I could, in principle, calculate the height of the building. Or, I could have waited for a sunny late afternoon, and measured the shadows of the barometer and the building. The height of the building would then be proportional to the known height of the barometer as the shadow lengths are proportional. Another way is to find the building superintendent and trade the barometer for the information about the height of the—"

"Stop," cried the professor. "I've heard enough!"

Creative thinking is the simple step of taking available ideas, being willing to combine them in different ways, and then recognizing the possible value of the new arrangement. Most of us think creatively all the time, and don't recognize it. Creative thinking does not always result in marvelous new inventions. Creative thinking results in someone saying or thinking *Aha!* And we've all done that many times.

Don't be afraid to go on a wild goose chase. That's what wild geese are for.

—Anonymous

Decision Making

All of this chapter has dealt with the process of making decisions. Applied well, the process will lead to better and lower-risk decisions. But there is one other aspect of decision making that is important—the courage to decide.

The fear of deciding comes largely from not being able to ensure the success of the eventual outcome. For many, this process may help alleviate that fear. For others, there are some techniques that may help.

First, recognize that few decisions that we make every day are life or death choices. Most are low-impact decisions, such as where to go to lunch today or which project to tackle first. For all practical purposes, no one will likely care 50 years from now which of these low impact choices you make today. But they are useful if they are recognized for what they are: decisions being made, and probably being made well. Each of us makes hundreds of decisions a day without fear. Except that they are low-impact decisions, they don't differ materially from the high-impact decisions that we face.

Second, we believe that the end result of the decision, an implemented change, is more important than the decision itself. A person who can make a decision without fear, and then be ready to modify and alter that course of action during its implementation to better fit changing needs and environment, will achieve the most success. So we move on to the skill of project management, the implementation of a selected course of action.

9 Project Management

Nothing comes from doing nothing.

—William Shakespeare

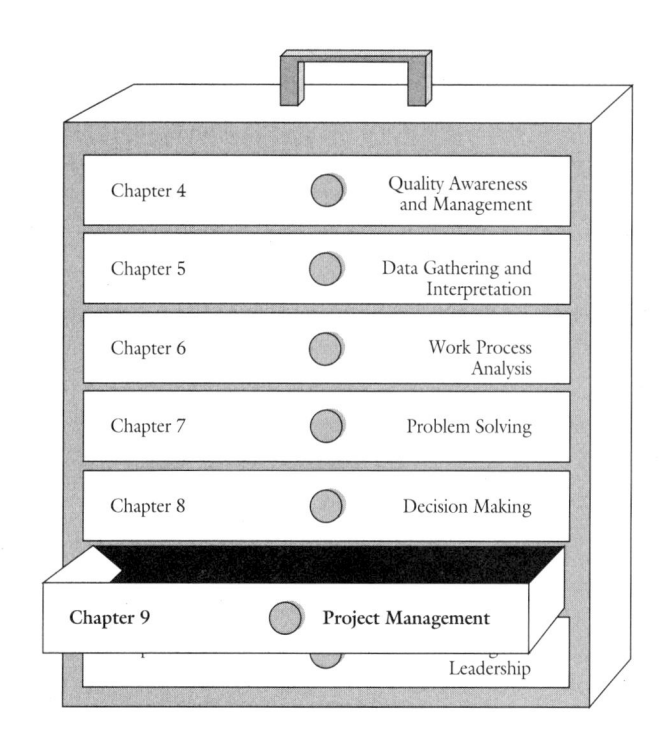

Project management is the culmination of sound work process analysis, problem solving, and decision making. Effective project management facilitates the smooth and successful implementation of a desired course of action.

When a project is poorly managed, the cause can usually be traced to a lack of careful planning. Many people who have cleverly identified a root cause of a problem, and creatively decided on a course of action to eliminate it, rush through the implementation of their idea as though the project is an afterthought. Planning at the front end of the project inevitably pays off later. The outcome of the project is more likely to be what is expected. It will arrive on time and within budget, and it will generate no unpleasant surprises for people who did not expect it or agree with it.

If this was a book about the construction of tall buildings in central Manhattan, the subject of project planning would, by far, be its biggest chapter. In fact, college courses are given on the subject. Our intent is to provide a simple framework appropriate to those occasions when your company's problem-solving network needs to implement a course of action considerably less complex than the construction of a skyscraper. Three steps will be discussed in detail: preplanning the project, the project plan, and executing/controlling the project.

> *Few people think more than two or three times a year. I have made an international reputation for myself by thinking once or twice a week.*
>
> —George Bernard Shaw

Preplanning the Project

When people are assigned to implement a project, they usually start by writing down all of the steps needed to fulfill the project. Whether these steps are correct or complete is dependent on the skill of the project manager and team. For example, if the project's intent is to implement a new computer system, we might expect the plan steps to include such things as select and buy the terminals, select and buy the software, install hardware, train users, and so on. But whether the steps are correct or incorrect or complete or incomplete, the project manager who starts here can rarely answer five fundamental questions without first giving them some serious thought.

1. What is the concisely stated purpose of this project, and what are its measurable outcomes?
2. Who will use the results of this effort, and who might be affected by them, whether they use the results or not?
3. What resources will be needed, in the categories of money, time, people, and materials?
4. What things can happen that will either cause the effort to fail, or at least give us some trouble in this implementation, and what steps are possible now to prevent these things from happening?
5. How will we know that we have achieved success, and how will we formally terminate this project?

These five questions comprise project preplanning.

Project Purpose and Outcome

A concise purpose statement provides an anchor for the project manager and team. It prevents a slow evolution away from the original purpose. Often people will ignore this step, assuming that they certainly know the purpose of the project. Write it down! A formal statement keeps everyone on track and is invaluable when presenting the project to senior management for approval or when responding to questions about it.

Think in terms of these questions: Why are we doing this? What exact course of action do we intend to pursue? When a statement of project purpose is complete, then the measurable outcomes can be added.

It is not enough to state the purpose alone. The outcomes must also be included. How will we know when we have succeeded? By what measures (and whose) will the results be judged? What distinct and measurable difference do we expect to see? What will these results replace? What will they enhance? If the project has no apparent measurable outcomes, then the key question to ask is, *Why are we doing this?*

For example, a project's purpose might be stated as: install the new computer network system and have it operational for all employees by June of next year.

Outcomes of this project that are measurable might be

- Reduce nonoperational time to no more than 2 percent.
- Improve the recovery time of records by 50 percent.

- Have 90 percent of all personnel fully trained.
- Reduce operating costs by $22,000 annually.

Together, statements of the project's purpose and outcomes will allow the team to know and then remember where it is going, and when it has gotten there.

People Who Will Use, and Be Affected by, the Product

Throughout this book, the importance of knowing customers' needs has been stressed. One of the best ways to meet these needs during project implementation is to involve those customers in the project in some appropriate way.

Project customers are of two types: the *user* community of customers and the *affected* community of customers. People and organizations that you expect to be using the results of your project (such as the new computer network system) have an *ownership stake* in the project. They will have to live with, and thereby they own, the system. The needs of these owners must be understood by including them in the project.

People and organizations who might be affected by the results of the project, but who may not use the results directly, have an *interest stake* in the project's results. An example of a group with an interest stake might be the management of a unionized employee group. If the labor relations department plans the project of contract negotiations, it needs to understand that the group's management is highly interested in the results, although not covered by the contract itself. It is equally important to involve the people with an interest stake in the project in some appropriate way.

The preplanning stage identifies people and organizations with both an ownership and an interest stake for possible inclusion in the project. Inclusion can mean several things. It might be appropriate to have one or more members of the ownership group on the project team. Alternatively, people who have an interest stake might not be on the team, but instead might be contacted periodically with updates on progress. Or, they may need to approve certain steps of the project. Either way, preplanning these involvements now forestalls a lot of embarrassment later.

Resources Needed

The complete list of resources, including time, money, materials, and people cannot always be totally anticipated at this point. Needs do change. But it remains useful to consider resources, especially people and materials, to the extent possible at this stage of the project.

Material needs for the projects we are considering (not the Manhattan skyscraper!) are easy. A short but mostly complete list would have headings of administrative (for example, computers and phones), space, ordinary office supplies, and raw materials for the system to be implemented.

The project's needs for people usually require more thinking. Both the expected input of team members and their responsibilities on the team must be considered. Typical expected inputs are

- Knowledge of the past practices that are to be replaced (to help the team understand when it is, or is not, improving things)
- Knowledge of systems similar to the one being implemented
- Knowledge of future needs (to recommend improvements along the way)
- Project desires of the future user community (for team members with an ownership stake)
- Project desires of the affected community (for team members with an interest stake)

Typical project responsibilities for any team members are

- Research of alternative ways to proceed
- Design of the new system
- Coordination between groups (intra- or interteam)
- Review and endorsement of results to date
- Technical guidance
- Administrative support
- Financial control
- Scheduling
- Quality assurance
- Leadership
- Oversight of pilot project

Best Case/Worst Case Scenarios

Suppose that you have just decided to take a vacation in Mexico, and you begin the enjoyable process of planning. The vacation is, of course, a project.

Its outcomes are to have a set of enjoyments and experiences (albeit they are sometimes hard to measure) within a preestablished budget (which is sometimes thrown to the four winds). You are the project manager. One night you awake and realize that so many things could go wrong with this plan! So you get up and make a list of all the things that could cause *project failure,* which by your definition is that the vacation doesn't happen. Here's your list.

Trip killers
Can't get airline reservations
Airline or controller strike
I get sick and can't go
Earthquake in Mexico
Hotel goes bankrupt

Now if you're a typical vacationer, you continue the list by jotting down next to each of these project killers a plan to cope with it.

Trip killers	Action to take
Can't get airline reservation	Book as early as possible
Airline or controller strike	Check into trains, driving
I get sick and can't go	Get trip insurance, go later
Earthquake in Mexico	Select alternative destination
Hotel goes bankrupt	Reserve two hotels as long as possible without penalty

You can control or eliminate some of the project killers, such as the inability to get airline reservations. Simply book the seats early and be sure to get to the airport with plenty of time to spare. Other trip killers, such as an earthquake in Mexico, might happen regardless of any precaution you might take. But a plan to counter this project killer can still be devised.

These kinds of events, which can cause project failure, are worst case scenarios. It is critically important when planning a project to identify these scenarios and to devise preventive actions, for those events you can control, and adaptive actions, for those events you cannot control.

What about other events that would not, by themselves, prevent your vacation in Mexico, but which could, nevertheless, cause real problems or annoyances for you. For example, you might continue your list this way.

Trip annoyances	Actions to take
Luggage gets lost	Carry-on bag with essentials
Get sick on water	Take water purification kit
Can't speak Spanish	Buy English–Spanish dictionary

None of these events or annoyances will result in project failure: the vacation will occur with or without them. But a perfect vacation could be defined as the elimination of all of these annoyances. Likewise, any perfect project is one that is implemented successfully without minor problems. We define the best case scenario as the absence of irritants or problems that, by themselves, don't cause project failure, but might demand extra time, resources, and/or attention.

Of course, to simply say that our best case scenario is the absence of all minor problems does not, in itself, serve the project manager and team very well. The probable minor problems have to be identified, and preventive or adaptive actions planned. Then the best case scenario is the absence of these specific minor problems.

Termination Needs of the Project

Early in the preplanning stage, the project's measurable outcomes were established. For example, one outcome might be the reduction of downtime to 2 percent on the new computer network system. These outcomes are often easily said and then somewhat forgotten. The last step of the preplanning stage is to determine how the outcomes will actually be measured. In this example, the plan might be to track downtime for two months following the completion of installation, debugging, and training at least 50 percent of the new users.

Other project termination factors that should be considered now are

- What are the training requirements for the user group? Who will do it? To whom? By when?
- What project materials will need to be transferred? To whom? By when?
- How will responsibility for the new system be transferred? To whom? By when?
- What resources (people and materials) will have to be redeployed? To where? By when?

- What kind(s) of presentations of results will be required? By whom? For what audience? When?

Of course, which of these factors are appropriate depends on the complexity of the project.

> *It is the function of creative men to perceive the relations between thoughts, or things, or forms of expression that may seem utterly different, and to be able to combine them into some new forms—the power to connect the seemingly unconnected.*
> —William Plomer

The Project Plan

With the completion of the preplanning exercises, the project plan itself can now be constructed. This is the document that provides the project manager and team a sequence of steps which logically move the activities from beginning to a successful finish.

Steps of the Project

As has been true with each of our core skills, there comes a point when the experience and judgment the project team's members are necessary. Of course, if the members have been chosen well during the preplanning stage, all the necessary skills are available. The team then notes all of the steps necessary to complete the project. They fall into several categories.

- The actual tasks necessary to complete the project. For the implementation of the new computer network, these would include such things as purchase terminals.
- Reviews with or input from user and/or affected communities. These people and organizations were identified in the preplanning stage.
- Reviews with supervisor or other person to whom the team is accountable.
- All preventive and adaptive actions. These were developed when best and worst case scenarios were identified during preplanning.
- All project termination steps that were also identified during preplanning. These include training, redeployment of resources, transfer of

responsibility, final presentation of results, and measurement of outcomes.

For each step, the team should note several important things.

- Who is responsible for this step?
- What resources are needed for this step?
- When should this step happen or start?
- When must this step be completed?
- What other steps must be completed before starting this step?
- What other steps cannot be started before this step is completed?

Preplanning activities will enable the team to answer each of these questions.

Critical Path

The last two questions recognize the fact that most project steps cannot be completed at once. Often, one is dependent on another (booking a seat for the trip to Mexico cannot happen until the airline is chosen). Also, resources are often constrained, requiring that steps which could be performed simultaneously be performed in sequence instead.

The *critical path* of a project is the shortest possible distance between beginning and end, which recognizes the limitations of dependencies and constrained resources. The path is the collection of steps that define that shortest distance in time. Any increase in time required for a critical path step increases the length of the project.

Arrangement of all the steps that have been identified into a sequence that will work most effectively defines the critical path. We will not go into a lengthy explanation here of how this can be done. One easy way that we have found is to place each of the project steps on one of those little pieces of paper that can be stuck to the wall, and to arrange the steps in such a way that makes sense. For example, for a project having eight steps (which we will simply number 1 through 8), the wall might look like Figure 9.1.

Step 2 cannot begin until step 1 is finished. Step 3 can begin about halfway through step 2 (as long as the same person isn't required for both). Step 4 can be done right away, or at any time during the project, again as long as there are no people constraints. Steps 5 and 6 follow respectively

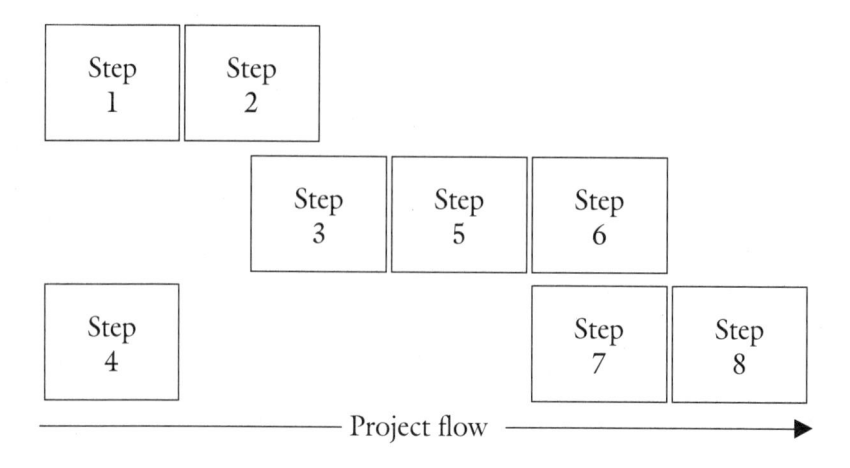

```
┌──────┐ ┌──────┐
│ Step │ │ Step │
│  1   │ │  2   │
└──────┘ └──────┘
            ┌──────┐ ┌──────┐ ┌──────┐
            │ Step │ │ Step │ │ Step │
            │  3   │ │  5   │ │  6   │
            └──────┘ └──────┘ └──────┘
┌──────┐                      ┌──────┐ ┌──────┐
│ Step │                      │ Step │ │ Step │
│  4   │                      │  7   │ │  8   │
└──────┘                      └──────┘ └──────┘
─────────────────── Project flow ──────────────▶
```

Figure 9.1. Project planning using small, self-adhesive papers.

from the outputs of step 3. And steps 7 and 8, themselves dependent on each other, can begin after step 5. The critical path in this example is steps 1, 2, 3, 5, 7, and 8.

Judgment is again required here. Consider the people on the team (who may or may not be able to do two things at once), the need to use the outcome of one step as input to the next, and then arrange the steps until they seem appropriate.

> *I'm a great believer in luck, and I find the harder I work the more I have of it.*
> —Thomas Jefferson

Executing and Controlling the Project

Now comes the exciting part, the implementation of the course of action. In many ways, if the planning was good, the implementation should almost be anticlimactic. At least, that's what the sensible project team hopes for! Even so, the smart team watches its progress carefully and understands at all times where it is against the plan.

Transfer of Steps to a Gantt Chart

The exercise with little pieces of paper stuck to the wall shows the general arrangement of the steps, but cannot show the time required for each. The steps must be transferred to a chart which is commonly called a Gantt chart, a simple bar graph of steps, their relationships, and the time required for each. For our example, the Gantt chart might look like Figure 9.2.

Now the specific time for each step can be judged, and the overall project length determined. If the time is too long, the team has to find ways to shorten critical path steps, or add more people resources, or both. Space is left under each bar to allow the team to track the actual length of each step, as shown for the first three steps in Figure 9.3.

Tracking actual progress this way is often sufficient. For more complex projects, teams sometimes use a method called an *S* curve.

The *S* Curve

We've all heard occasional reports from construction engineers engaged in a large project who say they are 45 percent complete, or some similar thing. Knowing that they too use Gantt charts, but even more complex ones than

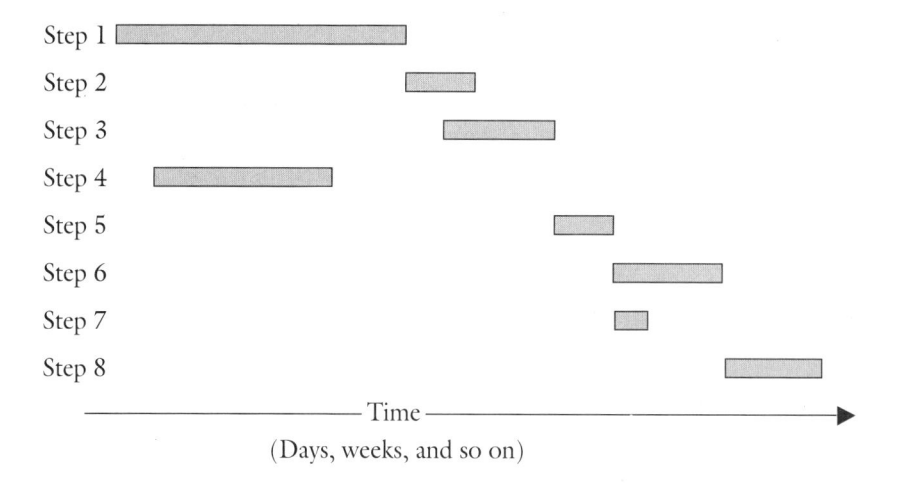

Step 1
Step 2
Step 3
Step 4
Step 5
Step 6
Step 7
Step 8

———— Time ————→
(Days, weeks, and so on)

Figure 9.2. Gantt chart—plan only.

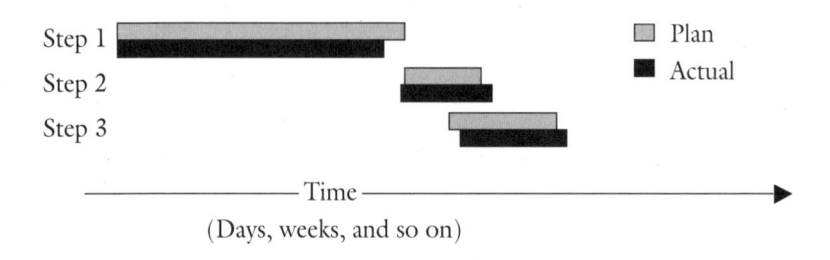

```
Step 1  ▓▓▓▓▓▓▓▓▓▓▓▓▓         □ Plan
Step 2           ▓▓▓▓          ■ Actual
Step 3             ▓▓▓
        ──────── Time ────────▶
         (Days, weeks, and so on)
```

Figure 9.3. Gantt chart—plan and actual.

we are likely to use on our quality projects, how can they determine that number? After all, when comparing actual to plan for a large number of steps, some are ahead of schedule, and some are behind schedule. The complexity of a Gantt chart is reduced to a single percent completion number using S curves.

Looking at the simple Gantt chart in Figure 9.4. There are five steps, some of which are performed simultaneously.

An S curve overlays this Gantt chart, using the same time axis, but a new vertical axis, which shows percent completion of the project. The percent scale always is the same height as all of the bars of the chart. If it is decided that each step represents 20 percent of the total project, then an S curve is constructed as shown in Figure 9.5.

At the start of the project, the percentage of completion is zero. When all steps are completed, the percentage of completion is 100. So the end points are easy. At the completion of step 1 in time, the project is 20 percent complete. (Remember that we have decided that each step represents 20 percent of the total project.) Step 3 overlaps step 2, so we can put a point at the completion of step 2 which is estimated to be 44 percent completion of the project (all of steps 1 and 2, plus about 20 percent of step 3, or 4 percent, yield a total of 44 percent). Continuing in this way leads to the S curve for the project plan.

The name of these curves derives from the fact that they typically resemble the letter S. In this example, each step was deemed to represent 20 percent of the total project. For a real project, the representation of each step is a matter of judgment: they simply need to add to 100 percent.

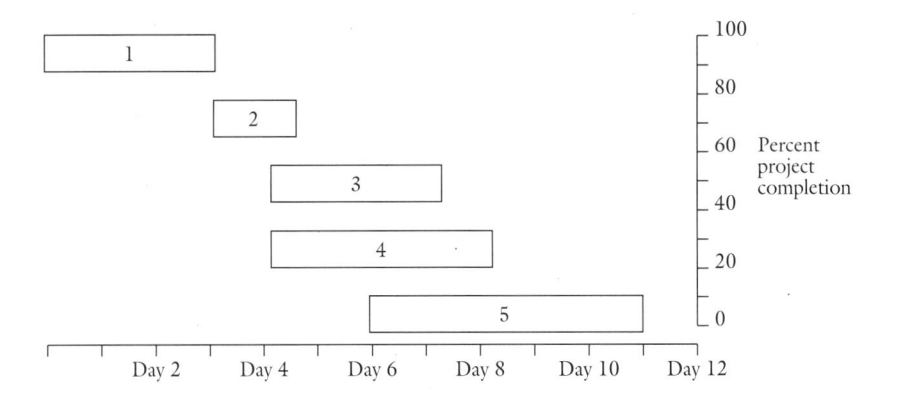

Figure 9.4. Gantt chart.

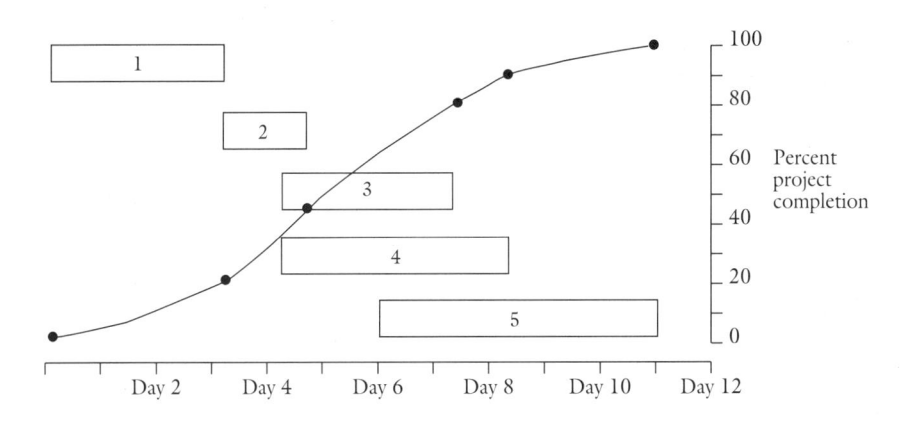

Figure 9.5. *S* curve.

Now, the planned percentage of project completion can be read off for any day of the project, using the right-hand *y* axis. Similarly, as the project unfolds, another *S* curve is constructed using actual data from the Gantt chart, and this second curve will show the overall project to be ahead of, behind, or in conformance with the planned schedule. Of course, the same weighting of each step must be used.

> *People should think things out fresh and not just accept conventional terms and the conventional way of doing things.*
> —Buckminster Fuller

Project Management

Good project management skills are essential to the completion of the tasks that all quality teams have: the implementation of actions that continually improve the business operation. Without them, the quality toolbox is incomplete, because all of the good work done in work flow analysis, problem solving, and decision making is not put into place effectively.

A good project manager is also one who can continually monitor the effects of the implemented project. Is it satisfactorily meeting the expectations that were established during the preplanning stage? Are there new issues that change the needs of the organization? Have superior alternatives been identified since the original decision was made? These and other things can require a change in the thrust or timing of the project.

10 Team Building and Leadership

Man's greatest discovery is not fire, nor the wheel, nor the combustion engine, nor atomic energy, nor anything in the material world. It is in the world of ideas. Man's greatest discovery is teamwork by agreement.
—B. Brewster Jennings

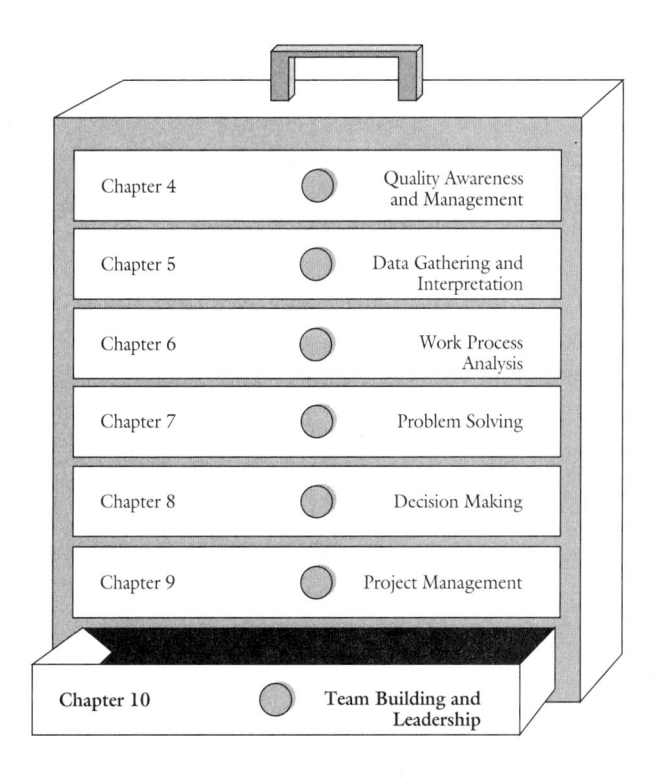

Chapter 4	○	Quality Awareness and Management
Chapter 5	○	Data Gathering and Interpretation
Chapter 6	○	Work Process Analysis
Chapter 7	○	Problem Solving
Chapter 8	○	Decision Making
Chapter 9	○	Project Management
Chapter 10	○	Team Building and Leadership

The final drawer of our quality toolbox recognizes the strength of teamwork in achieving continual quality improvement. But in most companies, teamwork doesn't just happen because it is desired. Teamwork that is truly effective results from some hard work and training about what makes a team strong, and why. Application of these tools helps achieve the old maxim—a total that is greater than the sum of the parts.

So far, we've discussed a number of the ingredients necessary for the success of quality teams. They include: senior management's recognition of quality teams as significant contributers to the company's profitability and future; the team's firm understanding of the strategic and tactical directions being taken, the necessary training in the use of quality tools; and proper management of the teams' quality efforts. Teams that enjoy these advantages have a significant head start over teams that do not.

Once a team is formed though, it must usually work without the constant intervention of supervisors or managers. Because of this fact, teams need to know how to work as a cohesive group, not as a collection of individuals. In our work we have found one more necessary ingredient, a team-building skill that enables diverse groups of people to identify and better utilize the significant strengths of their members. This team-building skill is the recognition and utilization of team interaction styles.

> *Leadership is action, not position.*
> —Donald H. McGannon

Team Interaction Styles

People do things for their own reasons, not ours. This basic law of human nature means that in any group of people, such as a quality team, the members usually differ as to what might motivate them to full participation. All of us have seen teams quickly align themselves into the active members, often thought of as the doers, and the more reticent members, the thinkers. Reticent members are sometimes thought to contribute less, because they are, by nature, less outgoing. Yet even the most reticent team members usually have much to contribute, and will do so in an environment that understands and responds to their needs. The smart team learns how to anticipate the needs or motivations of each of its members, and properly respond to them to ensure maximum effectiveness.

What does each team member see as important? In what ways might the strengths of each member's communication style support the team's efforts? What offends them? What turns them on? An understanding of basic team interaction styles by each member can help the team answer these and other related questions.

The model that we have found most useful identifies behavior by using four categories or styles. First introduced by Karl Jung, other researchers such as Anthony Allesandra, David Merrill, Katheryn Myers, and Isabel Briggs have used modified versions of Jung's work. Our model is similar, but further simplified for ease of understanding. Through study of their own styles and others, individuals begin to learn how they are perceived by others, what the needs of others might be, and how to modify their behavior to best meet those needs.

The Assertiveness Dimension

Two dimensions are used to form a profile of team interaction styles. The first is the assertiveness dimension. Assertiveness can be defined as the energy or effort one expends to control or influence others. Highly assertive people tend to make strong statements and positive declarations. They might be referred to as tell oriented because that is what they are typically more comfortable doing. Most of us would characterize a highly assertive person as direct and quick to act. People with high assertiveness strive to make their presence known, to take charge and use their power, and to have strong opinions that they are unafraid to voice. They challenge and confront others.

At the other end of the dimension are people with low assertiveness, sometimes referred to as ask oriented. We would view these people as reserved, easygoing, and anxious not to impose on others. They like to listen, and will support the views of others when they believe in them, but tend to keep their thoughts to themselves. They tend to ask many questions (thus ask oriented), and take more deliberate actions. On a simple scale, the assertiveness dimension can be shown in Figure 10.1.

Less assertive—ask oriented   More assertive—tell oriented

Figure 10.1. The assertiveness dimension.

Though everyone can, at times, move toward more assertive or less assertive behavior, most people are most comfortable in a relatively small section of the scale. Absent any unusual circumstances, or significant effort by themselves to change, they act accordingly.

The Responsiveness Dimension

The second dimension of the team profile is that of responsiveness, which can be defined as the extent to which the individual reacts to influences, appeals, or stimulations, and how he or she expresses feelings, impressions, or emotions. Highly responsive people are sometimes said to be emotive, or highly demonstrative of their feelings. We might find them warm and approachable, easygoing, personal, informal, and open. They may be emotionally expressive, dramatic, and somewhat undisciplined (especially about time), but also strongly concerned about how others feel in a situation.

People with low responsiveness can be called stern, guarded, and tough. We would describe them as precise, no-nonsense, and critical. Low responsive people see themselves as independent, self-sufficient, logical, disciplined, demanding, and rational. Their distance from others might make them stiff in social settings and lead to an avoidance of personal involvements.

The responsiveness dimension can also be shown as a simple scale, such as Figure 10.2. As was true with the assertiveness dimension, normal circumstances would find an individual most comfortable in a narrow range of this scale.

The Profile

At this point, many people see some key descriptive phrases (for example, stiff in social settings), decide that they don't want to be like that, and figure that one direction or another is best on each dimension. There are two good reasons not to do this. First, there is no right place to be. As will be shown, individuals at each end of the two dimensions bring significant, though usually different, strengths to a quality team or any other endeavor. Second, although it is possible to bend a style to meet the different needs of another style, as will also be shown, most people usually operate in their zone of comfort, that is, the style that is naturally comfortable to them. More benefit derives from maximum use of the strengths of one's normal style, than from efforts—usually unsuccessful over the long term—to change it significantly.

More responsive—shows more feelings (emotes)

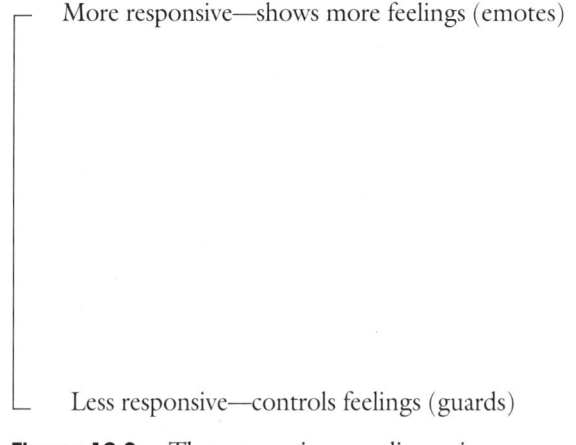

Less responsive—controls feelings (guards)

Figure 10.2. The responsiveness dimension.

The profile that is developed from these two dimensions is not a personality profile, a model of good–bad behavior, or a predictor of success or failure. It is simply a practical description of behaviors that are commonly seen and that can be observed in any person at any time. The profile helps us overcome biases about the behaviors of others, because it helps us understand those behaviors.

The profile is formed by simply combining the scales developed for the assertiveness and responsiveness dimensions, the former horizontally and the latter vertically, as shown in Figure 10.3. Framing these two axes creates the profile, a matrix of four quadrants. Each quadrant describes a combination of typical behaviors in the assertiveness and responsiveness dimensions. Each has a name: supporter, socializer, analyzer, and controller. Let's take a look at the characteristics, strengths, and weaknesses of each.

The supporter (see Figure 10.4) is one who tends to be ask oriented (low assertiveness) and emotes feelings (high responsiveness). These are the support specialists of teams, combining dependability, loyalty, sensitivity to the needs of others, patience, empathy, calm reconciliation of factions, and trust. They are diplomats, striving to build and maintain synergy in a group. Supporters can be excellent internal advocates for ideas. Sometimes, they avoid decisions that involve risk in unknown areas. Also, they may be slow

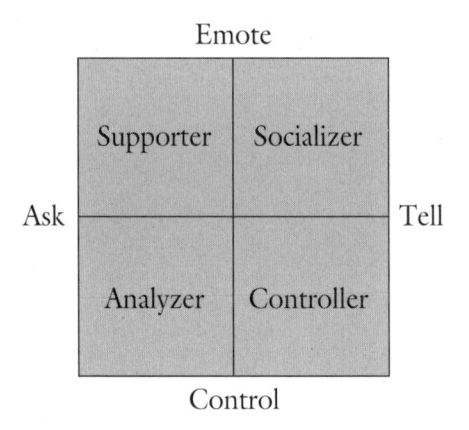

```
              Emote
      ┌─────────┬──────────┐
      │Supporter│Socializer│
 Ask  ├─────────┼──────────┤ Tell
      │ Analyzer│Controller│
      └─────────┴──────────┘
             Control
```

Figure 10.3. Team interaction styles profile.

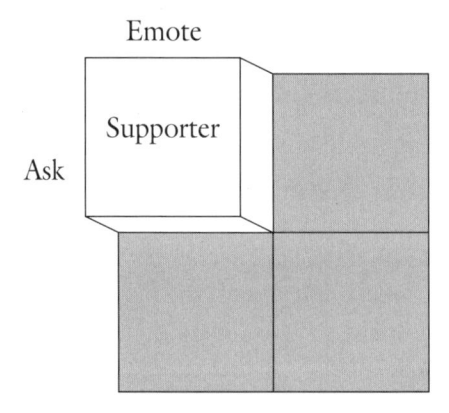

```
         Emote
       ┌─────────┐
       │Supporter│
  Ask  │         │
       └─────────┘
```

Figure 10.4. The supporter style.

to embrace significant change, especially when the situation being changed is known and comfortable to them.

Most of us remember presidents Gerald Ford and Jimmy Carter, who were both supporters. Another good example of a presidential supporter was Dwight D. Eisenhower (I Like Ike!), whom everyone liked. As the highest ranking general of the Allied armies in World War II, Eisenhower was able to create synergy by reconciling the needs of two very different generals—Montgomery and Patton—both of whom were controllers.

The socializer (see Figure 10.5) is tell oriented (high assertiveness) and tends to emote feelings (high responsiveness). Sometimes we call them vision specialists because they intuitively focus on various futures. Socializers are social experts because their high position on each scale is perfect for the formation of strong relationships. They bring to a team creative imagination, initiation of relationships, motivation of others, enjoyment, enthusiasm, risk taking, and persuasion. Their tomorrows are filled with glorious possibilities of success and progress. Ideas that lack excitement or don't shine are quickly discarded, even if they previously seemed totally committed to them. Socializers can be terribly wrong at times, because they tend to act out of hunches and intuition, rather than facts and the present reality.

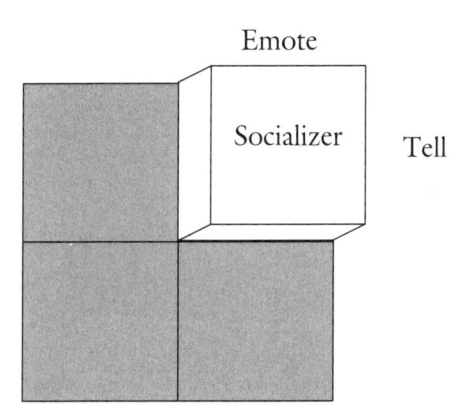

Figure 10.5. The socializer style.

Lyndon B. Johnson is a good example of a recent socializer in the White House. His vision resulted in significant domestic legislation, but some say led to trouble because of persistence in Vietnam. More of his business was allegedly conducted over the Texas barbeque than in Washington, because of the social nature of that approach.

The analyzer (see Figure 10.6) is ask oriented (low assertiveness) and controls emotions (low responsiveness). These are the technical specialists of the team. The common stereotype of the scientist alone off in a corner with calculators and charts doing unfathomable things is not far from the truth, at least for a strongly analytical person. Analyzers gather facts that enable them to examine all sides of a situation. They support a team by defining, clarifying, and evaluating, and by keeping the proceedings logical, systematic, and anchored in reality. They are administrators, with the ability to complete tasks others might find too boring. A high need for thoroughness and precision sometimes causes analyzers to become so consumed with the facts they forget that the problem needs to be solved now. Others can view them as cold, detached, or lacking in enthusiam, but drawing them out will provide the team with very consistent thoughts.

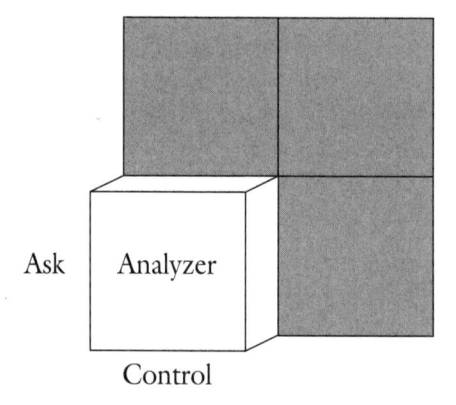

Figure 10.6. The analyzer style.

Lately, there have been few strong analyzer presidents (Calvin Coolidge was one, for example). But to the extent that he was neither very responsive nor assertive, George Bush somewhat fit the mold.

The controller (see Figure 10.7), as the name might suggest, is tell oriented (high assertiveness) and emotion controlling (low responsiveness). These people get things done. We call them the team's task experts, because

Team Building and Leadership 203

| | Controller | Tell |

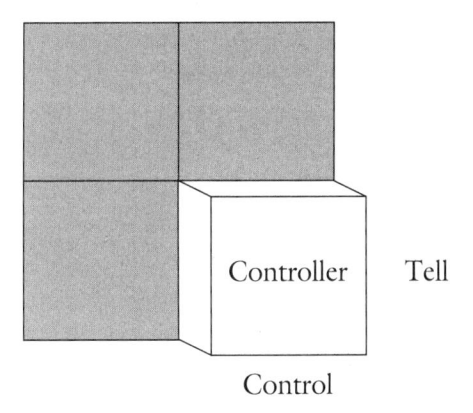

Control

Figure 10.7. The controller style.

they let little distract them from the task at hand and its swift, efficient solution. They are concerned with the now and have little patience for the past or the future. Controllers are accomplishers, results oriented, pragmatic, candid, and competitive. Several options from which they may choose, and an understanding of the impact of each option on the bottom line, are important to them. In trying to get their own way, they can dominate a team of more emotive and ask-oriented people simply by the force of their drive. They may appear harsh, impatient, critical, and uncaring of others' feelings in their effort to get it done now!

Richard Nixon may be the best example of a presidential controller in recent memory. He was very tell oriented yet hard to read emotionally.

The Benefit to the Team
What does all of this have to do with the successful operation of a team? Why not assemble a group of contollers and ensure that some sort of answer will be delivered almost immediately? One answer is that no one of these styles is as strong as the combination of them. Each brings to the team strengths that can't be found under normal circumstances in the other styles. Another answer is that a company's problem-solving network consists of all of these styles, just as it consists of people with many different colors of eyes and hair.

Let's consider a meeting of four people, each of whom is most comfortable in one of the four styles. The meeting was scheduled to start 15 minutes ago, but no one has discussed any business at all. Cathy Controlum is very angry.

What a waste of my time, she's thinking. *How does anybody get Sue Support and Sam Socialle to sit down and get to work? They've been yakking like a couple of long-lost friends for almost 20 minutes. Does he have to shake hands with everyone. It's not like we're strangers!*

Finally, she could contain herself no longer. "If everybody would please sit down, I'm sure you all realize that we've got some important work to do." The dripping sarcasm in her voice was not lost on Sam, whose face showed that he was both hurt and indignant about Cathy's dogmatic manners.

Life's too short, Cathy, he thought. *Lighten up and you'll feel a lot better.* But instead of voicing his thoughts, Sam just looked glumly down at the table.

Sue was getting very uncomfortable. She enjoyed Sam's company. He was fun, and made these meetings a lot more bearable. She could feel Sam's hurt and wanted to do something to reduce it. At the same time, she understood that Cathy felt a lot of pressure to get some results, even though she was not the formal team leader.

"Gee, Cathy, I know you want to get started, but I don't think anyone wants this group to get angry about it. What if we . . . "

"Oh great!" Cathy interrupted. "Why don't we just talk about our feelings all day. I'm sure that would be very useful to the company. At least, you all would be real happy! Can't we get started here?" Sue joined Sam in studying the tabletop.

Meanwhile, oblivious to most of what was going on, Ann Alytical was engrossed in a stack of computer printouts. She had not even lifted her head when Cathy was voicing her anger.

Cathy glanced at her three team members. *Well, at least I shut those two up!* she thought. *At least Ann seems to be doing something; who knows what it might be! Maybe if something important comes up, she'll honor us by telling us! Can't worry about that now, though. There's work to do!*

"OK, everybody," Cathy said brightly. "Here's what we need to do . . . "

This team's experience is not unusual. Three of the four members have been effectively shut out for the simple reason that they were behaving in a manner comfortable to them. Had their respective styles been understood, their unique skills probably would more likely have been effectively utilized.

Understanding the styles is important, and is usually easily done. Many people can readily identify their co-workers' interaction styles. But understanding is only a first step. How do we use this knowledge to improve the performance of teams?

There are two strategies to do so. The first moderates behaviors that are strongly oriented toward an extreme of one or both of the dimensions. The second shows team members how to better approach and work with others who exhibit a style different from their own.

The central theme of style modification is very simple. Do more of what you rarely do, and do less of what you usually do. This tends to move all team members toward a more common approach to the issues at hand. For example, people with low assertiveness take the lead more often, while people with high assertiveness reduce their desire to overpower the proceedings and get their own way. Figure 10.8 demonstrates some basic style-modification techniques.

The second strategy recognizes the reality that although each team member might develop significant capabilities to modify his or her extremes of style, the underlying comfort level of the desired style will remain. It is still important for each team member to recognize some dos and don'ts to guide ongoing relationships with other team members. Figures 10.9 through 10.12 provide some specific behaviors for dealing with each of the four predominant styles. They are not hard-and-fast rules, but simply methods that, if employed, will ensure that team members become equal, contributing partners in the endeavor of the team.

Twenty Other Questions

Team success can be greatly enhanced by understanding and recognizing team interaction styles and by applying the principles of that we have shown. But other factors that contribute to, or diminish the success of quality teams must also be considered. We have developed 20 key questions that should be asked whenever a team approach to problem solving is planned. Try them for your company, giving each question a score of 1 to 5, with 1 meaning *never* and 5 meaning *always*. Then add up the scores for the 20 questions.

To decrease responsiveness, strong supporters or socializers should
- Talk less
- Restrain enthusiasm
- Make decisions based on facts
- Stop and think
- Acknowledge the thoughts of others

To increase responsiveness, strong analyzers or controllers should
- Verbalize feelings
- Pay personal compliments
- Spend time on relationships
- Socialize and make small talk
- Use friendly, nonverbal language

To decrease assertiveness, strong socializers or controllers should
- Ask for opinions of others
- Negotiate decisions
- Listen without interruption
- Adapt to the time needs of others
- Allow others to lead

To increase assertiveness, strong supporters or analyzers should
- Get to the point
- Offer information
- Be willing to disagree
- Act on your beliefs
- Initiate conversation

Figure 10.8. Style modification techniques.

A total score of 80 or higher indicates that things are working pretty well. Remain vigilant for ways to improve toward a maximum score of 100. Don't relax: good team functioning can unravel without attention.

A total score between 60 and 80 shows that some work is needed to improve team functioning. Your teams are probably getting significant things done, but considerable advancements in their efficiency and effectiveness are possible.

Total scores below 60 signal some trouble. Teams are struggling against difficult odds, and their success is not very likely. Some major changes are required.

Team Building and Leadership

Do	Do not
1. Start the session with a personal comment: break the ice.	1. Rush headlong into business or the agenda.
2. Show sincere interest in supporters as people. Find areas of common involvement. Be candid and open.	2. Stick coldly and harshly to business. On the other hand, don't lose sight of the team's goals or reason for meeting.
3. Patiently draw out personal goals and work with the supporters' help to achieve those goals.	3. Force the supporters to respond quickly to your objectives. Don't say, "Here's how I see it!"
4. Present your case in a non-threatening way.	4. Dominate, demand, or threaten with personal or positional power.
5. Ask how questions to draw out supporters' opinions.	5. Debate facts and figures. Supporters will stop participating.
6. If you agree easily, identify and recognize areas of early disagreement or dissatisfaction.	6. Manipulate or bully supporters into agreeing. They will tend not to fight back.
7. If you disagree, be alert for hurt feelings or a belief that you are being personal.	7. Patronize or demean by use of subtlety or invective.
8. Move casually and informally.	8. Be rapid and abrupt.
9. Define individual contributions clearly, preferably in writing.	9. Be vague. Don't offer opinions and probabilities.
10. Provide some assurances that the decisions of the supporters will not engender personal risk.	10. Offer guarantees and assurances you can't fulfill.
11. Provide clear, specific solutions with maximum chance of success.	11. Decide for them: they will lose initiative.
	12. Leave supporters without backup support.

Figure 10.9. Specific behaviors for dealing with supporters.

Do	Do not
1. Plan interactions that support their dreams and intentions.	1. Lay down the law.
2. Leave time for socializing and relating.	2. Be curt, cold, or tight-lipped.
3. Talk about people and their goals. Share opinions they will find stimulating.	3. Drive on to fact, figures, alternatives, or abstract ideas.
4. Discuss the big picture, not the details.	4. Leave things hanging in the air. They will stay there.
5. Ask for opinions and ideas concerning people.	5. Waste time being impersonal, judgmental, or task oriented.
6. Provide them with ideas for implementing action.	6. Dream with them: you'll lose sight of the teams's objectives.
7. Use time to be stimulating, fun-loving, fast moving, and entertaining.	7. Kid around too much. But don't stick to the agenda too much either.
8. Provide testimonials from people that the socializer sees as important or prominent.	8. Talk down to them.
	9. Be dogmatic.
	10. Try to cover up.
	11. Offer stopgap solutions.
9. Offer special, immediate, and extra incentives for their willingness to take risks.	

Figure 10.10. Specific behaviors for dealing with socializers.

Do	Do not
1. Prepare your case in advance.	1. Be disorganized or messy.
2. Approach analyzers in a direct way. Stick to business.	2. Be circuitous, giddy, casual, informal, or loud.
3. Support their principles and thoughtful approach. Build your credibility by listing the pros and cons associated with your suggestions.	3. Rush the decision-making process.
	4. Be vague about what is expected of either of you. Don't fail to follow through.
4. Make an organized contribution to their efforts. Present specifics and do what you say you can do.	5. Dillydally.
	6. Leave things to luck or chance.
5. Take your time, but be persistent.	7. Provide special personal incentives.
6. Draw up a scheduled approach to implementing action with a step-by-step timetable. Assure them that there will be no surprises.	8. Threaten, cajole, wheedle, coax, or wimper.
	9. Use testimony of others or unreliable sources. Don't be haphazard.
7. If you agree, follow through.	
8. If you disagree, make an organized presentation of your position.	10. Use someone else's opinion as evidence.
	11. Use gimmicks or quick, clever manipulations.
9. Give them time to verify the reliability of your actions. Be accurate and realistic.	
10. Provide solid, tangible, practical evidence.	
11. Indicate guarantees over the long term, but provide options.	

Figure 10.11. Specific behaviors for dealing with analyzers.

Do	**Do not**
1. Be clear, specific, brief, and to the point.	1. Ramble on or waste time.
2. Stick to business.	2. Try to build personal relationships.
3. Be prepared. Bring all support materials, requirements, and objectives in a well-organized package.	3. Forget or lose things. Don't be disorganized, messy, or do anything that will confuse or distract the controllers from business.
4. Present facts logically through a well-planned program.	4. Leave loopholes or cloudy issues.
5. Ask specific, perferably what, questions.	5. Ask useless or rhetorical questions.
6. Provide alternatives and choices that will let the controllers make decisons.	6. Come to the meeting with a ready-made decision. Do not make it for them.
7. Provide facts and figures about the operations' probability of success or effectiveness.	7. Speculate wildly or offer gurantees or assurances.
8. If you disagree, take issue with the facts, not the person.	8. Let disagreement reflect personally on the controllers.
9. If you agree, support the results, not the person.	9. Reinforce the statement with "I'm with you!"
10. Motivate and persuade by referring to objectives and results.	10. Convince by personal means.
	11. Direct or order.
11. After talking business, depart graciously.	12. Do an epilogue after finishing business.

Figure 10.12. Specific behaviors for dealing with controllers.

The function of our team
1. Are team members clear about their goals?
2. Do team members demonstrate a sense of purpose?
3. Are team members committed to achieving their goals?
4. Does every team member understand his or her function and role on the team?
5. Is all the information necessary for the team to do its job accessible and effectively shared?
6. Are team members able to express feelings and ideas, even when they conflict with others?
7. When conflict arises, do the team members try to work it out in a cooperative way?
8. Do team members demonstrate respect and support for each other?
9. Are new ideas encouraged and valued by team members?
10. Do team members utilize each other's skills, experience, and expertise?
11. Is collaboration routine on the team?
12. Do team members consistently use and follow a formal and logical process to analyze work processes and other issues?
13. Do team members consistently use and follow a formal and logical problem-solving process?
14. Do team members make timely decisions using and following a formal and logical decision-making process?
15. Do team members have appropriate opportunities to influence team decisions?
16. Do team members apply a systematic, step-by-step approach to assigned projects?
17. Are team members given personal responsibilities that are in line with their expertise and experience?
18. Is the leadership style used in the team appropriate for the its needs?
19. Do team members consistently maintain high expectations regarding the quality of their performance?
20. Are recognition, rewards, and opportunity distributed to the team fairly?

If the blind lead the blind, both shall fall into the ditch.
—Matthew 15:14

Team-Leading Skills

Each quality team needs to have some form of leadership to ensure that it effectively applies itself to its assigned issues, and that it properly assembles and presents to senior management its recommendations for action. The team leadership is usually selected beforehand, and may or may not be an individual with prior experience leading a group. Also, the leader of a quality team often does not have positional power, that is, a hierarchical role of authority. (Of course, that should not matter, since in our view, the application of positional power is not the most effective form of leadership anyway!)

The effectiveness of any quality team is significantly improved through familiarity with a few simple, team-leadership techniques. The benefits to the present team leader are obvious. But other team members benefit too: they can readily support an inexperienced leader by knowing what he or she is trying to accomplish. And their turns as leaders will come. We will look at four aspects of team leadership.

The Team Leader's Role

The overall role of any team leader is to make sure that all of the resources available to the team, and especially its members' skills and experiences, are applied to the maximum extent and with the highest level of efficiency and effectiveness. How that is done usually depends on the circumstances at the time, but there are at least six key steps that any quality team leader should take.

1. The leader fully defines the problem to be worked on, the purpose of the team, the nature of the deliverable results (for example, a report, recommendation, or perhaps a complete change), and any time restrictions. The leader does not have to autocratically decide these items alone; the team can be very helpful. But the leader needs to ensure that they are done.
2. Everyone on the team should have knowledge of team interaction styles and use it to draw out and better relate to other team members. The leader, however, has the ultimate responsibility to

understand the most comfortable style of each member, and apply team interaction styles skill to create a well-working team.
3. The leader assigns special responsibilities as appropriate. These may include researching, co-leading, writing, piloting a process, or any other team need.
4. Proper application of the quality tools will give good results. The leader must insist that systematic methods of thinking are used and not let the team slip back into well-worn ways of dealing with issues. This often means argument, bias, and poorly formed but popular opinions. Recommendations of the team that applies well-worn methods are usually those that have been supported or advanced by the strongest or loudest.
5. The leader must watch the clock and get things done on schedule. Left alone, teams can get caught up in the fun of the mental exercise and forget the purpose of their efforts.
6. Finally, the leader must try to gain consensus on the results of the team's work. Teams divided in their belief in the results cannot effectively support them. And that leads to the last responsibility. No results are worth much if they are not reported. The leader's role is to coordinate the preparation of a presentation of the work. More will be said about this later.

Encourage Participation

There are many ways in which team members can encourage or discourage participation. Everyone on the team who encourages others to participate takes on an appropriate form of leadership. Conversely, those who discourage ongoing participation (sometimes without conscious knowledge that they are doing so) also lead; but such behavior is not useful.

Participation is discouraged in several ways. One that we have already looked at is the failure to draw out the more reticent members of the team, perhaps the analyzers. Another way to discourage participation is through responses to another team member's statements. For example

- "I don't think that's important at all."
- "That idea will never work!"
- "You're missing the point here."

- "There's not much we can do about that!"
- "OK, but that doesn't apply here."

All of these are cut-off statements. They all imply, in one way or another, that what has just been said is wrong, irrelevant, or even ignorant. They ensure that the person making the statement will think twice before risking another response of this type.

There are, of course, responses to statements that can encourage further participation. Sometimes these seem difficult to use, because the statement made is so clearly off base that the respondent does not want be encouraging. But few team members continue to make one irrelevant statement after another. Their next idea might be a jewel. And sometimes, the statement isn't so far off base after all. Encouraging statements might include the following:

- "That's an interesting point. How do the rest of you feel about that?"
- "Would you explain that further?"
- "How would that idea apply to the problem at hand?"
- "John feels that we should do . . . What other possibilities might there be to consider?"
- "Sue, how do you feel about that idea?"
- "How can we remove some of the apparent obstacles to that plan?"

Each of these encouraging responses is a question. It elicits further conversation. If there is a good idea hiding in what at first glance seemed preposterous, it will tend to surface. If the idea is a bad one, the group's responses will usually demonstrate that to its proponent in a way that is not demeaning—unless, of course, the response to one of the encouraging questions is a cut-off statement! The idea-generator might have a much better one next time, and would still be willing to voice it.

Dealing with Difficult Situations

The leader has a unique opportunity and responsibility to identify and deal with difficult situations that arise while working with the quality team. These can include a team's lack of desire, unwillingness to accept the leader in that role, wandering away from the issue at hand, or any number of other scenarios. Figure 10.13 shows some of the more common situations. In

Situation	Remedy
A member is passive or slow.	Ask the member provoking questions.
Members argue with each other.	Step between; draw attention to yourself.
A discussion out of control.	Assume more control. Ask directing questions.
A member gangs up on the leader.	Shift the topic; don't argue. Work out a compromise.
A member rambles on.	At pause, thank the person. Rephrase a statement made and move on.
A member talks too much.	Use a summarizing statement and direct a question to another member.
A member makes an insensitive comment.	State frankly what can and cannot be discussed.
A member is definitely wrong.	Don't tell. Ask group members for their opinion. Let them explain the error.
Personalities conflict.	Cut across conflict with a question on the topic. Frankly ask that personalities be left out.
A member is bored.	Find the member's interest. Call for his or her experiences.
A member just wants to listen.	Use direct, provocative questions.

Figure 10.13. Remedies for difficult team situations.

many ways, they are like the situations that a teacher, trainer, or facilitator must face. All of the remedies have one thing in common. They maintain the leader's respect of the individuals on the team and strive to work out the problem as a team.

Prepare an Effective Presentation

Finally, as was stated earlier, many fine efforts by effective teams are negated by poor presentations of the results. In reality, the team never has the time in a presentation to go over every fact gathered, or every conclusion discarded, or every action plan considered but rejected. If they did, the problem would not have been delegated to them in the first place! The presentation is a time for a succinct summarization of the results, and (hopefully) acceptance of the work. As such, it is both important and difficult, especially if the senior management for whom the presentation is intended is unlikely to embrace the team's output.

The team leader must coordinate the preparation of the presentation, because he or she is accountable for the results of the efforts made. Two broad areas must be considered: the variables of the audience and the physical setting, and the organization of the presentation.

The variables of the audience are, of course, fixed. Whatever they are must be dealt with. Also, unlike public speaking, considerations of special interests or hobbies, age distribution, memberships, and other similar factors are less important, because this is a business presentation. But there are a few factors that the leader should consider when deciding on presentation content.

- Audience size and physical location help determine the kind of presentation materials that may be best. Should overhead transparencies or handouts be used? Should a lectern with rear projection be used or is an informal sit-down delivery preferred?
- The specific positions and responsibilities of the audience can help establish detailed areas of questioning that may arise. For example, if the chief financial officer will attend, the presenter should be prepared to defend the cost estimates of the proposal.
- Senior managers are not always knowledgeable about all aspects of the business. If they aren't, be prepared to give a short background summary of the topic at hand. If they are cognizant, don't bore them with details. More commonly, you aren't sure, or the managers' knowledge is mixed. In such a case, be prepared with the background summary and ask the most senior person (preferably beforehand) how much background presentation would be appropriate.

Finally, organize the presentation. This step is especially critical for presentations that are sure to generate conflicting opinions or that will give unexpected recommendations. The presentation usually will consist of five discrete steps, which follow whatever introduction formalities are appropriate for the company.

- **Purpose of the team.** Why did the team meet? What problem or issue was addressed? Why is it important? What is going to be presented (for example, information, options, recommendations, or completed implementation results)? If the team has elected to include a summary background of the issue for some less knowledgeable managers, it would be done before or during this step.
- **Process of the team.** Who were the members? Why them? What were the specific responsibilities of the members? By what processes was the issue examined and a recommendation derived? This step should be short and should include only information that helps the audience better understand the body of the presentation. Generally, it is a mistake to use this step solely for the aggrandizement of the team members.
- **Results step.** What is the solution that satisfies the need which the team was assembled to address? This is the body of the presentation. It usually includes overall conclusions, options considered but rejected and the reasons why, the actual recommendation and its cost, implementation plans and other necessary information.
- **Consequences step.** What are the pros and cons, if any? What other systems or organizations might be impacted by the recommendation? How will these impacts help the company? How will they be minimized if they are negative? What clearly beneficial results can the audience expect from the implementation of the recommendation? The intent here is to move the audience from an attitude of it can't hurt, and it's not that expensive, to this would be an advantage to me!
- **Action step.** Request that the audience approve the recommendations and authorize the necessary implementation plan.

Not all of these steps are always appropriate, and sometimes others are necessary. But organizing all quality team presentations along these lines will result in significant increases in the speed in which improvements are made.

Summary

The principal mark of genius is not perfection but originality, the opening of new frontiers.
—Arthur Koestler

Quality Can Be Easy

Quality isn't a mystery. Nor does it have to be difficult to implement. It isn't the province of the Japanese, or any other group of people. It does not require expertise in mathematics, fancy charts, or a lot of money. It certainly does not require a specially trained employee group who are known as the quality people. It doesn't need millions of words of rhetoric, or large posters, or clever names. It shouldn't require a great deal of effort. It should come easily.

Quality requires a few key factors. One is a management group that has decided that quality is not a good thing to do for the business; it *is* the business. Another is that the company must reach a higher quality plateau, as was described in chapter 1. A third key factor is a management group that is willing to trust that the company's employees, at least most of them, *want* to do the best job they can. A management group that strives to make it possible for them to do so by providing the necessary training, and then letting employees apply it. Some call this empowerment, others use different names. The name is not as important as the act.

The importance of utilizing the incredible power within people to solve problems and create innovative new ways to do business is a central tenet of this book. That's why seven chapters have been devoted to the tools people need. Almost no one is trained in problem solving, decision making, work process analysis, or project management in typical school curricula. It must be provided on the job, and it must be continually improved.

But of all things that quality requires, perhaps the most important is a fundamental understanding of the simple word *customer*. In our work we have found no one who thinks he or she doesn't understand this word. Yet, few really do, or at least they do not act as if they do. Everyone can understand the idea of the external customer, the person or group or company that buys the product or service. Real quality arrives when each employee, from the lowest to the highest level of the company, understands as a basic rule that everyone with whom he or she comes in contact during the business day is a customer. That each of these customers has a set of musts and wants. That smart suppliers don't assume those must and wants, but work hard to identify them. That meeting and exceeding those musts and wants is what brings external customers back and is what helps internal customers run the business more effectively and efficiently.

> *Destiny is not a matter of chance, it is a matter of choice; it is not a thing to be waited for, it is a thing to be achieved.*
> —William Jennings Bryan

When Customers Aren't Identified

We once worked with a small hospital that was having difficulties with the relationship of its surgeons and the operating room (OR) staff, consisting of nurses, orderlies, and other support employees. The surgeons were not hospital employees and, at times, treated the OR staff with less respect than was warranted. Surgical schedules were battered by late-arriving surgeons. Heated arguments arose when certain tools were not available, even when they had been requested. It was, for the doctors and staff, a genuine us-against-them scenario.

Neither side was right, and neither side was wrong. In fact, there was often dissension within the OR staff itself. One nurse felt that her job description included more time-consuming and difficult work than another. The nurses could be short with the cleaning crew, and so on.

A study was undertaken by interviewing many of the doctors and most of the OR staff. Through those interviews the difficulties just described and others were identified. Interestingly, everyone focused on the customer. It was stated again and again. But notice that the phrase is singular: the customer. The customer referred to here is, of course, the patient, and thank goodness everyone was so concerned about this person, so helpless during surgery.

The thrust of our work with this group was to surface and gain acceptance of the notion of multiple customers. A matrix-style table was constructed, which enabled us to show the relationship of all possible combinations of doctor, scrub nurse, OR supervisor, and so on, both as a supplier and customer, similar to the mileage charts on maps. For example, the doctor is certainly a customer of the person who sterilizes equipment and provides surgical kits (the array of tools necessary for the planned surgery). Likewise, of course, the equipment sterilizer is a customer of the doctor. In this case our customer is supplied information: special needs, possible complications that may require different tools, personal desire for layout, and so on. Providing this simple information to the customer not only allows him or her to do the job more effectively, but builds an important bridge between the two people. Doctor, it might be interesting to you that during the last three gallbladder operations you used only three whatchamacallits, and always request eight in your kit. Since we have to sterilize everything after the surgery, even the tools not used, we could save some time and money if you'd consider reducing your kit content to five whatchamacallits.

Just once in this business we got nowhere, and this was it. The surgeons failed to accept the idea of multiple customers, and lost an opportunity to gain a much better working relationship with the hospital staff, and possibly in their private offices as well.

A New Start

Throughout this book, we have included some of our favorite quotations that seem to fit the topic being presented. Their intent has been to stimulate the readers' thinking about quality issues. If they have by any chance led to deeper philosophical inspection, great! Our final quote is for the readers who may have picked up this book hoping to find a way to set right a quality effort gone wrong. A quality effort that began with a lot of fanfare, many promises, perhaps a large budget line item, but which has just not met with the expectations of the company. A quality effort where many things are being done, but none seems to affect the outcome of anything important. A quality effort that runs the risk of disillusioning the employees who saw hope in it.

For this reader, we have outlined a set of tools and a process we are convinced will work if applied. While doing so, consider the words of Henry David Thoreau: *If you have built castles in the air, your work need not be lost; that is where they should be. Now put the foundations under them.*

Index

Adaptive alternative courses of action, 173
Adult learning. *See* Quality training
Affected community of customers, 184
Allesandra, Anthony, 197
Alternative courses of action
    adaptive, 173
    corrective, 172
    fit of, in decision making, 173
    interim, 172
American business cycle, 45
American Society for Quality Control, 48–49
Analyzer style of interaction, 202
    behaviors for dealing with, 209
Appraisal costs, 46–47
Assertiveness dimension of interaction styles, 197–98

Balance sheet model of decision-making, 166–67
Breakthrough, definition of, vii–viii
Briggs, Isabel, 197
Business cycle, 89–90
    American, 45
    in business doomed to failure, 94–95
    in business running on luck, 93–94
    in prospering business, 92

Cause-and-effect diagrams, 125–28
CEO, importance of, in organization, 26–28
Check sheets, 104–5
    multiple-variable, 105–7
    transferring results from
        to histogram, 114, 115
        to Pareto chart, 109
    trend charts, 105
Coin flip model of decision making, 166
Communication
    common language as key to superior quality, 62–65
    importance of, 55–56
Consultant, in quality process, 80
Control charts, 119–25
    R charts, 125, 126
    $\overline{X}$ charts, 125, 126
Controller style of interaction, 202–3
    behaviors for dealing with, 210
Corrective alternative courses of action, 172

Cost of quality audit, 45–49
  appraisal costs, 46–47
  failure costs, 46
  prevention costs, 46–47
Creativity, in decision making, 176–78
Critical path of project, 189–90
Culture
  definition of, 65
  and language, 65
Customer(s)
  affected community of, 184
  adjusting to change in needs, 8
  and business success, 90–95
  definition of, 10
  employee role as, 10–15
  external, 6–7, 26–28
  identifying, 15–26
  internal, 6–7
  meeting needs in, 4–5, 8–9, 34
  musts and wants in, 7–8, 15–26
  rating of, in process evaluation, 144, 146
  self-evaluation as, 144
  steps in analysis of, 184
  understanding needs of, 6
  user community of, 184
Customer cycle, 91
  in business doomed to failure, 94–95
  in business running on luck, 93–94
  in prospering business, 92

Data gathering and interpretation, 57
  cause-and-effect diagrams, 125–28
  check sheets, 104–7
  control charts, 119–25
  flowcharting, 131–38
  histograms, 111–16
  Pareto charts, 108–11
  rules for collecting data, 107
  scatter diagrams, 117–19

Decision making, 58, 179
  collecting range of alternatives, 172–73
  considering solution after next, 171–72
  creativity in, 176–78
  determining purpose of decision, 168–70
  establishing criteria of decision, 170–71
  evaluating choice for strategic fit and risks, 175–76
  investigating fit of each alternative, 173–75
  levels of decisions in, 169
Decision-making models
  balance sheet, 166–67
  coin flip or hunch, 166
  decision tree, 167
  point-scoring, 167–68
Decision statement, parts of, 169–70
Decision tree model of decision making, 167
Deming, W. Edwards
  demonstration by, 119–21
  14 points of, 64
Department needs, flexibility for varying, 59–62
Diagnostic problem solving, 160

Employees
  meetings with management, 54–55
  multiple role of, 9–15
External customer, 6–7
  importance of, in organization, 26–28
Externalized appreciation plateau of quality, xii

Failure costs, 46
Fishbone diagrams, 125–28
Flowcharting, 57, 131
  benefits of, 138

elements of, 131–32, 133
level of detail in, 132, 134–36, 137
useful rules for, 136, 138

Gantt chart, for project management, 191, 192, 193

Histograms, 111–12
alternating distribution, 116
bell-shaped pattern, 112–14, 122
emergence of, into control chart, 122–23
formation of, 112–13
plateau distribution, 114, 116
skewed pattern, 114, 116
two-peak pattern, 114, 116
uses of, 114
Hunch model of decision making, 166

Implementation skills, 58
Interest stake in project results, 184
Interim alternative courses of action, 172
Internal customers, 6–7
Internalized understanding plateau of quality, x

Job descriptions, and quality improvement, 29
Jung, Karl, 197
Juran, Joseph, 108

Management
changing attitudes of, about quality management, 44–49
commitment of, to quality, 35–36, 42–44
meetings with employees, 54–55
need for top-down, 68–69
in quality antagonistic environment, 36–40
in quality environment, 40–44
responsibilities of, 69

role of, 96, 148
Manufacturing activities/organizations
versus nonmanufacturing activities, 130
productivity in, 60
Manufacturing quality council
versus nonmanufacturing councils, 97–101
process of, 99
Meetings, between employees and management, 54–55
Merrill, David, 197
Montgomery, Bernard, 201
Multiple-variable check sheets, 105–7
Musts
as criteria for decision making, 170
definition of, 7
versus wants in customer needs, 7–8, 15–26
Myers, Katheryn, 197

Nonmanufacturing activities/organizations. *See also* Service organizations
versus manufacturing activities, 61, 130
Nonmanufacturing quality council
versus manufacturing quality councils, 97–101
process of, 100

Organization
defining function of, 30–33, 34
pyramidal view of, 26–28
role of, 28–33
Ownership stake in project, 184

Pareto, Vilfredo, 108
Pareto charts, 108–11
Pareto principle, 108
Patton, George, 201
Pictures, value of, in quality training, 77

Point-scoring model of decision making, 167–68
Presentation skills, 58
  deciding content of presentation, 216
  steps in presentation, 217
Prevention costs, 46–47
  definition of, 46
  high, 46
  low, coupled with appraisal costs, 46–47
Problem solving, 58, 148, 150
  common elements of problem, 150–51
  and common language, 66
  day-one problem, 161
  diagnostic, 160
  importance of process for, 162
  identification of possible causes, 156–57
  multiple problem, 160–61
  organization of relevant data about problem, 153–55
  problem recognition, 150–53
  questions for team approach to, 205–6, 211
  reduction to probable cause, 157–58
  requirements of good, 149
  research of changes, 155–56
  testing for root cause, 158–60
Process description, 138
  customer analysis, 139–40
  key questions in, 142–43
  steps in, 130–31
  supplier analysis, 141
  throughput analysis, 139
Process evaluation, 143, 145
  customer and supplier ratings, 144, 146
  self-evaluation as processor, supplier and customer, 143–44
  steps in, 131

Process observation and data-gathering tools. *See* Data gathering and interpretation
Processor
  definition of, 10
  employee role as, 10–15
  self-evaluation as, 144
Professionalism, 5
Project failure, causes of, 186
Project management, 182, 194
  executing and controlling project, 190–94
  Gantt chart, 191, 192, 193
  preplanning project, 182–88
  project plan, 188–90
  S curve, 191–94
Project plan
  critical path of project, 189–90
  steps in, 188–89
Project preplanning, 182–83
  best case/worst case scenarios, 185–87
  persons using and/or affected by product, 184
  purpose and outcome, 183–84
  resources needed, 184–85
  termination needs of project, 187–88

Quality. *See also* Superior quality
  appropriateness of, 80
  definition of, 3–9, 15
  disillusionment with, 51–52
  key to continual improvement in, 15–26
  superior, 81
    common language, 62–65
    flexibility for varying department needs, 59–62
    good start, 53–56
    problem-solving network's involvement in common language, 66–68

process appropriate to company, 80
quick results versus quick fix, 78–80
system of top-down management, 68–69
training for adult learners, 69–78
useable tools, 56–58
Quality antagonistic environment, 34
management's attitude in, 36–40
Quality awareness, 86
process knowledge, 88–95
traditional versus new views of quality, 87–88
Quality councils, 96–97
manufacturing versus nonmanufacturing, 97–101
role of, 98–99
Quality efforts
in manufacturing versus nonmanufacturing organizations, 61
plateaus of, viii–xi, xii
reasons to embrace total, xi
Quality management systems, 95
management's ongoing role in quality, 96
quality councils in, 96–101
Quality supportive environment, 34, 49
management's attitude in, 40–44
Quality tools
data gathering and interpretation, 57, 104–28
decision-making skills, 58, 166–79
flowcharting, 57
implementation skills, 58
presentation skills, 58
problem-solving skills, 58, 148–63
project management, 95–102, 182–94

quality awareness, 86–95
guidelines for, 57
team building and leadership skills, 58, 196–217
usability of, 56–57
work process analysis skills, 58, 130–46
Quality training
adult learning versus child learning, 70–71, 77–78
needs for effective adult learning, 72
Quick fix, as impediment to quality improvement, 78–80

Random distribution, depiction of, 112–13
R charts, 125, 126
Responsiveness dimension of interaction styles, 198, 199
Risk in decision making, 175–76

Scatter diagrams, 117
incomplete, 117
negative relationship in, 117, 118, 119
no apparent relationship in, 118, 119
positive relationship in, 117, 118
Scattered thinking, 162, 163
S curve, for project management, 191–94
Service organizations. *See also* Nonmanufacturing activities/ organizations
assigning processes for analysis, 101
identifying problems in, 59–62
productivity in, 60
Socializer style of interaction, 201
behaviors for dealing with, 208
Social skills, balancing, with technical skills, 76–77

Solution after next, in decision making, 171–72
Statistical process control (SPC), 57
    application to service organizations, 62
Strategic fit in decision making, 175
Stressful situations, practicing techniques for handling, 75–76
Structured thinking, 166
Studied indifference plateau of quality, viii–ix
Style modification
    central theme of, 205
    techniques for, 206
Supplier(s)
    definition of, 10
    each employee's role as, 10–15
    identifying, 15–26
    rating of, in process evaluation, 144, 146
    self-evaluation as, 144
Supplier analysis, 141
Supporter style of interaction, 199–201
    behaviors for dealing with, 207

Team building and leadership
    problem-solving questions for, 205–6, 211
    team interaction styles, 196–205
    team-leading skills, 212–17
Team interaction styles, 196–97
    analyzer, 202, 209
    assertiveness dimension of, 197–98
    benefit to quality team, 203–5
    controller, 202–3, 210
    profile development, 198–203
    responsiveness dimension of, 198, 199
    socializer, 201, 208
    style modification, 205, 206
    supporter, 199–201, 207

Team-leading skills, 58, 212
    for difficult situations, 214–15
    encouraging participation, 213–14
    presentation skills, 216–17
    role of team leader, 212–13
Team members
    encouraging participation of, 58, 213–14
    expected inputs from, 185
    responsibilities of, 185
Technical skills, balancing, with social skills, 76–77
Throughput analysis, steps in, 139
Top-down management, need for system of, 68–69
Total quality management (TQM), general requirements for, xiv–xv
Trend chart, 105

User community of customers, 184

Wants
    definition of, 7
    as criteria for decision making, 170–71
    versus musts in customer needs, 7–8, 15–26
Weighted score (WS), calculating, in decision making, 174
Work environment
    quality antagonistic, 34, 36–40
    quality supportive, 34, 40–44, 49
Work process, understanding, 88–95
Work process analysis skills, 58, 130, 146
    and flowcharting, 131–38
    process description, 130–31, 138–43
    process evaluation, 131, 143–46

$\overline{X}$ charts, 125, 126